WKK HIGH SCHOOL.

ENGLIS

D0581913

R. 50

THE ROAD TO MEMPHIS

'Statler Aames and his brothers got a big kick out of teasing coloured folks, and for the most part all coloured folks could do was stand and take it.'

But what happens in 1930s Mississippi when coloured folks don't stand and take it? Even Cassie Logan and her community who know all the white folks' rules could not have imagined the terrible consequences of Moe Turner's action.

So begins the flight to Memphis which for Cassie Logan is more than just a journey. The events which overtake her yield experiences of such intensity that her life will never be the same again.

ABOUT THE AUTHOR

Mildred D. Taylor was born in Jackson, Mississippi, and grew up in Toledo, Ohio. After two years with the Peace Corps, she enrolled at the School of Journalism at the University of Colorado, where she worked with university officials and fellow students in structuring a Black studies course at the university. She now lives in Colorado.

Other titles by Mildred Taylor in New Windmills:

Roll of Thunder, Hear My Cry
The Friendship and Other Stories

The Road to Memphis

Mildred D Taylor

HEINEMANN
NEW WINDMILLS

Heinemann Educational
a division of
Heinemann Publishers (Oxford) Ltd
Halley Court, Jordan Hill, Oxford OX2 8EJ
OXFORD   LONDON   EDINBURGH
MADRID   ATHENS   BOLOGNA   PARIS
MELBOURNE   SYDNEY   AUCKLAND   SINGAPORE   TOKYO
IBADAN   NAIROBI   HARARE   GABARONE
PORTSMOUTH NH (USA)

First published in Great Britain by Victor Gollancz Ltd 1990

First published in the New Windmill Series 1993

93 94 95 96 97 10 9 8 7 6 5 4 3 2 1

ISBN 0 435 12395 5

British Library Cataloguing in Publication Data
for this title is available from the British Library

Typeset by Cambridge Composing (UK) Ltd, Cambridge
Printed and bound in England by Clays Ltd, St Ives plc

Dedication

*This book is dedicated to the memory of my beloved father,
who lived many adventures of the boy, Stacey,
and who was in essence the man, David.*

*This book is also dedicated to my uncle, Mr James Edward
Taylor, who has always been like a second father,
who has always encouraged me, and since the death of my father,
has been my greatest resource in the writing of my books about the
South and the Logan family.*

Contents

Author's Note

I am indebted to many people for their generosity of time
and expertise in my writing of *The Road to Memphis*. I
thank Mr Don Nodtvedt for allowing me to view his
splendid 1937 Ford firsthand and for answering so many
questions about automobiles of the 1930s; Mr and Mrs Bob
Sisemore for identifying the make and model of one of my
father's first cars from a family photograph; my cousin, Mr
Edwin Taylor, for doing the same; Mr Ed Frank and Mrs
Bobbette Walker of the Mississippi Valley Collection at
Memphis State University for providing so many resources
during my research visit to Memphis; Mr Bruce Greene, a
lawyer and friend, who checked all my legal references;
and Mr Norman Early, Jr., another lawyer and friend, who
has checked legal references for my other work. I am also
deeply grateful to Ms Janet Chenery, my editor at Dial
Books; Mr Skip Skwarek, General Manager at Dial; Ms
Phyllis Fogelman, President and Publisher of Dial; and
Ms Regina Hayes, editor of my first books about the Logan
family.

As always in the writing of my books, my family has
supported me in my efforts and have been invaluable
resources. I am especially thankful to my uncle, Mr James
E. Taylor, who has provided so much encouragement and
understanding. I am also thankful to his wife, my aunt,
Mrs Curtis Lee Taylor, and to my mother, Mrs Deletha
M. Taylor, and my sister, Ms Wilma M. Taylor, without
whose support I could not have gotten through the writing
of this book or any other. I thank as well all the other
members of my family who have contributed so much to
my storytelling by relaying their memories of the South to
me. Most of all, as in the writing of all my books about the

Logan family, I am thankful and grateful to my father, the storyteller, for without his words my words would not have been.

M.D.T.

A Fine New Car

It was hot. Mississippi hot. Although it was October, the day was unusually muggy and sticky and everything seemed to sweat. Overhead the sky was thinly streaked in pale runner clouds that did nothing to block out the sun, and little stirred along the rusty roads and in the cotton fields. Most folks with good sense, and that included Christopher-John, Little Man, and me, had found themselves a shady spot and settled there. Sitting in the mule-hitched wagon under the wide-spreading branches of a white oak at the corner of Soldiers Bridge Crossroads, we were thankful for the shade as we waited for the bus from Jackson to arrive. We were waiting for our eldest brother, Stacey. He was supposed to be coming home today.

I glanced impatiently up the road. 'Wonder what's taking that bus so long?' Neither Christopher-John nor Little Man said a word, though I knew they were as tired of waiting as I was. Christopher-John, alone on the wagon seat, didn't even bother to turn around and look at me. Little Man in back with me, both of us perched on the sideboard of the wagon for a better view of the road, didn't look at me either. They both just kept gazing east, up the road. 'Now, this is just ridiculous!' I grumbled. 'Having to wait this long! Been here more than an hour. I could've been home. I got things to do!'

Christopher-John now glanced back. 'You know, Cassie, bus most times is late.'

'Maybe so, but that doesn't make it right!' I argued, knowing perfectly well that what he said was true. Still, what I said was true as well. The bus should have been here on time and I did have plenty of things to do and should have been home doing them. After all, tomorrow

1

when Stacey headed back to Jackson, I would be going with him, for I now attended school in Jackson and had been doing so for the last two years, since the fall of 1939. Actually, I should have already been in Jackson, for school there had started some weeks back, but just before I was to go, I had come down with what Big Ma called the walking pneumonia and I was only now feeling good enough to leave home. Once I got to Jackson, there would be a lot of school work for me to make up if I was going to be graduated at the end of the school year, and that had me worried a bit. I couldn't afford to fail. Thinking on that, I snapped out another condemnation against the tardiness of the bus. 'Bus supposed to be here at a certain time, it ought to be here!'

Christopher-John, a stalwart-looking boy of fifteen, was not much one for arguing, especially not arguing some useless point. He just looked at me, shrugged, turned, and faced the road again. I gazed at the road as well, hoping to see the rising dust and then the Jackson bus.

But the bus didn't come.

I sighed and looked around. We sat at the northeastern corner of the crossroads just east of Soldiers Bridge that crossed the creek called the Little Rosa Lee. As on two of the other corners of the crossroads, forest land of white oaks and long-leaf pines and bushes of heavily ladened hazelnut grew densely upon it. Across the road on the fourth corner of the crossroads stood the Wallace store, central to most of the community and frequented by most folks around. On this Saturday morning the store was doing slow business. There were only a pickup truck and a wagon parked in front of it. Several grey-board houses belonging to the Wallace clan stood behind the store, while in front was one lone gas pump. Standing under the shading of the porch, looking as if they were also waiting for the bus, were two ruddy-skinned men with travelling bags at their feet. They had been waiting as long as we had.

'I expect they're tired of waiting too,' I surmised.

Little Man, also known as Clayton Chester, the name he more and more insisted upon being called these days, glanced over at the store; then he stood in the wagon and stretched. Little Man was a handsome boy of fourteen, slight – a bantamweight – with reddish-pecan brown skin like Papa's and Indian-like hair combed straight back. He looked halfway cool despite the heat, but then again, he most times did look cool. He worked at it. 'Maybe we should've gone to Strawberry and picked Stacey and them up,' he suggested.

'Would've taken us all morning in the wagon,' Christopher-John pointed out.

Little Man sat back down. 'Too bad Papa didn't get back with the truck. Could've driven it.'

I laughed. Strawberry was the nearest town, twenty some miles away, and the bus would be stopping there before coming here, but I knew that convenience wasn't the only reason Little Man wanted to go to Strawberry. 'Aw, you just want to get up to town and see that little ole girl live there you call yourself liking.'

Little Man grinned, not denying that was partly true. Little Man was becoming quite a ladies' man. 'Leastways we wouldn't have to be waiting here.'

'Naw, we wouldn't. We would just be sitting up there in Strawberry doing mostly the same thing.' I knocked away a fly buzzing annoyingly close to my face. 'I tell you one thing. That bus doesn't come on, I'm going back home.' Both Christopher-John and Little Man nodded as if that was to be expected and didn't try to dissuade me. I wiped my brow with the back of my hand and grumbled on. But with neither of the boys paying attention now, I soon grew silent. I placed an elbow on each knee and propped my chin in my hands. A slight breeze stirred and my skirt, which had draped between my legs, billowed up. Irritated, I slapped the skirt downward. That was one of the things I hated about wearing skirts and dresses on a day like today when a body should have been in pants. A person couldn't even sit the way one wanted in a skirt, but that made no difference to Mama and Big Ma, who forbade me to wear pants. They said pants weren't ladylike. More than likely, they would have said the same about my sitting on the side of this wagon, but it seemed to me, nothing much I did these days was ladylike, now that I was seventeen. I sighed at the miseries of ladyhood.

3

Christopher-John suddenly turned. 'Y'all hear that?' he said. 'Something's coming.'

Little Man and I both listened, for Christopher-John had a keen ear. We heard an engine, but the sound was coming west from the bridge, not from the east. 'Wrong direction,' I said. Still, we all looked toward the bridge waiting to see what was coming, and soon a pickup truck appeared. It came up the road and parked in front of the Wallace store. Two young men hopped down from the back, and two others got out of the cab. One of the young men was blond and slight. He was Jeremy Simms. The other three were his cousins, Statler, Troy, and Leon Aames, all brothers. Jeremy glanced across the road at us as he stepped onto the porch of the store and gave a nod. We nodded back. Jeremy was all right, but I wouldn't have taken a nickel for the other three put together. The four of them went into the store. Still looking at the store, I said, 'Hope we get away from here before Statler and them come out messing.'

Christopher-John agreed. Little Man, though, said nothing as he turned moodily away. Little Man had a strong dislike for the Aames brothers as we all did. He was silent for some moments, then looking southward, he said, 'That Harris coming up yonder?'

I turned to look and saw a figure lumbering slowly up the road. 'Can't be anybody but Harris,' I quickly noted, for Harris Mitchum could hardly ever be mistaken for anybody else. Harris was a right sizeable boy. The same age as I was, and at about the same height, Harris weighed a good three hundred-fifty pounds. Wearing a pair of giant, baggy overalls and no shirt, he moved awkwardly up the road, dabbing at his face and neck with a dishtowel-sized hand-kerchief. As he drew closer, we yelled out to him. "Ey, Harris!'

"Ey!' he returned. He passed the store and came over to the wagon. 'What y'all doin' here?'

'Waiting on Stacey,' replied Little Man.

'They ain't come in yet?'

'Bus is late,' I explained. 'What you doing here? Figured you'd be in the fields what with all the cotton to pick.'

Harris grinned sheepishly. 'I . . . I kinda sneaked off. Too hot to work.'

4

'Well, you right about that. We left the fields a good two hours ago.'

'You know you lucky, Cassie. No more picking cotton for you after today. You still leaving for school tomorrow, ain'tcha?'

'Tomorrow afternoon sometime. Papa and Mama, they're going to be driving me up in the truck.'

'Stacey and them, they goin' back with you then?'

The 'them' he spoke of were two of Stacey's best friends, Moe Turner and Little Willie Wiggins, both of whom were from down here too, but who, like Stacey, now worked in Jackson at the box factory. 'How else you think they're getting back?' I said. 'Bus won't be here again until midweek. Fact, they couldn't've even come home today if Papa wasn't going to be driving back, not if they're going to be at work come Monday morning. They took off work today as it is. They're supposed to work Saturdays.'

'Yeah, I know,' said Harris, stepping away. 'Well, I best get on in this store. Gotta get me some shells for my shotgun.'

Little Man's interest was quickly whetted. 'You going hunting?' he asked. Little Man loved to hunt.

'Yeah . . . gonna hunt me some squirrel.'

'When you going?'

'I get me a break from my grandmama, next week sometime. Goin' huntin' for coon t'night, though, me and Clarence.' He was silent a moment, then looked at us with anticipation. 'Y'all wanna come? Me and Clarence, we done got the traps ready and everything. We could have ourselves a good time. Stacey and Moe and Willie come, why, it be like old times, 'fore y'all gone t'Jackson, Cassie. All us huntin' down on the Rosa Lee . . .'

'Well, it depends on Stacey and Willie and Moe, what they want to do,' said Little Man, 'but I figure they'll most likely want to come along.'

'Well, y'all let me know.'

'Yeah, sure will.'

Harris gave a wave. 'I see y'all in a bit. Bus come and I'm in the store there, tell Stacey and them not t' get 'way from here 'fore I holler at 'em.'

As he started across the road I jumped off the wagon and

5

stopped him. "Ey, Harris! Wait up a minute. I'm going in with you.'

Christopher-John scowled down at me. 'Cassie . . . you know you're not supposed to be going in that store.'

Yes, I did know that. 'I want to find out about that bus. See if those folks in there know something we don't about what's keeping it.'

My reason did nothing to quell Christopher-John's disapproval. 'Every time we set foot in there, Cassie, there's trouble, and we don't need any more trouble. You know we got no business in that store.'

That was sure enough the truth, all right. Our family and the Wallaces had had more than one run-in. Besides that, long ago Mama and Papa had set the store off limits to us; they didn't want us going in. Yet, too, more than one time we had defied that ruling. 'Don't worry, won't be any trouble,' I said as Little Man also got down. Christopher-John, frown lines furrowing, said nothing more as Little Man and I joined Harris and crossed the road to the store. At the steps we heard laughter coming from inside, stopped, and glanced through the screen doors. We saw the storekeeper, Kaleb Wallace, leaning against a counter doing the talking, and Jeremy Simms, the Aames boys, and some other white men seated at a table drinking soda pop. Everybody in the store was white, and except for Jeremy, we had no good words for them.

Little Man now hesitated. 'You know, Cassie, maybe Christopher-John's right,' he said, calmly assessing the situation without the heat of his sometimes fiery temperament. 'Maybe we best not go in, not with Statler and them in there anyway. You know how they like to start messing.'

I glanced back into the store, knowing he was just as right as Christopher-John had been. 'But I want to find out about that bus – '

'I'll find out for ya, Cassie,' Harris volunteered. He had no restrictions set on him about the store. 'I gots to go in for my shells anyways.'

'Thanks, Harris. We'll wait here for you,' I said, and he went on in.

As Harris stepped into the store, Kaleb Wallace glanced over, then paid no more attention to him. Kaleb Wallace was in the middle of telling a story, and despite his new customer, he went on with his story in a most leisurely fashion. Harris didn't say a word. He just stood at the far end of the counter, away from the others, patiently waiting for Kaleb Wallace to conclude. When the story finally ended, Kaleb Wallace turned to Harris and greeted him. "Ey, there Harris! What bring you in here, boy? Your Grandma Batie needin' herself some more snuff already?'

'No, suh,' answered Harris, ignoring Kaleb Wallace's belittling tone. 'Come in for some shells.'

'Shells?'

'Yes, suh. Figures to go huntin'.'

'That a fact? Wheres 'bout?'

'Down 'long the Rosa Lee.'

'Well, what ya huntin'?'

'Squirrel,' said Harris.

'Squirrel?' retorted Kaleb Wallace. 'Why, boy, don't you know it's coon huntin' season now!'

'Yes, suh, sho does. Already gots my traps ready to set. We be huntin' coon t'night – '

Statler Aames let go a laugh, taking a sudden interest in the conversation. 'Coon! That's a good one. Coon huntin' coon! You ever heard the story 'bout the coon and the monkey, boy?'

There was a pause from Harris before he answered. 'N-no, suh, Mr Statler . . . I don't believes so.'

'Oh, Lord,' I muttered to Little Man, 'he's about to start up.' Little Man concurred with a nod. Statler Aames and his brothers got a big kick out of teasing coloured folks, and for the most part all coloured folks could do was stand and take it, for white folks ruled things, and talking back to them with a smart mouth could only get you into big trouble. Hitting one of them could get you killed. That was the way of things.

'Well, seems there was this monkey was hunting this coon,' said Statler, getting on with his story, 'and this ole monkey, he chases the coon up a tree. Then he gets the coon cornered, but he ain't been able to get his hands on him. 'Stead, the coon, he shines a light on the monkey and say, you lookin' for me? And the monkey, he says, yeah, I'm lookin' for you all right, and see I done got ya too. And

7

the coon, he says, well, come on up! Well, then the coon, he turns off the flashlight, and the monkey, he hurries after him. When he gets to the top of the tree, he hollers to the coon, where are ya, coon? And the coon, he shines a light on the monkey, and the monkey looks down and sees that ole coon is out the tree and standing on the ground. And the coon says, I guess it's true what folks say. And what's that? asks the monkey. And the coon, he says, monkey see, monkey do!' With that Statler howled with laughter; so did Leon and Troy, Kaleb Wallace, and the other men, all except Jeremy Simms, who fingered his soda bottle and looked down solemnly at the table. Harris smiled politely. Then Statler said to Harris, 'Now, just which one are you, boy? The monkey or the coon?'

Harris grinned awkwardly and stepped away from the counter. Statler laughed again and didn't press him to answer. But Kaleb Wallace said, 'Where you goin', Harris? You ain't yet got your shells.'

Harris apologized. 'No, suh, I guess I ain't,' he said, and stepped back to the counter. Kaleb Wallace got the shells, and Harris thanked him, paid for them, and turned to leave. He got as far as the door, then Statler started in on him again.

"Ey, fat boy!' he called. 'You sure you wanna be huntin' coon, hot as it is?'

Harris looked around. 'Gets hungry, Mr Statler, no matter what the weather.'

'Yeah, well, we can tell that. See you got a mighty fine appetite there.'

Harris nodded in silent agreement and again turned away.

'Boy!' Statler got up and stepped toward him, 'Ya know, my brothers and my cousin here, we been thinkin' on doin' some huntin' ourselves tonight. How'd you like to join us?'

Harris looked baffled at the invitation. 'Well, suh, that's kindly of ya, but Clarence Hopkins and me, we was gonna go down to the Rosa Lee – '

'Clarence and you, huh? You sayin' you ain't wantin' to hunt with us?'

I knew Statler was only teasing. Maybe Harris knew it, too, yet he looked cautiously around at the others before he

replied, and when he did, fear was in his voice. 'Why –
why, no, suh, I ain't sayin' that – '

'I find that insultin'.'

'Why, no, suh . . . ain't meant it t' be. I was jus' sayin' – '

'Or maybe you too dumb to know when you insultin'
somebody. Listenin' to you here, I'm thinkin' maybe you
make a better monkey than a coon. Seem like to me you a
bit too dumb to make a good coon. I'm figurin' a coon's too
smart for you, boy. But you tell me, Harris, which one you
figure you be?'

Harris stared at Statler in fearful silence, his mouth
agape.

'Well, answer me, boy!'

'I – I – '

'He can't answer, Stat,' said Leon, grinning, 'Maybe he
can show ya.'

Statler smiled at the suggestion. 'Yeah . . . yeah, that's
an idea, all right. Harris, go 'head and show us how good a
monkey you can be. Show us how a monkey act.'

Poor Harris just stood there with his bag of shells, not
knowing what to do. Little Man looked at me and I looked
at him and we were uncertain what we could do to help
Harris. But then Jeremy got up and said, 'Ah, Stat, leave
him be.'

Statler turned. 'What you say there, Cousin?'

'Said . . . said, leave him be. He ain't done nothing.
Harris, you go on.'

Harris looked from Jeremy to Statler and waited for
Statler's approval. Statler silently studied Jeremy, then
said, 'How come you always defending niggers, Jeremy?'

Jeremy shook his head. 'I – I ain't defendin' him. He just
wasn't doin' nothin'. Just figure you oughta let him go on
and leave.'

Statler stared long at Jeremy, then gave Harris a nod.
'All right, boy, you go on.'

Harris gratefully hurried out, passed Little Man and me,
and crossed the road to the wagon. We followed. Christopher-John took note of our faces and got down. 'What is it?'
he asked, but Harris didn't answer. So I did.

'Statler Aames and them were in there messing with
Harris,' I told him. 'Somebody needs to knock him out!'

9

'Wish it could be me,' said Little Man vengefully, then slammed the flat of his hand against the side of the wagon.

'It ... it don't matter,' said Harris, shrugging off the humiliation. 'He ain't meant nothin'.'

'He'd've meant something if you'd've talked back to him!' I surmised.

'Cassie,' said Christopher-John, shaking his head in sympathetic admonishment for Harris.

I looked at him and was quiet. I knew he was right. Again. Harris probably was feeling bad enough without hearing from me.

Harris looked meekly at me in apology. 'I ... I'm sorry I ain't found out 'bout the bus, Cassie.'

'Ah, don't worry about it,' I said with a sigh. 'They probably didn't know anything anyway.'

'Jeremy, he wasn't messing, was he?' asked Christopher-John as Jeremy came out onto the porch.

Harris looked over. 'Naw. He don't never mess.'

We watched Jeremy speak to the ruddy-faced travellers, then start across the road toward us. As he neared, Harris stepped around to the other side of the wagon.

'How y'all doin'?' asked Jeremy, joining us.

'All right. Yourself?' we said.

'All right, I 'spect, 'ceptin' for this heat.' He pulled out a handkerchief and wiped his neck. He looked at the wagon. 'Y'all here pickin' up a load?'

'We waiting on Stacey,' said Little Man.

'Stacey? He coming in from Jackson?'

'S'pose to be. Got a letter from him the other day, and he said he was. Little Willie and Moe coming, too, but the bus is late.'

'Well, it most times is.'

I turned, disgusted at that same fact being pointed out. 'Anybody say anything inside about how come it's late?'

Jeremy shook his head. 'Don't figure there's cause for worry, though.'

'Suppose not.'

He glanced up the road, as if expecting the bus any minute, then looked again at me. 'You going back to Jackson with Stacey this time, Cassie?'

'Suppose to.'

"Spect you lookin' forward to it.'

I shrugged. 'Not all that much. I get homesick way up there in Jackson.'

'Well, you been going up there the last two years. Figure you'd be used to it by now. Y'all stay with kin up there, don't ya?'

'Yeah, but I still get homesick. It's not home.'

"Ey, Cousin!' Jeremy turned. Statler, Leon, and Troy had just stepped out to the porch. 'Thought you said you had to go!' called Statler. 'See you got time to talk and pass a spell with that gal Cassie there.' He grinned over at me, ignoring the fact that all the boys were standing there too. 'Course, I don't much blame you for that, now.'

Little Man's jaw tightened, and I cut him a hard look, warning him to keep his silence. He balled his fists, jammed them into his pockets, and looked away.

Jeremy's face reddened, and he stepped back. 'I'm . . . I'm headin' home now.'

'Want us to run you up there?'

'No. I'll walk.'

'All right, then. See ya t'night?'

'Yeah, see ya.' Jeremy nodded us a silent good-bye, turned, and walked away to the south. Statler, Leon, and Troy remained on the porch awhile talking to the two travelling men, then they got into their truck and headed west, back toward Soldiers Bridge.

Harris, too, prepared to leave. 'Was hoping to holler at Stacey and them, but 'spect I best get on home,' he said, "fore Ma gets t' missin' me.'

'Wait,' said Christopher-John gazing back up the eastern road. The rest of us including Harris looked that way too and waited for we figured Christopher-John had heard something, and he had. Soon a bus was speeding toward us. It passed the wagon, pulled in front of the store, and stopped, and Christopher-John, Little Man, and I hurried over. Harris stayed by the wagon. Impatiently, we waited as the bus door opened and the bus driver and several people got off; Stacey, Willie, and Moe weren't among them. We kept on waiting, checking the windows all the while to see if maybe they were just slow in gathering up their things. But then when the two men who had been

11

waiting on the store porch picked up their bags and got on, and so did the driver, who shut the door, turned the bus around, and continued on west toward the bridge and Smellings Creek, we realized that Stacey, Moe, and Willie weren't coming home.

'Now, just where the devil are they?' I exclaimed as the bus sped away.

Christopher-John shook his head. 'Maybe they're still in Jackson.' Disappointment was all across his face.

We returned to the wagon. 'They ain't come?' said Harris.

'You see them standing here?' I snapped.

'I don't understand it,' said Little Man, his voice flat. 'Stacey said he was coming, and it's not like Stacey to go change his mind, not after he said he was coming.'

Christopher-John nodded agreement with that, then frowned and stared again up the road. 'Y'all ... y'all don't s'pect maybe something done happened to them?'

I sighed and climbed back onto the wagon seat. 'Boy, don't go to worrying, now. They probably still sitting up in Jackson, doing just fine. In any case, they won't be coming now. Let's go.'

Little Man took one more look up the road, and then got on in back. 'Come on, Harris,' he ordered. 'We give you a ride far's your road.'

Harris nodded his thanks and heaved his tremendous body up and sat on the edge of the wagon bed with his legs hanging over. Christopher-John turned to climb on as well, but then stopped and glanced again at the road. 'Boy, stop wasting time,' I said, not in the best of moods and certainly not wanting to spend any more time here.

'Something else coming.'

'Well, that's got nothing to do with us.' We all knew that there would be no more buses from Jackson, and I wasn't interested in anything else. 'Boy, get on this wagon and let's go!' I ordered.

Christopher-John obeyed. As he settled down beside me and took up the reins, a car came into view. Christopher-John waited for it to pass before heading the mules out. The car, wine-coloured and with chrome shimmering in the October sun, came full speed up the road. As the car drew near, it slowed, then pulled right in front of the mules and stopped. In silence, we stared at the car, wondering what it was doing stopping in front of us. Then the driver's door opened and a handsome young man, tall and slender, wearing a short-sleeve shirt, dress pants, and a fedora stepped out.

It was Stacey.

'Well, aren't you all going to speak?' he said.

I spoke, all right. 'Boy, what are you doing driving that car?'

Stacey just grinned as Moe Turner, tall, thin, and cocoa skinned, got out on the other side, and Little Willie, a runt of a young man, got out the back. They were grinning too.

Little Man jumped over the side of the wagon and ran to Stacey. 'Where'd you get the car?' he asked eagerly as Harris and Christopher-John got down too. 'What you doing with it?'

'You like it, Clayton?'

'Why, sure I do, but – '

'Then, that's good!' Stacey slid his hands into his pants pockets and leaned toward Little Man as if to share a secret. 'Because I bought it. It's mine.'

Little Man let go a whoop of a yell and got inside. Christopher-John walked slowly around the car in awe. Harris, too, eased closer. Now I got down from the wagon and took a better look. The car was a Ford, I knew that, and it looked like new. Despite the road dust that had settled on it, there was a shine to all the chrome and a soft sheen to its wine colouring. It had whitewall tires and there wasn't a dent or a scratch anywhere on the body. Inside, the felt grey upholstery was spotless and unworn and the dashboard was all wood and chrome and gleam. Even the rug mats hardly looked stepped on. It was a fine-looking car.

I turned to Stacey. 'Where'd you get the money to buy a new car?'

'Car's not new,' he replied. 'It's a '38.'

I looked again at the Ford and frowned. 'Well, it sure looks like new. Where'd you get the money for it?'

'Saved it. Told you I was going to get a car.'

'Yeah, but I thought you were talking about next year sometime.'

Stacey wiped the dust from the right sideview mirror with his fist. 'Was. But that was when I was thinking to pay cash.'

'When'd you change your mind about that?'

Little Willie laughed. ''Bout ten o'clock this morning, wasn't it, hoss?' Then he took over answering my questions, and that was just as well since Stacey could be awfully tight-lipped sometimes. 'That was 'bout the time when Stacey got tired of riding that bus!' Little Willie was some eight inches shorter than Stacey and Moe, both of whom measured a little over six feet. I was even taller than Willie, but height didn't bother Willie. He talked as if he were eight feet tall. Like Stacey and Moe, he was twenty, near to twenty-one, an assured young man with all the world before him. 'Ya see, lotta coloured folks was on the bus travelling today, and the back seats got all filled up. So some folks had to stand. Course, now, there was some empty seats up front, where the white folks sit, but you know we couldn't hardly sit up there, so folks had to stand and that done included the three of us. By the time we got to Strawberry, ole Stacey, he was mad as a dog! Wasn't you, hoss?'

'You telling the story,' Stacey said quietly.

'Yeah, you was mad all right! We got into Strawberry, and Stacey said he wasn't going one more foot on that bus, and my boy got off!'

Stacey laughed. 'See you got off too.'

'Yeah, course we did! Had to keep an eye on you, man! Thought you'd gone mad, talking 'bout buying yourself a car! Moe and me, we followed the boy, not knowing how we was gonna get ourselves home. Followed him straight to Mr Wade Jamison's office and listened to him bargain himself a deal for this car right here! Used to be Miz Jamison's!'

I studied the car anew. No wonder the car looked so good. Mr Wade Jamison was a lawyer in Strawberry whose wife had died two years ago. I turned to Stacey, 'Well, what kind of deal you make?'

Stacey smiled modestly. 'Well, I told Mr Jamison I knew he most likely wouldn't want to part with the car, seeing it belonged to Mrs Jamison, but if he was willing to part with it, I'd like to talk about buying it. He said he'd sell it to me on time, so I put every penny I had in my pocket on it, and Mr Jamison said he'd give me a year to pay off the rest. I figure to pay it off 'fore the year's out, though.'

Little Man sat behind the steering wheel. 'Well, it sure is something, all right.'

'Yeah ...' murmured Christopher-John in admiration. 'Yeah ...'

'It's got a few little problems,' said Stacey. 'Heater doesn't work very well, and the engine seems to be missing.'

'Well, I can take a look at that for ya, Stacey,' Harris volunteered eagerly. 'Maybe the carburettor just needs adjusting a bit.'

'Well, I'd be obliged, Harris,' Stacey said, and put up the hood.

Harris was good at mechanical things. Though there weren't those many coloured folks with cars in the community, a few had trucks and farming equipment that needed fixing from time to time, and for the last couple of years Harris had managed to keep mostly everything running. He studied under the hood, then asked Stacey if he had a screwdriver. Stacey got him one from a toolbox in the trunk and Harris adjusted the carburettor with it. 'Give that a try,' Harris said, grinning. 'Oughta help.'

Stacey told Little Man to start the car. It sounded good. Stacey smiled his appreciation. 'Why, thank you, Harris.'

Harris carefully lowered the hood. 'It's a fine car you got here, Stacey,' he said, wiping a spot with his handkerchief that his fingers had smudged. 'One of these days I'm hopin I can get me a car and fix it up. Got that ole wreck of a truck runnin' my grandpap used to have. Only thing is, can't 'ford no gas for it.' He looked longingly at the Ford. 'Sure would like t' see how this one runs.'

'You on your way home?'

'Yeah.'

'Well, I'm going to take Little Willie up to his place. Seeing yours on the way, be glad to take you too.'

Harris was elated at the offer. He grinned widely, then hurried into the back.

'I best take the mules on home,' said dutiful Christopher-John, although he looked at the car with some regret that

15

he wouldn't be getting to ride in it, not now, anyway. 'I'll let Mama and Big Ma know y'all here.'

'How's everybody?' asked Stacey.

'Fine. Papa's not home, though. He went down south of Smellings Creek early yesterday morning to do some work. S'pose to be back late today sometime.'

Stacey looked at me. 'Speaking of how folks doing, how you feeling, Cassie?'

'Good enough to be going back to Jackson tomorrow,' I said.

He smiled. 'Good. Now I can take you in my new car.'

Christopher-John climbed onto the wagon. 'S'pose I'll see y'all in a bit.'

'All right,' Stacey said, giving him a wave, then he opened the car door to get in. Little Man slid over, and I got in on the other side, leaving Little Man to sit in the middle.

I turned around and looked at Moe as he got in the back to sit beside Little Willie, and said, 'Got something to tell you, Moe.'

'What's that?' asked Willie, as if I had been talking to him.

'Your name Moe?' I questioned.

Moe flashed his sweet, dimpled smile at me and my upbraid of Willie. Little Willie just shrugged. 'What is this? Something I can't hear?'

'I want you to hear it, I'll tell you,' I said.

'Well, be that way,' shot back Willie, as if I had hurt his feelings; but I wasn't worried that I had. Willie and I were always speaking our minds to each other, and neither one of us took offence to what the other one had to say. Being with him and Moe was the same as being with my brothers. We were all too close and knew each other too well to go taking offence.

'What is it, Cassie?' asked Moe quietly, still smiling. 'What you got to tell me?'

I cut my eyes at Willie. 'I'll tell you later.'

'Yeah, she tell you later,' said Willie, ''cause she ain't decided yet if she want me to hear it. But don't you go feeling bad now, Moe, 'bout you and her keeping secrets

16

from me. I'll find out sooner or later what she feel so important I can't hear.' He grinned. 'I got my ways.'

'Uh-huh,' I said as Moe shook his head and Little Man and Stacey laughed at my usual duel of words with Willie. Then Stacey started the car, honked the horn in good-bye to Christopher-John, and sped south down the road, past Jefferson Davis School, where the white students attended, then turned east. Soon we passed the grounds of Great Faith, where mostly everybody in the Negro community attended church and where children of the community attended school. Not too far from Great Faith was where Harris lived. As we neared the trail leading to Harris's place, we saw Clarence Hopkins standing on the road talking to Harris's sister, Sissy. Sissy was Harris's twin, though you'd never know it to look at the two of them. They didn't look a thing alike. Stacey honked the horn, and Little Willie poked his head out the window and called, "Ey, you two! What y'all know good?'

Sissy turned, stared at the car, then hollered at Harris as if she hadn't even noticed the rest of us or the new car we were riding in. 'Harris! You come on! We got work!'

Obediently Harris got out of the Ford. As big as he was, Harris was afraid of his sister and most always did her bidding. 'Well, I thank ya, Stacey, for the ride,' he said, running his fingers softly over the side chrome. 'It sure is nice . . .'

'Harris! Ma's waitin'!' Sissy shrieked, then without a wave or hello, she turned and switched up the trail.

'I best go on,' said Harris regretfully. He turned toward the trail, then looked back. "Ey, almost forgot, Stacey, what with the new car and all, but Clarence and me, we goin' coon huntin' t'night. Y'all gonna come 'long with us?'

'Coon hunt?' said Willie. 'Yeah, I'll be on there. Feel like some good coon eatin'.'

'Harris!'

'More than likely, we'll join you too,' said Stacey as Harris backed off. 'We'll talk to you later.'

We said good-bye, and Harris followed Sissy up the trail. Clarence glanced after them.

"Ey, man!' called Willie, his head still out the window. 'You and Sissy fighting again?' Although it wasn't any of

17

Willie's business if they were, the fact of the matter was that Sissy and Clarence had been seeing each other steady for the last two years and they always seemed to be fighting.

'Ah!' scoffed Clarence, dismissing Sissy with a wave of his hand. 'Don't even wanna talk 'bout that girl!' He hurried over to the car. A good-sized boy, well built, and standing some six and a half feet tall, Clarence was another of Stacey's closest friends. He looked the car over. 'Now, whose car is this?' he demanded. 'Tell me, Stace, whose is it?'

'Who you see driving it?' Stacey returned with a wide grin across his face.

'Yours?' Clarence hit the roof of the car and laughed. 'Man, you don't say!'

'It's the truth, hoss!' proudly testified Little Willie, as if the car were his. 'Our boy done signed the papers just this mornin'!'

'Well, I want me a ride!' declared Clarence. 'Y'all move over in back there.' He opened the door and started to get in, but then a truck came roaring crazily up the road, and he slammed the door quickly and jumped out of the way behind the car. The truck passed us, hit a deep pothole, and went careening off to one side and into a muddy ditch. Stacey immediately turned off the car engine and jumped out. The rest of us followed and dashed over to the truck, its right wheels in the ditch and lying almost flat on its side. As we neared, the door exposed to the road opened and a big, red-bearded man attempted to get out. When we saw him, we stopped. We knew the man. He was Charlie Simms. He was Jeremy's father.

Mr Simms poked his head out the window and glowered at us. 'Well, come on! Help us with this door!' he ordered. 'Can't lift it from the inside.'

Clarence climbed onto the truck and lifted the door upward. Mr Simms scrambled out. Jeremy followed.

'Y'all ain't hurt none, are you?' asked Clarence.

Jeremy looked at his father and shook his head. 'Don't think so. Seem like the brakes just gone out on Pa.'

Mr Simms went to the front of the truck, checking the

ditched side, and Stacey said to Jeremy, 'Look like you'll be needing a team of mules to get you out.'

Jeremy sighed. 'Yeah, look that way, all right. S'pose that what come from hurryin'.'

His father came back. 'Whose car is that sittin' there yonder?'

Stacey glanced up the road as if he didn't know what car Mr Simms was talking about. Then he turned back and looked at Charlie Simms. 'It's mine.'

Mr Simms did not look pleased. 'Ain't know'd you had a car, boy,' he said, as if he were supposed to know everything. 'You earning that much money up there in Jackson? When'd you get it?'

His was not a friendly inquiry. 'Just recently,' said Stacey, not bothering to fill him in on the details. The less white folks knew about our business, the better.

Mr Simms stared malevolently at the car, then he went to his truck and pulled out some rope from the back. 'Truck'd do better, but I 'spect y'all can still help. Come on, give us a hand,' he ordered. 'Three of y'all get on down in that ditch, lift the truck level to the road. We'll get this rope here tied to the back end of that car and the other end to the front of the truck, and y'all can pull us out.'

Jeremy stared at his father. 'But, Pa, Stacey, he could tear up his car thataway – '

'Got no time for discussin',' said Mr Simms as he tossed Stacey the rope.

Stacey caught it, glanced at his new car, then looked again at the truck and shook his head. 'I try pulling that truck with my car, Mr Simms, I'll likely tear up my rear end gears.'

'No, you won't,' replied Mr Simms, all knowing. 'Just go 'head, tie that rope on like I said, put it in low gear, and you'll be all right.'

'Pa, we can't ask him to do that. I'll go on home and get the mules.'

Mr Simms turned red-hot. 'Don't you dispute with me! I don't wanna hear 'bout no mules! I got no time to go back for no mules! We needs to make that run to Strawberry, and we needs to make it now! Now, Stacey, you hitch up that rope, boy!'

19

Stacey did not move. Calmly he said, 'Mr Simms, you need a pair of mules to pull that truck out of that ditch.'

'Pair of mules or an engine. Thing is, though, I don't see no mules, and I got no time to go fetchin'. Now, nigger, you do like I say.'

The look in Stacey's eyes hardened as he stared at Mr Simms, but he said nothing. We all knew that there was little he could say, that for the most part, there could be no disputing white folks, despite their insults. If a person did, the repercussions could be terrifying.

'Ain't you heard me? Move!'

In silence, Stacey turned and walked back to the car. Standing beside it, he took off his hat, his shirt, his shoes, his socks as well, and rolled up his pants.

'Hell, boy, wh-what you doin'?' sputtered Mr Simms.

Stacey looked at him again and replied quietly, 'Getting ready to get your truck out.' Returning to the truck, he handed the rope back to Mr Simms. 'But we won't be using my car.' He glanced at the rest of us and stepped into the ditch. Willie, Clarence, Moe, and Little Man, too, all followed his lead. They took off their shirts and shoes and socks, rolled up their pants, and joined him. So did Jeremy. Then together they lifted the truck level to the road and pushed it out of the ditch. Mr Simms stood aside, the rope in his hand, watching stone faced. Once the truck was back on the road, he got in without a word and tried to start it. At the first attempt, the truck sputtered and died. He tried again, and the engine roared to life. He barked for Jeremy to get in.

'We thank y'all for what ya done,' Jeremy said.

Stacey looked at him, glanced at Mr Simms, and replied, 'Well, that's what neighbours do.'

'Jeremy!'

Jeremy looked around, left us with a nod, and got into the truck. Before the door was closed, Charlie Simms stomped on the gas and tore up the road toward Strawberry. He never even said a word of thanks. But that was the way of Charlie Simms. He had been that way for as long as we had known him. There was no changing him now, and we sure weren't going to try. We weren't going to

20

worry about him either. The boys cleaned themselves up as best they could, put their shirts and shoes back on, and we again went on our way. It was too hot a day to worry about the likes of Charlie Simms. Besides, we had a fine new car to celebrate.

Friendships

Moe Turner propped his arms on the wooden fence and stared out at the cotton field stretching flatly toward the woods that separated the Turner plot of farmland from the next plot over. Beyond the woods, beyond that next plot of land, vast acres of the Montier Plantation swept southwards past Smellings Creek. Most of the Montier acreage was farmed by sharecropping families, folks like Moe's family, who lived on the land and gave half or more of their crops to Mr Joe Billy Montier for the right to farm his land.

Standing there beside Moe, I noticed the frayed cuffs and collar of his shirt. The shirt had been perfectly clean before our run-in with the Simmses and their truck – Moe always kept his clothes clean; he washed and ironed them himself. The thing was, though, he never bought himself anything. All his money, except for rent money in Jackson and a few dollars for living up there, went straight to his father. He was the oldest of seven and he took that position seriously. I glanced into his face, noticed how proud he was of the cotton, and I propped my elbows on the fencing and stared out too. 'It's been a good crop,' I said.

'Yeah,' Moe agreed. 'Papa maybe even make a little something after he give Joe Billy Montier his half and pay the expenses.'

'Hope so.'

Moe sighed, his eyes still on the field. Then he turned, looking first at me, then over to where his widowed father stood by the Ford talking to Stacey, and Little Man strutted casually around the car, showing it off to Moe's six younger brothers and sister. Little Willie and Clarence weren't with them. We had already dropped them off. 'That car of Stacey's, it's pretty nice, huh?' Moe said, smiling now.

I took a moment to look at that deep-set dimpled smile of his before I answered. I loved Moe's smile. Moe wasn't what most girls would have called a good-looking boy. He wasn't a bad-looking boy, just all right-looking, except for that smile; it was wonderful. I looked again at the car. 'Yeah, it is. He's certainly proud of it too.'

'Well, he got a right to be.'

'Like that time Uncle Hammer came down from Chicago with that new Packard,' I said, speaking of Papa's older brother who lived in Chicago. Stacey had gotten a lot of his car-loving ways from him. 'We all were sure proud of that car too.'

Moe laughed. 'Y'all weren't the only ones. Every Negro 'round here was proud of that car . . . almost like it was theirs. I know I was.' He turned to the fields once more. 'One of these here days I'm figuring to get myself a car. First, though, I'm gonna buy me that land and give it to my daddy.'

I didn't say anything to that. Moe had been talking this same talk about land for his daddy for as long as I could remember.

'I get the money, I'm going to buy us a nice little piece of land, then there won't be no more sharecropping for this family. Course, I know we probably won't ever have a place big as y'all got. Y'all was lucky, you know, your grand-daddy buying up them four hundred acres all them years ago. Y'all ain't had to worry 'bout trying to get land.'

'No . . . just worry about trying to keep it.'

He nodded, still looking at the fields. 'One day we're gonna have something too. I got my mind set.'

'I know that, Moe.'

He turned suddenly and smiled generously. 'I got my mind set on something else too.'

'And what's that?'

'You.'

I heaved an exasperated sigh. Moe sometimes liked to tease about courting me, but I didn't pay much attention to it. Moe and I were best friends, not courting partners. Besides, up in Jackson he already had himself two girls he was courting. 'Boy, don't be talking that talk to me. I got other things on my mind.'

He folded his arms across his chest and laughed. 'I know. High schooling and college.'

'You're right about that.'

Moe laughed again. 'Yeah . . . so what's this you said you had to tell me? It got to do with schooling?'

I grinned, pleased at my news. I always shared my school news with Moe. 'Got my application from Tougaloo and Campbell College the other day.'

'Already?'

'What do you mean, already? It's October.'

'But you not going off to college till next September.'

'Got to start early on this kind of thing, Moe. I don't want September to roll around again and I don't have all my stuff together. I have to get myself some scholarship money, you know that.'

'Wish I could help you.'

'Well, I thank you, Moe, but you be helping anybody, you best be helping yourself. Besides, I've got plenty of help. Stacey and Uncle Hammer, they're both planning on letting me have some money, and Mama and Papa, they'll do what they can. I get a scholarship, though, I won't have to put a hardship on anybody.'

'Still, wish I could help you.'

I gave him a hard look. 'You know you ought to go ahead and put some money on yourself, maybe even finish school.'

He shrugged. 'Too late for that, Cassie.' He looked past me out to nowhere.

I didn't say anything further. He and Stacey and Willie, too, had all dropped out of high school at tenth grade to go to work. They had all figured that working and earning some money was better than going to school, and I could hardly fault them for thinking that way. There weren't all those many jobs open to educated coloured folks except to teach, and none of the boys had an inclination for teaching. Besides, there were some other jobs around that paid a whole lot better than teaching.

'Cassie!' Stacey called. 'We best be getting home now.'

'All right, I'm coming!' I called back, then looked at Moe. 'You mind what I say, Moe. It's not too late.'

Moe smiled at my persistence and shook his head, and we left the fence and headed over to join the others. Before we reached them, several of Moe's brothers came running up all excited about the car. 'Y'all sure y'all like it, now?' teased Moe at their elation. He wasn't at all bothered that they seemed to have forgotten about the bags of licorice drops he had given each of them upon his arrival. But that was like Moe. It didn't bother him what other folks had or the praise that was coming to them. He had his own goals set.

Mr Turner laughed. 'Mos' likely we ain't gonna hear nothin' else 'ceptin' 'bout this car and them gettin' that ride!'

Moe looked at his father. 'We'll have ourselves a car one of these here days, Papa. Have a car and land too.'

Mr Turner's hard-lined face softened somewhat, and he put a hand on Moe's shoulder. 'All I wants is for y'all young-uns to get grow'd and off this place. Make yo'selves good lives. I ain't worryin' 'bout no car, no land neither.'

'Still, you gonna have 'em. I promise you that.'

I don't know if Mr Turner actually believed that he would ever have either, but he patted Moe's shoulder just the same. The land and the car were Moe's dreams, not his.

Stacey opened the car door. 'Well, we best be getting on. Folks at home probably been looking for us these last couple hours.' He glanced across the car at Moe. 'You going with us on the coon hunt tonight?'

'No, don't 'spect so. Best stay on home and visit.'

'All right, then. Comin' up to church in the mornin'?'

Moe smiled that dimpled smile. ''Spect so.'

'See you in the morning, then,' Stacey said.

Little Man and I said good-bye to Moe and his family and got into the car. Then Stacey started the Ford and we rolled away toward home. We again crossed the Rosa Lee, but this time, instead of taking Soldiers Bridge Road, we took the Harrison Road, which cut east through the Harrison Plantation and onto Logan land. Our land. Coming up from the west, we passed forest on both sides of the road, but as we drew nearer to the house we began to pass fields planted in hay, soya beans, and sugarcane to the right side of the road. To the left of the road the forest still stood. Then the fields ended, and we turned up a long, dusty drive.

To the east of the drive was the house Grandpa Paul-

Edward Logan had built some forty years ago. The house was wood, had a tin roof, and five large rooms. Like many of the other houses in the area, each room had an outside exit. One room, Mama and Papa's room, which also served as the living room, had two exits, one to the front porch and the other to the small side porch which faced the side yard and the driveway. Doors from the kitchen and the dining area opened onto the back porch that stretched along the full rear of the house. Deep green lawns and Mama's flower garden were at the side and front of the house. Beyond the eastern fence the cotton field stretched on and on to a sloping meadow and the magnificent old oak that marked the eastern boundary of our land.

Stacey drove to the barn at the end of the drive, stopped in front of it, honked the horn, and we all got out. Immediately the side door was thrust open, and Christopher-John came bursting out, excited that we had finally made it home. The kitchen door slammed shut, and Big Ma ran down the back porch. Mama came up from the vegetable garden beyond the backyard. Big Ma fussed at Stacey for taking so long to get home, then hugged him tight. Mama looked at the car, looked at Stacey, and worried about his spending so much money. Christopher-John took his turn at the wheel. Then, despite Mama's protests and Big Ma's fussing, Stacey cajoled them into the car and we all went for a fast, dust-spreading ride up the road.

Papa wasn't home yet.

It was near to suppertime when Jeremy Simms came walking up the road. The boys and I were in the side yard washing the dust off the Ford. Stacey wanted the car looking its best on Sunday morning. Although I was supposed to be in the house helping prepare supper, I much preferred scrubbing on the car to standing in the hot kitchen stirring up food on the wood-burning stove. Besides, I was as fascinated by the car as the boys were. As Jeremy came up the drive Stacey stopped to greet him. Christopher-John, Little Man, and I said our hellos and kept on working. Jeremy folded his arms across his chest and nodded undeniable approval of the Ford. 'It's a mighty fine-looking car, all right,' he said. 'Always did admire it.'

26

'So did I,' admitted Stacey.

'That wine colouring, it's right rare.'

'Mr Jamison said he special ordered it for Mrs Jamison. Said it was her favourite colour.'

'Well, Miz Jamison, she took mighty fine care of this car. Course, I don't 'spect she drove it that much, seeing she died a year after she got it.' He paused for some moments, gazing at the car, and the silence with him was not unusual. 'Heard Mr Jamison got it for her 'cause he was doin' so much work in Vicksburg and Jackson these here last few years and he wanted her to have a way to get 'round when he wasn't home there in Strawberry.'

'Yeah, that's what he said.' Still holding the chammy, Stacey leaned against the fence that separated the drive from the side yard and the house and openly admired his new acquisition. 'Course, it's got no radio, and the heater needs fixing, but I figure I can do without a radio, and if I can't fix the heater, I can stand a little cold. Main thing is the engine's good and it runs fine. It was missing a bit, but Harris, look like he fixed that.' He took a pause. 'Got to admit, too, I do like how it shines.'

'Yeah . . . it do shine pretty,' Jeremy agreed. 'Ain't got a scratch on it.' Then he also leaned against the fencing. 'How she ride?' he asked.

'Fine. Just fine,' Stacey answered.

Again Jeremy was silent. He started to speak, then hesitated. Finally he cleared his throat and got on. 'You know, I – I want to thank y'all for helping us out today. On the road, I mean . . . with the truck.' We all looked at him. Jeremy's eyes were dead set on the car as he spoke. 'Couldn't've got outa that ditch without y'all, 'less'n we'd've got hold of some mules.'

Stacey, too, kept his eyes on the car. 'Well, anybody would've done the same.'

'I know my pa, he ain't a easy man. He don't give much to saying thanks, but I just wanted y'all to know we obliged just the same.'

Stacey stepped from the fence. 'Don't matter about your pa. Like I said, anybody would've done the same.'

Jeremy looked at him and nodded. 'Yeah . . . yeah.'

I glanced over at the two of them and once again studied

on Jeremy Simms. That boy had been a puzzlement to me since I had first known him. He had always been friendly; he was like no other white boy I knew. In fact, he was the only white person of manhood age whom we addressed face-to-face directly by his first name without setting a *Mr* in front of it, but we only addressed him at those times when there were no other white folks around, for addressing him so familiarly could get us all, including Jeremy, into trouble. When other white folks were around, we usually did not address him at all, and though we never spoke of it to him, we knew Jeremy understood why.

From childhood Jeremy had seemed to understand. From childhood and days of fishing on the Rosa Lee, days of chasing deer and squirrels through the forest pines, days of just lazing back on soft grass watching puffs of brilliant white clouds and dreaming of nothing more than fried chicken and sweet potato pie, we had had a friendship with Jeremy Simms. It was a cautious friendship. We all treated Jeremy as a distant friend, and Jeremy treated us pretty much the same way too; yet, there was a closeness between him and us that ran deep and was never spoken.

Stacey said nothing else as he left the fence and came back over to the car and dipped his chammy into one of the water pails. Jeremy came over too. 'What she look like under the hood?'

Stacey squeezed the water out of the chammy and glanced back at him. He seemed to understand Jeremy's curiosity about the car. It was a male thing, I supposed, this passion for cars, and in that there was no distinction between black and white. 'You want to take a look?'

Jeremy looked at him with a wide grin. Stacey put up the hood, and the two were soon immersed in talk of carburettors and engines and horsepower. I wondered at them. Stacey, usually almost monosyllabic in his talks with Jeremy, was in his pride, being most expansive as they discussed the car's mechanisms. Jeremy, most times stumbling in his speech in search of words that did not offend, talked almost without pause. Then, amidst it all, Jeremy, his blue eyes bright and his face lit in eager excitement, turned to Stacey and asked: 'You . . . you think maybe I could get a ride in it?'

Stacey's smile faded. White folks most times didn't ride with coloured folks unless the coloured folks were in the white folks' employ and were driving the white folks' car as a chauffeur. Under those circumstances white folks sat in the back seat. There were those times, of course, when white folks gave black folks a lift, but on those occasions black folks sat on the bed of the truck or on the back seat of a car or on the rumble seat, if a car had one. That was just the way it was, and since most coloured folks didn't have cars or trucks to be giving rides, there was never that much question of coloured folks giving white folks a lift. Now Jeremy was asking for a ride in Stacey's new car, and it was an awkward thing.

'Just 'cross the pasture there, back of the barn,' said Jeremy, knowing what he was asking. No one could see them riding in the pasture.

Stacey hesitated, glanced at Christopher-John, Little Man, and me; then he nodded. 'All right,' he said, and opened the driver's door and got in. Jeremy, grinning, ran around to the other side and slid in beside him. Then the two of them took off through the pasture gate onto the meadow grass. Stacey raced the Ford up the pasture and down the pasture and around in circles, and as he did Jeremy's laughter was so loud and hard at the speedy ride that we could hear him from where we stood by the gate. I had never seen Jeremy more joyful. Then they came back through the pasture gate, hollering something we couldn't understand, and continued on down the drive and across the road and up the forest trail on the other side.

'What they say?' asked Little Man.

'I don't know,' I replied, staring after them.

Christopher-John and Little Man stared out at the forest as well, then tossed the water from the buckets and took them into the barn. I started to return to the house and my kitchen chores before Big Ma came out calling for me, but then I looked back to the forest again, and without hesitation I, too, went down the drive, crossed the road, and started up the forest trail. I was curious where Stacey and Jeremy were headed.

I wound my way through the forest. Years ago unwanted lumbermen had come onto our land and cut the trail, but they had cut more than the trail. They had cut down trees that had stood virgin strong for centuries untold. I followed the trail of rotting logs to within several feet of the Caroline, the pond Grandpa Paul-Edward Logan had named for Big Ma. There I stopped, for parked on the bank facing the pond was the Ford. Jeremy and Stacey were inside, and to my surprise Jeremy was now sitting behind the wheel. The front doors to the car were wide open. I stepped behind a pine and didn't show myself. Neither Stacey nor Jeremy saw me.

Jeremy motioned toward the pond and spoke softly. I strained to hear. "'Member how we used to come down here, lay on the bank for a while, and then go wadin' in that water? 'Member how we used to fish?'

Stacey turned so I saw the profile of his smile. 'I remember, all right.'

'And 'member that ole tree house I used to have, just up the ways a bit?'

Stacey grinned. 'Remember you wanted to build us one.'

'Yeah, but ole Cassie, she wouldn't hear of it. She always figured I was kinda crazy sleeping up in that tree – '

'Well . . . you know Cassie – '

'But she was right! I was crazy! I was sleeping up there when it was thunderin' and lightnin' and carryin' on – '

'Yeah, and you kept on sleepin' up there – '

'Till that lightnin' strike hit that ole tree, I sure 'nough did.' The two of them laughed, remembering childhood. Then Jeremy sobered. 'Them was good days, wasn't they, Stacey?'

'Yeah . . . they was,' Stacey conceded.

'Sometimes . . . sometimes I wish they could come back. I mean . . . so's we could still do them things . . . could still do 'em and folks wouldn't mind.' He looked again at the pond. 'I don't know how come things can't be like this all the time.'

Stacey was silent for a moment, then said: 'What you mean?'

'Well . . . just us taking the time like this now . . . talking . . . like when we used to sit here and fish . . .'

'Well . . . that was some years back . . .'

'Yeah . . . I know, but . . .' His voice waned. 'Stacey 'bout my pa . . .'

Stacey looked away from him. 'You already said your words about your pa.'

'Yeah, I know, but . . . he's a hard man sometimes . . . and I – I just ain't wanted y'all t' take no offence. I mean . . . he just got his ways.'

Stacey looked at him again but didn't speak.

'I . . . I know them ways don't set well with some folks . . . coloured folks in particular . . . but, well, Pa's just Pa. He just set in them ways of his, and ain't nothin' to be done 'bout 'em. Him and me, we ain't never much seen eye to eye, but Pa, he believe in his way. Can't see no other. He done tried to make me see his way, too, but it just don't make no sense to me, the way he look at things. Way he look at folks. He got himself a one-set mind, and it don't change.'

'What 'bout yours?'

'Mine?' Jeremy's voice and his face were openly frank as he said, 'Well, to me . . . folks is just folks.' He leaned forward, his arms against the steering wheel. 'I recollect tellin' my pa that one time when he caught me down here playin' with y'all.' He laughed. 'He liked t' wore me out.'

Stacey smiled.

Jeremy shook his head. 'Pa, he been trying to make me see his way long's I can 'member. I was more like my cousin, Stat, he'd be a proud man. He crazy 'bout him.' His arm hugged the wheel, and there was silence between them. Stacey didn't say a word. Jeremy glanced at him, as if embarrassed by his confession, then looked again to the pond.

'Course, now, don't want you to be thinkin' me and Pa buttin' heads all the time. I mean, we ain't much like you and your pa, but we have us our good times. Pa, he a mighty good hunter, and he done learned me good 'bout huntin'. Why, sometimes him and me, we go huntin', be gone all the night, jus' him and me. We bring us home a bagful ever' time, and Pa, he be right proud 'cause I'm a good shot, and I set my sights on something and it don't hardly get away from me.'

Stacey confirmed with a nod that he understood the

feeling Jeremy was talking about. 'Used to hunt a lot these last few years with Papa 'fore I moved up to Jackson. Still like to hunt with him whenever I get a chance.'

'Yeah ... well, you and your pa, even when he was off workin' on that railroad most the year, y'all always was close. Used to see y'all talkin' and jus' a-laughin' with each other.' He clung to the wheel. 'All y'all's close. I done always been admirin' of that ...'

Stacey thumped his hand on the dashboard, and his silence accentuated his awkwardness at Jeremy's confidences.

Suddenly Jeremy released the wheel and sat back, grinning. ''Member that time I give you that old wind pipe I done made? Give it to you one Christmas ... back ... oh ... near to eight, ten years ago now.'

Stacey smiled. 'Yeah ... I remember. Still got it.'

'You don't say!' Jeremy laughed with delight. 'Thought it would've rotted away by now!'

Stacey shrugged. 'Always keep things.'

'What it sound like?'

'Oh, I don't know. Haven't blown it in a spell.'

'But you say you still got it, huh?'

'Yeah ... I still got it.'

'How 'bout that?' Jeremy exclaimed, sounding childlike happy. 'How 'bout that?' Then he looked again at the pond, rested his arm once more on the wheel, and was silent.

In the silence I left the tree and moved away, back toward the house. Jeremy had seemed so happy about Stacey still having that wind pipe, and Stacey hadn't told him that he had put that wind pipe away in a box under his bed that same Christmas Jeremy had given it to him and had not played it since, or at least to my knowledge he hadn't. I certainly hadn't seen it again.

It was some time before Jeremy and Stacey came back up the drive. When they did, Christopher-John, Little Man, and I were waiting at the barn. Stacey was again at the wheel. He parked the car, and as he and Jeremy got out Jeremy looked fondly at the Ford and noticed mud on the newly cleaned tyres. Jeremy frowned, then called to Little Man. "Ey, Clayton, hand me a rag, will ya?"

Little Man went to the backyard where the newly

washed chammies were hung, returned with a couple, and tossed one to Jeremy, who stooped by the front wheel to wipe off the mud. Stacey took the other chammy and told Christopher-John to pull up some water from the well. Then, with Jeremy's help this time, we again wiped down the car. By the time we finished, the car was gleaming once more, and all five of us stepped back proudly to admire our work.

It was then that Papa came home.

He drove the truck up the drive and parked it behind the Ford and got out. Papa was a tall man, lanky, with pecan-brown skin and with a way about him that demanded respect. The boys and I hurried over to greet him. Jeremy, though, backed away, away from the car, and us.

'Well, see you made it home,' Papa said to Stacey.

'Yes, sir, I did,' Stacey returned; then the two hugged in greeting.

With his arm still around Stacey, Papa nodded to Jeremy but did not speak his name. Jeremy nodded back; then, looking like that awkward little boy from years ago, he moved toward the road. 'Best I be gettin' on home now . . . Ma's most likely got supper waitin'.'

Stacey went over to him. 'Well, we thank you for coming.'

'No matter.' Jeremy pushed his hands into his pants' pockets, glanced at Papa, and looked again at Stacey. 'When – when you going back up to Jackson?'

'Tomorrow sometime.'

'Well, I don't see ya, safe trip to y'all.'

'Thank you.'

He nodded farewell to the rest of us, took a few steps, and turned. 'Stacey, it's a fine car, all right. Gonna remember that ride.'

Stacey nodded. 'I'll . . . I'll be remembering it too . . .'

Jeremy nodded again, glanced at Papa once more, then walked down the drive, hands stuffed in his pockets and bouncing on the soles of his feet. Papa watched him, his eyes disapproving. When Jeremy was gone, walking down the road past the cotton fields and out of our hearing, Papa turned to Stacey. 'What was he doing here?' he asked quietly.

Stacey looked after Jeremy and answered just as quietly.

'His pa and him ditched their truck on the road just past Great Faith, and we helped get them out. You know how Mr Simms is. Didn't show any appreciation. Jeremy just came by to thank us for what we done.'

Papa nodded and said nothing else about Jeremy. It wasn't that he didn't like Jeremy; he did. Jeremy always showed him respect. But to Papa's way of thinking friendships that got too close between black and white could only lead to trouble. Papa always kept his distance with white folks, figuring that was the best way. He didn't trust getting too close. He had told us he figured that was the best for us too. He had said long ago that he figured when childhood was over and Jeremy was a man, he would change toward us and go his own way. Even though now Jeremy was twenty, a man grown, and remained the same, Papa still was wary. He figured as long as there was breath, a body could change on you.

Christopher-John stepped forward and sliced the silence. 'Papa! You not going to say anything 'bout the car?' He knew Papa's thinking about Jeremy, as did we all.

Papa glanced at him, at Stacey, then stepped closer to the Ford. 'Well, now, what's this here?'

'It's a '38 Ford, Papa,' I announced proudly, 'and it belongs to Stacey.'

Papa seemed not a bit surprised. His back to Stacey, Christopher-John and Little Man, he smiled at me and winked, then studied on the car and was silent.

'It's something, huh, Papa?' asked Little Man, coming along side him.

Papa didn't answer. Hands in his pockets, he walked slowly around the car, saying nothing.

Stacey looked a bit anxious. He came closer, waiting on Papa's assessment of the car. But Papa, after rounding the car, just grunted and still said nothing. Stacey looked at the car, then back at Papa. Papa's good opinion was a mighty precious thing, not only to him, but to all of us. 'Papa?' he said finally. 'What do you think?'

Papa didn't crack a smile. 'Well, now, I been hearing 'bout a new car all up and down the road. Got stopped three different times by folks braggin' on it . . . Seems you been showin' it off.'

Stacey looked away, his face solemn. 'Wasn't showing off, Papa. Was just taking folks for a ride.'

'You sure 'bout that?'

Stacey looked back at him, 'Well, I suppose the truth is I was showing it off . . . a little.'

Papa grunted again and walked once more around the Ford, giving it another close inspection. Stacey, Christopher-John, and Little Man all stood aside, awaiting his decision, but I knew how Papa felt. The wink had told me all. Finally he came back around and joined us. 'Well, I'd say folks are right. It is something!' He smiled wide and put his arm around Stacey's shoulders. 'Now, when I'm gonna get me a ride?'

Stacey gave Papa a joyous hug, then tossed him the keys, much as Uncle Hammer always did whenever he came down from Chicago with his new cars. 'Right now, Papa!' he said.

'Ah, now, son, look like you just finished cleaning it – '

'Don't matter! We'll clean it again – '

'That's right, Papa!' volunteered Christopher-John, though I, myself, had no intention of chammying down this car one more time. 'We don't mind.'

Little Man opened a back door, eager for another ride. 'Papa, come on!'

Papa laughed and got in the driver's seat. Stacey got in the front with Papa, and I was about to get in, too, when Big Ma came down the back porch. 'Now, where y'all goin'?' she yelled, hand on her hips. Then she squinted. 'David, that you?'

'Yes, ma'am, Mama!' Papa called back. 'We're just gonna take us a ride.'

'Son, don't y'all leave from here! Supper's 'bout on!'

'Won't be but a minute, Mama! My son just done bought himself a car, and I got to take me a ride in it!'

'Well, Cassie, don't you leave from here! You gotta get this here table set and mix up some corn bread – '

'I'll be right back, Big Ma!' I yelled, and got into the car. If all the boys were going, I knew I was going too. While Big Ma continued to fuss Papa turned the car around and we rolled down the drive to the road. It was another glorious ride.

When we got back, more than an hour later, Big Ma was still fussing, but that wasn't unusual. By the time we settled down for supper, she had finally quieted, having vented all her displeasure at having to hold up her supper and about my being no help at all. But then I announced that I was going coon hunting with the boys, and she started up again. My grandmother loved to fuss. 'David, y'all jus' spoils this girl!' she declared, glancing with disapproval down the table to the other end, where Papa sat at the head. She passed the hot platter of golden-fried chicken down to Stacey, then let Mama, sitting next to Papa, have a condemning look too. 'I done told y'all and told y'all time and time again, a hunt ain't no place for a young lady! This girl, she got no business goin' huntin'! That's what menfolks s'pose to do!'

Christopher-John glanced over at her as he helped himself to another slice of corn bread. 'But, Big Ma, it wouldn't hardly be a hunt without Cassie.'

Little Man concurred in that opinion. 'Cassie, she always go when she's here.'

'Go too much, ya ask me!' Big Ma got up and pulled another pan of corn bread from the stove. She slid the bread onto the already near-empty platter, then sat again and went on fussing. 'Boys s'pose t' go huntin', not girls! Boys got men things t' be talkin' 'bout on these hunts, and girls, they jus' ain't s'pose t' have no ear for that kinda thing!'

Papa smiled. 'Well, seems like to me, Mama – and you tell me if I'm wrong here – but seems like I remember the time when Papa was away from home and we ain't had meat for the table and we gone hunting. Now, I recall rightly, it was you gone with me and Hammer down into them woods to hunt us a coon. You recall that, Mama?'

Big Ma got contentious. 'Well ... that was different. Y'all was just little boys and we needed us some meat. Your papa and your brothers Mitchell and Kevin, they was all gone off workin' 'way from here, lumberin' up near that Natchez Trace. Somebody had to put meat on this table!'

Papa took a slice of corn bread. 'I recall, you were a mighty fine shot too.'

'Yeah, I was,' Big Ma admitted, looking a bit prideful

about the thing. Then she frowned at Papa's teasing. 'But that got nothin' to do with Cassie here! She always been too much like these boys as it is. Time she started taking on womanly ways.'

'I got womanly ways,' I contended, not too concerned about where this conversation was headed. I heard it every time I wanted to go on a hunt. 'I cook and I wash dishes.'

Everybody but Big Ma laughed. 'Girl, don't you get smart with me! You knows what I mean!'

'Don't worry, Big Ma,' said Stacey. 'Up in Jackson, Cassie's not so bad. Most times she can be a real lady, and you'd be proud. Suppose, though, that's because she doesn't have any mules to ride up there.' He grinned over at me. I rolled my eyes at him and went on eating.

Papa smiled at the two of us, then said to Stacey, 'Now, Son, what's this you were sayin' 'bout a truckin' job earlier?'

Stacey wiped at his mouth and spoke eagerly. 'Looks like we could be getting on at the trucking company pretty soon now, Papa. Moe, Willie, and me, we all went down and talked to a man over there, and he was saying he was expecting to take on a lot of new workers. He said with all the Army camps opening up and all this defence building going on what with that war over in Europe, they'd have to soon have men pulling overtime.'

'I thought you were doing some overtime work at the box factory,' said Mama, looking a bit concerned at this talk of changing jobs.

'Well, yes, ma'am. But the thing is, Mama, I never planned on making a life's work at the box factory. Trucking pays more money. It'd be a good job, I can get it.'

Mama slowly nodded. 'Well, anytime you can improve yourself, you need to do that, but I think you need to think about the fact you've been at the box factory for over two years now and you've had steady work. Also, you need to keep in mind you just bought yourself a car. Maybe now isn't the best time to quit the box factory.'

'Can't be a better time, Mama. All kind of jobs are opening up and all kind of factories for defence. Now, you know the white folks, they get first crack at all those defence jobs, but they're leaving some good jobs to take those on. That means we get a chance at some of the jobs they're leaving. Some good jobs, too, and I figure to get myself one. Course, I don't figure to quit the box factory until I actually get hired on at the trucking company. Could get hired next week. Could be a couple months yet, but I can wait.'

Papa nodded his approval. 'Leastways that's something good coming out of this war talk.'

'Maybe,' said Mama. 'But I still don't like this talk of sending our boys to fight.'

Stacey shrugged off the possibility. 'We aren't going anyplace, not yet, anyways, Mama. It's just talk.'

Big Ma grunted disparagingly. 'It was just talk, too, when your uncle Mitchell and your Uncle Kevin gone off to fight some twenty odd years back and got theyselves killed, and your Uncle Hammer, he gone off and got hisself all shot up in the leg.'

Stacey reached for more chicken. 'Well, it's not going to be that way with me. I'm going to have myself a good job soon. I'm not planning on anything spoiling that.'

'I hope nothing does,' said Mama. 'I don't want my boys in a war.'

'I wouldn't mind going to fight,' said Little Man. 'Seem mighty adventuresome to me.'

'Not to me,' said Christopher-John. 'Things adventuresome enough right here. 'Sides, I wouldn't want to be pointing a gun at anybody.'

'Would if I had to,' said Little Man.

'Now, boy, you hush!' ordered Big Ma. 'You ain't going to fight no war! Ain't none of y'all boys goin'!'

Stacey laughed. 'Just make sure you let President Roosevelt know that, Big Ma.'

Big Ma grunted. 'Maybe I'll do jus' that!' she said. Then she laughed. We all did.

We were still laughing when there was a knock at the back door. It was Sissy and Harris Mitchum. 'Have some supper with us,' Mama said as Christopher-John and Little Man got chairs for them.

'No, thank ya, Miz Logan,' said Sissy, sitting down. 'We just come back from takin' some cookin' up to Reverend

Gabson's place, and we headed home. Just thought we'd stop by and holler at y'all.'

'Reverend Gabson?' said Stacey. Reverend Charles Gabson was the pastor of Great Faith Church, and he had been ailing for some weeks now. 'He still not up yet?'

Big Ma shook her head. 'Fact to business, he doing right poorly. I been up to they place trying to help out most everyday this week myself. Like for you to run by and see him while's you here, Stacey. He always askin' 'bout you.'

'Yes, ma'am, I'll sure do that. I'll go on by there tomorrow after church.'

'Harris,' I said, 'what time you and Clarence going hunting?'

Sissy took it upon herself to reply. 'Why you askin', Cassie? You not going, are you?'

'I was figuring on it.'

'Well, you gonna figure yourself right out of a boyfriend pretty soon here, Cassie, goin' huntin' all the time.'

I turned on Sissy. 'Well, that don't make me no never-mind!' Mama cast me a reproving look, not because of my pronouncement, but because I had totally fractured my speaking. Mama, being a teacher, had been hard on the boys and me – especially me – these last few years about speaking correctly. She said if we were going to be educated people, we needed to speak that way. 'As I said, it doesn't make any difference to me,' I corrected, as Christopher-John and Little Man grinned at me knowingly. Mama nodded, satisfied, and I turned back to Harris. 'Harris, what you say? What time?'

'Well, I got no mind for huntin' myself,' Sissy went on, not giving Harris a chance to respond.

'Leastways, somebody actin' like a lady 'round here!' said Big Ma, heartily approving of Sissy's attitude. 'I been tryin' t' tell this girl she got no business goin' huntin'!'

'I was talking to Harris,' I muttered.

Big Ma laid a fierce glance of suffering on me, then said to Sissy and Harris: 'Y'all not gonna have any of our supper, least have some of my blackberry cobbler. There's plenty.'

'No, ma'am, thank ya, Miz Caroline,' said Sissy. 'We don't care for anything.'

'What 'bout you, Harris? I know you loves my blackberry cobbler.'

Harris looked at Sissy as if expecting her to answer for this, too, since she took it upon herself to do so much of his talking for him. When she didn't say anything, he looked back at Big Ma and kind of halfway smiled. 'Yes'm, Miz Caroline, I surely do.'

'Then have some. Cassie, go get a plate for Harris.'

I started to rise, then saw Sissy give Harris a poke. The smile left his face. 'No ... no, ma'am, Miz Caroline, don't ... don't y'all bother.'

Big Ma put her hands on her hips. 'Boy, you gonna insult me and my cobbler?'

Harris looked at her wide-eyed. 'Why – why, no, ma'am, I sure ain't! I – '

Sissy took up the talk. 'We just done got up from the table, and we're plumb full,' she explained. ''Sides, we watchin' Harris's weight, and he done had enough. Ain't that right, Harris?'

Harris looked at the floor and agreed it was.

'Girl, why don't you let Harris speak for himself?' I said, feeling right irritated with Sissy about the way she was always talking for Harris.

'Cassie,' Mama admonished, reminding me with one sharp look that this was none of my business.

I heeded the look and kept my silence, though I felt like saying more. Sissy and Harris were such an opposite pair of twins. Sissy was a little bit of a thing and a spitfire of a girl. Harris, despite his tremendous size, was a retiring kind of soul. He messed with no one if he could help it. Their mother was dead and they had never known their father. They lived with their grandma Batie and their great-aunt, Mrs Sarah Noble. I supposed that having no parents was one of the reasons Sissy was always bossing Harris around. But as bossy as Sissy was, she was mighty protective of Harris, too, and would take on anybody who messed with him, especially if somebody teased him about his weight.

'Well, y'all know y'all always welcome to our table,' Papa said and we went on talking about other things.

After a while, when supper was over, Papa and the boys

went out to tend to the evening chores and Harris went along with them. Mama returned to the garden and Big Ma joined her. I was stuck with clearing the table and doing the dishes. As I stacked the dishes, Sissy sat right where she was, not offering a hand, and prattled on and on about my going on the coon hunt. 'Well, Cassie, I just don't know how come you always wanting to go huntin' with them boys,' she said. 'They wanna talk 'bout men things, 'bout they personal business, and how they gonna do that with you sitting all up there?'

I laughed for I could see right through Sissy. She had always been jealous of my friendship with Clarence, with Moe and Little Willie, too, and I knew it was her jealousy that was trying to keep me from the hunt. Still, despite her devious and jealous ways, I liked her. Big Ma said that was because we were so much alike. 'What's the matter, Sissy?' I asked. 'Clarence didn't invite you?'

'Ah, I'm not thinking 'bout Clarence!'

'What he do now?'

She looked sullenly away, her arms folded across her chest, and thought a moment. 'You know what he come telling me today? Said he goin' off and join the Army.'

I picked up the now empty chicken platter. 'Well, you know he's been talking about it.'

Sissy ignored that. 'Talkin' about leavin' me and just going off like we ain't been nothin' to each other. Here I am wantin' to be gettin' married, and he 'round here talkin' 'bout takin' off.'

'Well, maybe you ought to let him. There's other boys around here besides Clarence.'

She turned a hostile gaze on me. 'What do you know? And how come you always takin' his side?'

'Girl, don't be putting me in the middle of this! I got nothing to do with you and Clarence. All I'm saying is there are other boys and other things to be doing, too, besides getting married. You only seventeen.'

'Well, who's askin' you? You got your dreams, and I got mine. You up there studying in Jackson, talkin' 'bout you going to college, thinkin' on the law. It's crazy, but that's your dream and I don't mess with it. You need that dream.

41

Me, I need my dream too. I need my Clarence. He the only dream I got, so don't come messin' with it!'

I laughed. 'Girl, you crazy,' I said, and took a load of dishes to the dishpan. 'Crazy to be worrying about that boy like he's the only one out there.'

'Don't you be laughing!' she chided. 'You seventeen now. You need to be thinking on somebody to marry –'

'Maybe, then, I'll think on Clarence,' I teased.

Sissy gave me a dead stare. 'Naw, not Clarence. I whip anybody mess with Clarence.'

'Now, see, that's just what I mean 'bout this love business. Makes you go crazy. Makes you say and do crazy things. Girl, don't nobody want Clarence but you.'

Now there was a burst of laughter from her. 'Well, then, that's good, Cassie, that's good. 'Cause that way he stay mine.'

'Well, you can sure have him too.'

She got up and gave my arm what was supposed to be a friendly slap. 'Girl, I gotta go,' she said.

I rubbed my arm. 'Well, if nothing else works out and you just set on marrying, you can always get Harris to go take a shotgun to Clarence.'

Sissy laughed once more. 'Harris? Shoot! Harris afraid of his own shadow. He ain't got the backbone of a flea. We going.' I followed her as far as the back door. 'See you at church in the morning, Cassie.'

'All right, see you,' I said and as Sissy went down the porch hollering for Harris, I went back to doing my dishes. When they were finished and the floor was swept and everything was clean in the kitchen, I went off to the room I shared with Big Ma to decide upon a dress to wear to church in the morning and iron it before I left for the hunt. After all, there could be no ironing on a Sunday. I opened the chifforobe and pulled out my two favourite summer dresses, one blue and one red, which were yet to be packed. Standing in front of the mirror, I propped one, then the other against myself. I tossed the red dress on the bed; then, still holding the blue one, I pushed the lone braid hanging at the nape of my neck up to the top of my head and held it there. I always felt sophisticated when I had my hair up. Also, when it was up, I looked even more like

Mama. As it was, I was tall like Mama, slender, tan-skinned, and had the same high cheek bones and long, crisp, thick hair. Mama always wore her hair up, and this time of year on a Sunday, so did I. I held the dress against me again. I liked what I saw.

'Blue one looks mighty nice.' I turned as Mama came in. She felt the soft cotton of the dress. 'Always did favour blue.'

'Yes, ma'am, I know. I like red myself.'

She stood behind me and gazed at me in the mirror. 'You know, sugar,' she said, pulling my braid back down, 'we're going to miss you. We were thinking we weren't going to have to say good-bye until after we took you to Jackson but now that Stacey's come home with a car, you'll be going with him. Have to admit, though, I'm a bit sorry that your Papa and I won't be taking you back. I was rather looking forward to it.'

'Well, Mama, you and Papa can still come.'

'No. There's the cotton to pick so it's better we stay here. We'll get up to Jackson another time.' She smiled, reconciling herself to that time to come, then moved away and sat on the bed. She glanced at the red dress. 'One of these dresses for church tomorrow?'

'Yes, ma'am. Wanted to wear something real nice.'

'That couldn't have anything to do with Moe, could it?'

'Aw, Mama, you know I've got no mind on Moe!'

'I know that's what you keep saying.'

'Well, I keep saying it because that's the truth.' I put the blue dress down, hung the red dress in front of me again, and bragged, 'I do look so good in red.'

Mama laughed and agreed. 'But you also look good in blue, and if I recall, Moe is right partial to blue.'

I laid the red dress on the bed again. 'I'm not dressing for Moe.'

Mama smoothed out the hem and said nothing.

Then I, too, sat on the bed, the dresses between us. 'Mama, you know how I feel about Moe. Moe likes to tease about wanting to court me, but he knows I know he's teasing. Besides, girls start courting, they're thinking on getting married, and pretty soon that's what happens.'

Mama studied me. 'Thought you wanted to get married one day.'

'Yes, ma'am, one day. But I figure to do like you. You went ahead and got your teaching degree before you even met Papa, and you've been teaching ever since, except for that bad spell. You'd've been married, you most likely never would've gotten that degree.'

'Maybe not.'

Mama spread her fingers over the bodice of the red dress, then looked at me. 'Listen, sugar, I want you to go to college as much as you want to go yourself. Wanted that for Stacey, too, but he chose to go to work.' She spoke those words evenly, without emotion, though there had been a time when she had gone 'round and 'round with Stacey about staying in school. 'But I also want you to be honest about Moe and how you feel about him. He's such a fine boy, and you should watch out for his feelings too.'

'Well, I don't have anything to do with his feelings!'

Mama didn't accept that. 'Of course you do.' She glanced at the dresses again. 'Any girl who looks for a special dress to wear for a young man has got to know that.'

'He's my friend,' I said quietly, 'and I want things to stay that way. I've seen how sometimes a boy and a girl be getting along just fine, and then they start seeing each other seriously, and then they break up, they can't hardly speak to each other after that. Been better if they hadn't even gotten together.'

'Well, I don't think Moe would act that way, and I certainly don't think you would.'

'Well, I still figure courting can get in the way of a good friendship. And most times I think that's all there is with us. I mean, I really like being with Moe, and I like it when he pays me some attention. I can talk to Moe about just anything. But, Mama, Moe doesn't stay on my mind like I figure a boy's supposed to, and top of that I don't go getting all excited when I see him. I miss him when he's not around, but I don't be crying about it. I miss him like I miss Stacey, and I figure Moe feels the same about me.'

'And what if he doesn't?'

I grew solemn. I hadn't thought about that. I had just always figured Moe did feel the same. 'Ah, Mama . . . I'd hate to think Moe was feeling something different from the way I feel. I ever thought he was, it'd spoil everything.'

'Spoil what?' asked Big Ma, coming in.

'We were talking about Moe,' I said.

Big Ma just looked at me, then she looked at the dresses. 'Moe got somethin' t' do with all these here dresses on the bed?'

'Cassie's trying to decide which one to wear tomorrow,' Mama said, turning to look again at the dresses herself.

'She oughta be in here packing,' asserted Big Ma, even though she knew perfectly well that my packing had been done for weeks now, since before I was sick. She came over to the bed and scrutinized the dresses, then picked up the red dress. 'I like this one. Moe will too.'

I jumped up and slammed my hand to my hips in vexation. 'Now, what I want to know is how come Moe's name keep coming up about these dresses?'

Big Ma ignored me and thrust the dress toward me. 'Try it on!' she ordered.

Mama laughed. 'Go ahead. Let's see which one shows you off best.'

Feeling a bit exasperated, I took off my blouse and skirt, then slipped on the dress. Mama got up and undid my braid, then combed it out and tied my hair with a ribbon. When she was finished, she and Big Ma stood back satisfied as I pranced around in front of the mirror admiring myself. I was pretty and I knew it. I didn't think much about it, though. It was just one of those things I was, and I didn't dwell on it, except for when I had on something especially nice and was wanting to look my best.

'Don't wear out that mirror, now,' admonished Big Ma, knowing I was thinking I was looking pretty cute. 'Here, try on the blue one here.'

I laughed and started to take of the dress. As I pulled it over my head there was a crisp knock on the door and Little Man called: "Ey, Cassie! Harris and Clarence and Willie, they're here! You still going hunting with us?"

'Course I am!' I hollered through the material, and hurried to get out of the dress.

Big Ma slapped at my arm. 'Girl, hang on there! You

gonna tear this thing.' She helped me out of it, then cast Mama an accusing glance. 'Y'all still gonna let her go?'

Mama smiled at Big Ma's continued disapproval. 'Mama, now, you know she's gone plenty of times before.'

Big Ma sighed in disgust. 'Y'all jus' spoils this girl!' she declared once more. 'Here, give me that dress, Cassie! Whiles you out prancin' 'round them woods, s'pose I best run the iron over one of 'em for ya, you gon' wear it in the mornin'. Which one you gonna wear?' She didn't give me time to answer as she took up both dresses. "Spect I best go and iron 'em both. Knowin' you, you likely to change your mind come mornin'.'

'Thank you, Big Ma,' I said cheerfully, and gave her a quick hug.

'Humph!' she grumped and went on out.

I laughed and hurried into my blouse, then started to pull on my skirt. 'You going hunting with the boys,' Mama said, 'you best wear that old, faded flowered skirt. This one's too nice.'

'What I need to be wearing is a pair of pants.'

'You know how I feel about that.'

'But, Mama, it just makes sense to wear pants!'

'That flowered skirt is washed and ironed and hanging up there in that closet somewhere. You best find it and put it on if you're going. Hunting is one thing, but wearing pants at your age is another. You planning on arguing with me about it, I've got the time. Do you?'

'Suppose not,' I grumbled. 'Wouldn't do any good anyway.'

'I think you're most likely right about that,' she said, heading for the door. 'Be sure you hang up that other skirt before you go. You can take it to Jackson with you and wear it again before it's washed.' She reached the door and looked back at me. 'You look mighty pretty in both those dresses, sugar.'

I smiled. 'Thank you, Mama.'

'You're welcome,' she said, smiling too. Then she left.

Little Man hollered for me again from the porch.

'All right, all right, I'm coming!' I shot back. I grabbed the flowered skirt from the closet and threw it on. Underneath it I pulled on a pair of Stacey's old pants that I kept well tucked away at the back of my drawer, rolled them up above my knees, and hurried out to join the boys. I was eager for the hunt.

The Hunt

The thing about going on a coon hunt was that a body had to be totally prepared, and that included taking along every item of importance. Before we left the house, we made sure we had ourselves a goodly size bag of peanuts, some potatoes for baking, a couple of jugs of cider, a kerosene lantern, matches, a flashlight, hunting knives, hunting bags, a rifle, and an ax. Then we set out for the cane field, where we chopped ourselves some cane. Now that we had all the essentials, we were ready. With three hound dogs along and with Stacey carrying the rifle, we set off for the woods.

The hunt had begun.

Clarence Hopkins led the way into the moonlit forest. The day had cooled considerably and was no longer miserable. A slight wind stirred. When we reached the Caroline, I slipped off my skirt, folded it lengthwise, and hung it neatly on the branch of a pine. The boys paid no attention and walked on. I had done this same thing plenty of times before. I rolled down my pants legs, then ran to catch up with the boys.

Wearing rubber boots to protect our feet from the damp of the forest floor, for some time we walked single file along the trail. Finally we came to the ridge leading down to the Rosa Lee and stopped. Earlier Harris and Clarence had baited several traps with fish, covered the traps with leaves and brush, and secured them to tree roots at the edge of the creek. We decided to wait until later to check them. We left the ridge and moved back into the forest to set up a camp that would be far removed from the traps, so that the dogs wouldn't be drawn to them. Then the hounds picked up a scent and we released them to track the coons. Now we got down to the fun part of the hunt. We gathered some wood and built ourselves a fire, then roasted our peanuts and potatoes, peeled our sugarcane, and settled back around the fire to await the barking of the dogs.

'Won't be long now,' predicted Harris, sipping at a cider jug. 'Ole T-Bone gonna soon be on the scent.'

The rest of us laughed. T-Bone was Harris's dog and had lost whatever hunting skills he was supposed to have practically the day after he was born.

'Ah, man,' said Little Willie, 'that ole T-Bone couldn't smell a coon if you put it right up under his nose.'

'Shoot, I don't even think he know what his nose is for!' declared Clarence.

'Excepting to get him into trouble,' I contended. 'Remember that time we came down hunting with Mr Morrison and old T-Bone was stupid enough to follow that coon down to the water and that coon near to drowned him – '

'Would've too,' said Little Man, 'Mr Morrison hadn't've come along! Old coon just sitting there in the water, holding T-Bone's head under!'

Christopher-John shook his head. 'Poor ole T-bone,' he uttered; then he couldn't keep from laughing.

We all laughed again, and Harris took our teasing in stride. He even smiled himself. He was accustomed to our ridiculing his dog. 'That's all right,' he said. 'Y'all jus' keep on talkin' 'bout T-Bone 'cause he gonna make y'all eat y'all's words. Y'all jus' wait and see. He gonna be the first dog down there barkin'. Why, even Mr Morrison said he had a nose – '

'You know, Harris,' said Stacey, joining in the fun, 'even Mr Morrison could be wrong. He said so himself.'

'But he wasn't often, was he, now?' asked Harris.

Stacey looked at him for a long moment while we all were silent, thinking on the giant man, Mr L. T. Morrison. Mr Morrison had come walking along the road one day with Papa years ago when we all were very young, and had stayed. He had become a part of our family and a part of the community too. He had been special to all of us. Now he was gone. Stacey answered Harris quietly: 'Naw, Harris, naw, he wasn't often.'

'Yeah, but he was that time!' cracked Little Willie, and laughter came back. 'He was here, he'd tell you so!'

We all laughed on, and that included Harris. Then we were merciful and let the subject of poor ole T-Bone rest. For some time after, we ate and laughed and drank our cider, told stories about days past, about hunts with Papa and Uncle Hammer and Mr Morrison, and hunts with Clarence's papa, J. D., and Willie's papa too. We talked and teased each other about days present, including everybody's love life – or lack of it – and gave little thought to raccoons. Then Clarence turned to Stacey on a sudden and said: 'Stacey, like to get me a ride up to Jackson with y'all tomorrow. There room?'

'What you wanna go to Jackson for, boy?' inquired Willie. 'You gonna get a job?'

Clarence grinned. 'Gonna join the Army.'

'What?'

'Yeah. Y'all remember my cousin El live over the other side of Strawberry? He come down here a few summers back.'

'El,' said Stacey. 'Yeah, sure – '

'Well, he done joined the Army!'

'That a fact?'

'Uh-huh, and he come down here on leave couple weeks ago, and we got to talkin' 'bout the Army, and he say it's all right. He talked so good 'bout it, I been figurin' maybe I'd join up myself. What you think, Stacey?'

Stacey took his time before he answered, and that was good, because Clarence thought a lot of his opinion. After all, since childhood, Stacey had pretty much been the leader of their small band of friends that included himself, Moe, Willie, Clarence, and at one time long ago, a boy named T. J. Avery. Willie, though, took no time for pondering. 'I think you a fool,' he said.

'I ain't askin' you!' retorted Clarence.

'Didn't need to ask me. Was happy to tell you without you asking.'

Clarence turned away from Willie, ignoring him. 'Stacey? What you say, man?'

'Well, I tell you, Clarence,' said Stacey, taking the cider jug, 'joining up, it's not something I'd do.'

'Well, you got no cause to!' exclaimed Clarence, defending his action. 'Shoot! Your folks always done had somethin'! And now you up workin' in Jackson, bringin' back that paycheck. You makin' so much money, you can 'ford to go 'head and buy a car! Me and mine, we ain't never had much of nothin' 'ceptin' that plot of land of Mr Harlan Granger's! I join the Army, I get me a uniform, then I belong to Uncle Sam!'

'That what you want, Clarence,' said Stacey, 'I'm not talking against it, I'm just saying, me, I'd never join. Don't see the need of it.'

'But you'll take me to Jackson?'

'Course, that's what you want.'

Clarence seemed relieved, not only for the ride but that by giving him one, Stacey had also given him his approval. 'Well, good, then! Give me a chance for a nice long ride in that new car of yours!'

'What your folks got to say 'bout all this?' questioned Willie. 'Or ain't you told them?'

'I told 'em all right, but you know Papa, he ain't wantin' me to go. He wantin' me to stay on and help him. But I got me a mind for the Army. I like them uniforms!'

'Well, you better be liking them a whole lot,' I advised. 'A war break out and you have to go fight, you might end up being buried in one.'

Clarence laughed. 'Shoot! I know how to use a gun and I ain't afraid to fight! Ain't nobody gonna shoot me!'

'Well, what about Sissy, then?' said Stacey. 'I know she can't be liking the idea.'

'Ah, Stace, that girl, she ain't even talkin' to me. Said she ain't studyin' me, I go off and leave her. That's what we was arguing 'bout when y'all come 'cross us on the road today. Said I can just forget 'bout her, I do.'

'But you going anyway?'

'Why, shoot, yeah! Ain't no woman the boss of me!'

'No woman 'cepting your mama and Sissy,' I muttered.

Clarence glanced over at me and laughed. 'Well, we just see 'bout that, Cassie. We jus' see 'bout that, 'cause I got my mind set. I'm goin'! And, Harris, you can jus' tell yo' little ole sister that for me too!'

Harris shrugged. 'You tell her. Got nothin' t' do with me,

and I ain't wantin' her comin' down on my head for telling her what you been sayin' 'round – ' He stopped abruptly and got up.

'What is it?' asked Christopher-John.

'Sounds . . . that sounds like T-Bone done bayed a coon.'

Willie shrieked with laughter. 'Boy, sit on down and enjoy these here peanuts! You know that ole hound ain't got nothin'!'

'He got reason for barkin',' contended Harris.

'Poor ole dog,' I commiserated. 'He probably got reason all right. He probably down there barking because he got himself cornered in that water again.'

Harris frowned, looking a bit worried at the thought. 'Y'all jus' wait on here,' he said, grabbing a flashlight. 'Me and T-Bone be back 'fore long.'

''Ey, don't you wanna take along a rifle?' called Clarence. 'Case you want to shoot down that coon T-Bone got treed?'

Harris glanced back in silence, then, as we laughed again, he hurried off as fast as he could without the rifle.

''Ey, Harris, wait up!' I yelled and got up and followed him. I certainly wasn't worrying about T-Bone. I just had a mind to go along with Harris because he seemed worried and was so ridiculously crazy about that dog of his. 'I expect you're going to miss Clarence now that he's going off to the Army,' I said, trailing behind him.

'Yeah. Worst thing 'bout him goin', though, is Sissy. That girl, she 'bout fit to be tied. Ain't no livin' with her now.'

'Suppose not.' We walked on. As we neared the ridge leading down to the banks of the Rosa Lee, Harris stopped. 'What is it?' I said.

He was silent a moment, then looked to the north. 'Somebody else huntin' in these woods, Cassie. Listen.'

I did and heard someone too. 'Maybe that's Stacey and them.'

Harris shook his head. 'Naw, sound comin' up from the wrong direction.'

'Well, anyway, whoever it is, they don't have anything to do with us,' I decided and moved on down the ridge.

'Wait, Cassie.'

I was getting irritated. 'Boy, what for?'

'Wanna see which way they headed. May be best not to run into 'em.'

'Harris, come on! Thought you wanted to see if that ole hound of yours got himself a coon.'

Harris seemed uncertain but came on anyway. We reached the banks of the Rosa Lee, and Harris pointed out some fresh coon tracks. 'Look at how big they is, Cassie. Gonna have us some fine coon tonight!' I nodded in anticipation for I loved coon meat as much as anybody. Smothered in onions and garlic alongside great, golden-coloured yams, baked coon was a grand feast.

Harris, his eyes to the ground, followed the tracks, and I followed him. We were so intent on the tracks that we forgot that someone besides us was in the forest. Then someone yelled: "Ey, Harris! Cassie! This here ole coon dog b'long to y'all?' We looked around. From down the bank came Statler, Leon, and Troy Aames, and Jeremy Simms. All four carried rifles, and Leon and Troy each were holding on to two hunting dogs. Statler had hold of T-Bone. 'Where y'all headed off to in these woods?'

Harris glanced at me and stuttered an answer. 'We ... we doin' us a bit of huntin', Mr Statler.'

'Just you and this gal here? That seems mighty cozy like to me. Thought you said it was you and Clarence s'pose to be goin' huntin'.' He grinned in that offensive way he had at me. 'What? You like fat boys, Cassie?'

Leon and Troy laughed. Jeremy just stood there. I didn't say anything to them. I just told Harris to come on and turned away.

'Now, wait a minute, wait a minute,' ordered Statler. 'Y'all say y'all goin' huntin'? How's 'bout we all go huntin' together? 'Specially since we got your dog here. Always did like me a coon hunt. Harris, tell you what. You be the coon.'

Harris's eyes grew wide. 'S-suh?'

'What? Ain't you heard me?'

Harris looked at me, then back at Statler. 'I ... I don't know what ya mean.'

'Sure ya do! We gonna have us a coon hunt, and you gonna be the coon. You make a nice fine fat one too!' He turned. 'Leon! Troy! Y'all let them dogs get a smell at Harris! We gonna hunt us some coon t'night!'

53

The dogs came in close. Harris backed away. Leon and Troy laughed. I looked at Jeremy, wanting him to say something to stop this, but he looked at Statler and didn't speak. 'Harris,' I said, figuring to shoot up that ridge and get back to Stacey and the others, 'come on, let's go.' But Harris didn't move.

Leon nudged Statler. 'Seem like to me, Stat, maybe it be more enjoyable it was Cassie there the coon. Sure would be delightful we was to get her cornered.'

My heart was already beating fast. Now it began to race. Again I looked to Jeremy. This time he spoke up. 'Ah, Stat, leave 'em be – '

'We just funnin' 'em, Jeremy! They know that.'

I stepped away, and Harris turned to follow. Statler released T-Bone and cocked his rifle. 'You hard of hearin', boy?' he asked as T-Bone ran off into the night. 'You actin' like you don't wanna hunt with us. I take offence to that. Here I am bein' all friendly. Second time I done invited you to join our company, and you just walking off – '

'No, suh, I – '

'Offendin' me and mine.'

'No, suh, I ain't meant no offence! I – '

'Then you gonna 'cept our invite and go huntin' with us?' Statler fondled the rifle as if about to use it.

Harris gasped for air. 'Yes . . . yes, suh . . . th-that what ya want – '

'Then, run, boy! Go 'head! Run!'

Harris looked at me. 'Harris, don't – '

But Harris, with the dogs leaping dangerously near, backed fearfully away.

'I said run!'

Harris did run. He turned away from the dogs and, his whole body shaking, ran as fast as he could down the banks of the Rosa Lee. But he was too heavy to run far, and he soon began to falter. Leon and Troy and Statler laughed. Harris looked a comical figure, but there was nothing funny about his fear. He fell, and Statler called, 'Get on up, boy, and go on! Don't let the dogs get ya now!'

'Y'all leave him be!' I cried as Harris looked back wildly, struggled up, and ran on, leaving his flashlight behind still shining on the ground.

Statler looked at me. 'You know, I'm thinkin' maybe Leon's right. We oughta be chasin' you. You got more fight . . .'

"Ey, Stat!' called Troy, drawing his attention. 'He gettin' away!'

I took my chance, turned, and dashed up the ridge.

Statler laughed.

'We goin' after him?' asked Troy.

'Gotta go after somebody,' said Leon as the dogs strained at their ropes. 'Can't hold these ole hounds here much longer.'

I reached the top of the darkened ridge, hid behind a tree, and looked back.

'What ya say, Stat?'

Statler was looking up the ridge, but I didn't figure he could see me now. Still, I backed away, farther into the shadows. 'Yeah, sure. Y'all go on after him.' Leon and Troy and the dogs took off. 'But y'all get him cornered, y'all leave him be till I get there! Y'all hear me?'

'Yeah! Yeah!' Leon and Troy hollered back and ran on.

Statler looked over at Jeremy. 'You comin'?'

Jeremy hesitated. 'Look, Stat, you done had your fun with him –'

Statler's voice hardened. 'I said, you comin'?'

Jeremy didn't say anything.

Statler turned in disgust. 'Sometimes I don't know 'bout you, Jeremy. Uncle Charlie, he always did say you got a streak of nigger lovin' in you –'

'You got no call t' say that!' Jeremy shot back.

'That right? Sometimes I get t' wonderin' how you could be Uncle Charlie's boy. I got me no notion.'

'Statler, you got no call –'

'You gonna prove me different?'

Jeremy just looked at him, and Statler walked off. Jeremy watched him, then gazed up the ridge, as if he could see me watching, then, rifle in hand, he turned and followed Statler. As they headed down the bank I ran back toward the camp, hollering as loud as I could for the boys, and they came running. 'Cassie! Cassie, what is it?' they cried.

'It's Harris! They got the dogs after him!'

'Who?' said Stacey.

'Statler Aames and his brothers!' My words were a winded rush. 'They were making fun of Harris, and Harris took off running, and now they're chasing him with their dogs along the Rosa Lee!'

'Ah, Lordy!' Clarence exclaimed.

Stacey grabbed hold of both my shoulders. 'They do anything to you?'

'I'm fine, but poor Harris, they've got him scared to death!'

Stacey looked off to the woods, and Christopher-John, frowning, said, 'Maybe we oughta go back and get Papa.'

'You, Man, and Cassie, you go on back. Clarence, Willie, and me, we'll go on after Harris.'

'I'm not going back to the house!' I said. 'I'm going with you!'

'Me too!' declared Little Man, and the thing was settled. There was no time for arguing.

We headed down the ridge. As I trailed Stacey I told him about Jeremy. 'He's with them,' I said.

Stacey stopped and turned, his eyes not wanting to believe. 'What you say?'

I didn't want to repeat it, but I did. 'Jeremy ... he's chasing Harris too.'

Stacey looked at the others, and we all paused in that moment, then nothing more was said. Stacey turned back to the trail, and we all hurried on.

As we neared the water we heard the baying of the dogs. 'Them dogs yappin' so, sound like they got ole Harris cornered,' said Willie.

We ran along the bank, and the barking grew louder. We made our way up a heavily foliaged knoll and saw the Aames brothers and Jeremy, their flashlights shining, watching their dogs yelping and leaping at poor Harris standing in an upper fork of a tree. How Harris had managed to get his massive frame up in that tree I had no idea. Maybe his fear and the nearness of the dogs had hefted him up. The dogs had been given free rein. Leon and Troy no longer held them. We came down the knoll, and

56

Statler turned. 'Well, now,' he said, smiling amiably, 'y'all out huntin' t'night too?'

Stacey glanced at Statler, then turned to Harris and shouted: 'Harris! Harris, get down from there!'

'Can't,' said Statler. 'He's our coon and we got him cornered. He get down and them dogs'll tear him up.'

Stacey looked back to him. 'Then call the dogs off.'

The mocking look of good nature left Statler's face. 'Nigger, you issuin' orders to me? Maybe you oughta be up that tree yourself – '

Suddenly there was an awful crack, then an ear-splitting yell as Harris toppled from the tree and crashed to the ground. The dogs immediately made for him. Stacey moved the quickest, dashing right into the midst of the hounds and slashing at them with the butt of the rifle. Clarence, Willie, and the rest of us grabbed up sticks and shot down behind him. Leon ran after us. 'Y'all niggers, y'all harm one hair on them dogs and I'll see all y'all dead! I swear!'

'Leon!' hollered Statler. 'Call them dogs back! Get them dogs off that boy! Get 'em off, I say!'

Leon and Troy called the dogs back and took hold of them again. We went to Harris. He was all in a mangle and out cold.

Statler came over. 'How he be?' he asked. We didn't answer. Harris was bleeding badly and a sharply broken bone stood straight up through the flesh of his left leg, cutting through the threadbare overalls and jutting upward into the night. His face was badly scratched and it was obvious that he had been bitten by the dogs. 'Y'all know we ain't meant Harris there no harm. We was funnin' with him, that's all . . . I said, how he be?'

Stacey looked at Statler, and his eyes said it all. 'We take care of him,' he voiced and turned again to Harris.

Statler backed away. 'Yeah . . . all right, y'all do that. . . . Like I said, ain't meant the boy no harm. Just funnin' with him . . . He ought've not gone up that tree, not with all that weight on him.' He gestured to Leon and Troy. 'Come on. Leave Harris to them. Jeremy, you comin'?'

Jeremy, eyes on Harris, mutely shook his head. Statler looked at him but didn't say anything else, and he and his brothers left with the dogs. For several minutes Jeremy stood aside as we worked over Harris, then, his face pale in the shadowy light, he took a hesitant step toward us. 'Anything . . . anything I can do?' he offered in a low voice that was hoarse and shaken.

Stacey's back had been to him. Now Stacey turned and looked at Jeremy. 'You were hunting Harris down. I don't expect so.'

Jeremy said nothing else and backed away.

Christopher-John grimaced at the ugly wound. 'How we going to get him home, Stacey? You figure we can carry him?'

'Best not move that leg before it's set. Cassie, you and Man go on home, get Papa and the wagon. Bring Big Ma up here, too, so she can set this leg. She'll know better how to handle him. Go on, hurry now!'

Little Man and I took off. We ran all the way back to the house. Mama, Papa, and Big Ma were sitting on the porch; they saw us coming. As we ran up the lawn Big Ma hollered: 'Girl, what you doin' in them pants?'

'Harris fell!' I cried, giving no thought to the trouble I would be in later about the pants.

'He's hurt bad too!' added Little Man.

Papa got up. 'What happened?'

We told him.

'Clayton, help me with the wagon,' Papa said; then he and Little Man went out to the barn. Mama, Big Ma, and I followed, and as soon as the mules were hitched we all got on the wagon and headed for the woods.

When we reached Harris, Big Ma looked him over and shook her head. 'Lord have mercy!' she exclaimed softly. 'Look like this here leg got more'n one break. Got some broke ribs too. No tellin' what else. Have mercy.' Then, under the glow of the flashlight, she set Harris's leg with branches that the boys and I gathered from the forest ground, and tied it with strips ripped from Harris's already torn overalls. Then gently, very gently, we lifted Harris onto the wagon and took him back to the house.

As soon as we had settled Harris on the bed in the boys' room, Stacey took out his newly polished Ford and drove over to get Ma Batie, Mrs Sarah Noble, and Sissy. There was no sense in taking Harris, Big Ma said; it would be too rough a ride, and Harris shouldn't be moved. Stacey was gone about half an hour, and when he came back with Harris's family, Harris was still unconscious. Big Ma said that wasn't good.

Through the night we all waited for Harris to come to himself. No one went to bed. Sissy stayed inside, sitting by Harris's bed with the older folks, while the boys and I sat on the front porch. Since the bedroom opened onto the front porch, we were able to observe Harris and all that went on through the window. We could see Harris lying unmoving on the bed and we could hear Ma Batie and Mrs Noble and Big Ma praying. We were silently praying too, or at least I knew I was. As the night drew toward dawn and our eyelids grew heavy, Harris finally awakened. It was a blessed relief.

We hurried in to see him, but Harris wasn't saying anything. He was awake and in pain. He started to cry. Clarence, Willie, Christopher-John, and Little Man went back out. Stacey and I remained inside, wanting to say something, to do something to make things better for Harris. There was nothing we could do, but we stayed anyway. Then Clarence stuck his head into the room and called Stacey to the door. 'Jeremy's out here,' he said. 'He say he wanna see ya. He was askin' 'bout Harris, and I told him how he was, but he say he wanna talk to you.'

'Jeremy?' Sissy was bent over Harris. She raised her head and looked out past Clarence into the night. 'Jeremy Simms?' Then, suddenly, she jumped up like a body possessed and ran outside.

'Girl, get back here!' yelled Ma Batie, but Sissy didn't stop. She was headed straight for Jeremy.

Clarence caught her, but that didn't keep her from screaming at Jeremy. 'You ole two-faced cracker! Messin' with Harris like that! Was it funny t'ya? *Was it funny?* Was it funny seein' the fat boy run? Was it funny seein' the fat boy fall? Was it – '

'Hush up that girl!' Big Ma ordered from deep inside the room.

'Clarence,' Papa said, 'bring her in here.'

Clarence nodded and, picking Sissy straight up, took her

kicking and still screaming back inside the house and off to the kitchen.

Papa glanced out at Jeremy staring up from the lawn and said to Stacey, 'You best go talk to him.'

For a moment Stacey didn't move. Papa didn't rush him. But then Mama did; I knew she didn't like Jeremy's being out there any more than the rest of us. 'Stacey,' she said. Stacey looked at her, at Papa, and stone faced, went out to the porch and down the steps. I followed him out and leaned against a porch post. Christopher-John and Willie, seated on the swing, and Little Man, seated by the door, remained silent, their eyes on Jeremy.

Jeremy looked at us, then at the open door and Harris lying on the bed. 'How – how is he?' he stammered. His words were not much more than a whisper.

There was no warmth in Stacey as he answered. 'Got a broken leg busted up more'n one place.'

'But . . . but he gonna pull through?'

'He just come to. Big Ma says time'll tell how he heals.'

Jeremy nodded. 'I'm prayin' he'll be all right. I been out here all the night prayin' for that.'

Stacey said nothing.

'Stacey, I . . . I'm really sorry 'bout Harris. Sorry as I can be. Things just done sort've got outa hand. I ain't never meant Harris no harm. I know Statler always be funnin' Harris, but that's just his way. Him and Leon and Troy, they ain't meant no harm neither.'

'And that's supposed to make things all right?'

'Well, naw . . . I 'spect not. But you know I wouldn't never do Harris no harm – '

'From what I could tell, you didn't try to stop it.' Jeremy didn't reply to that, and Stacey took his silence as an answer. 'If you didn't, then don't come up here telling us you're sorry.'

'You . . . you don't understand – '

'Yeah, I understand. You didn't mean Harris any harm. Y'all was just funning.'

Jeremy stepped back. 'I want y'all to understand. Asking you to understand . . .'

'Told you I understood.' Stacey's words were cold and unforgiving.

60

Their eyes fixed on each other and didn't waver.

'Asking you to see how it is for me, Stacey. Things ain't so easy for me, neither, always tryin' to help y'all out – '

'Always tryin' to help us?' Stacey repeated, his words like an ice-cold torrent. '*Always trying to help us?* When we ever ask your help 'cept for that one time, and that was to help a white man? You recall, that was when Mr Farnsworth, the county agent, got beaten up so bad some years back, and, you recall, he was beaten up by white men. You recall, we were fearful coloured would be blamed. You recall, we could've left him there on that road to die, but we didn't. 'Stead, we asked your help to get him to some white folks so's he could get some doctoring. Now, you blaming us for that? We suppose to thank you for that?'

The rush of hostile words shoved Jeremy backward. He retreated a few steps as far as the magnolia tree midway down the lawn; but he didn't leave. He looked off into the night, turned his back to Stacey with words spoken so softly I could hardly recognize them. 'I . . . I ain't never know'd a time I done lied to y'all, on a purpose done none of y'all no harm. Need y'all t'believe me on this here now.'

'You asking something too hard of me to believe, Jeremy. You hunted Harris down. That's all I know . . . or need to know.' Those were Stacey's final words.

Jeremy looked again at him and accepted them as final. He turned and walked down the lawn. Once he reached the road, he looked back. 'I swear to the Lord God Almighty, Stacey, I ain't never meant that boy no harm. I swear to God.' Then, hands buried in his pockets, his head bowed, he crossed into the woods and was gone.

Stacey came back to the porch. I didn't say anything to him. Little Willie, Christopher-John, and Little Man didn't either. I looked out to the woods and figured maybe it was just as well that this had happened. After all, Jeremy was a man now, and childhood was over. Appropriately, I supposed, so was our friendship.

61

Down Home Farewell

By Sunday night Harris seemed some better. On Monday morning, long before dawn, Stacey, Moe, Little Willie, and I got into the Ford and headed for Jackson. Clarence went with us. When we reached Jackson, Clarence did as he said he would. He went to the Army recruiting office and joined up. A few days later he went to Camp Shelby for training. Stacey, Moe, and Little Willie went back to working their six-day shifts at the box factory, and I settled in, started school, and tried to adjust again to living in Jackson.

I wasn't all that crazy about Jackson. It was the capital, and it was big, too big for me. There were sixty some thousand people in the city and more folks coming all the time, what with all the military bases opening up in the state and jobs too. That was fine, I supposed, for folks who liked city life. As for me, I preferred the country, where things were open and clean and there weren't people the next house over practically sitting on your doorstep. But the schools were better in Jackson, and Mama and Papa wanted me to have the best education they could afford to give me. They had wanted that for all of us. Stacey, too, had attended a Jackson school until he had quit at the end of his tenth grade year and Christopher-John and Little Man, though still attending school at Great Faith, would most likely be attending a Jackson school next year. I realized that living in the city was necessary to getting a good education, so I didn't complain. Not too much, anyway.

One good thing about living in Jackson, in addition to the schooling and the jobs, was that Little Willie and Moe were close by. We all lived on Rose, a quiet little street, unpaved, with no sidewalks, but with decent houses, some plumbing, and sensible folks. Stacey and I lived with Cousin Hugh Reams, Big Ma's sister's son, and his wife, Sylvie, and their family, and that included Oliver, who at twenty-one was only a year older than Stacey. Little Willie and Moe lived two houses down with Mrs Mabel Stalnaker, a neighbour lady. Another good thing about Jackson was that most places I needed to go were close by. Campbell College, which I attended and which boasted both a Negro college and a high school, was only a few blocks away, and Lynch Street, where Cousin Sylvie and Cousin Hugh owned a little cafe and also ran a barber and beauty shop, was within walking distance.

My last two school years in Jackson I had worked at the cafe after school and most weekends too. I soon found, however, that I wasn't going to be able to keep that same schedule this year. Our first weekend back Stacey decided to return home again, and I was glad of that. I missed everybody. Just about every weekend after that as well, the two of us, along with Willie and Moe and sometimes Oliver, made the trip home as soon as the boys finished up their Saturday shift at the box factory. Now that we had our own transportation, Stacey figured there was no reason for us not to go back. Besides, he loved driving that Ford of his, and the rest of us certainly weren't complaining about it. Going back so often kept us all from being so homesick. But then, as luck would have it, just after Thanksgiving, Stacey, Moe, and Willie got put on the night shift, and we figured that was the end to our weekend trips home, for a while anyway, since the boys would now have to work Saturday nights. Yet, one week later we were headed home once again, for the Thursday following Thanksgiving, Papa called us from Strawberry with the news that Reverend Charles Gabson, pastor of Great Faith Church, was dead and was to be buried on Saturday.

There was never any question that Stacey, Willie, Moe, and I would go to the funeral. All of us had grown up under the pastorage of Reverend Gabson; he was the only pastor of Great Faith we had ever known. So on Saturday morning, as soon as the boys got off work, we dressed in our Sunday best, got into the Ford, and headed for home. The boys all wore their best dark suits, and I wore a navy blue two-piece outfit that looked more like a dress than a suit. The jacket was fitted, the skirt was flared, and both the collar and the buttons were black. I also wore my last year's Christmas coat, the one Uncle Hammer had brought me from Chicago. It was a luscious, deep dark brown and had fur sleeves and fur covered buttons. It fit me almost like a dress, snuggly around the bodice and waist and flared nicely around my hips and legs. My pumps, hat, gloves, and purse were all black. I was quite pleased with how I looked, even if I was going to a funeral.

Clarence, now in uniform and on an overnight pass from his base at Camp Shelby, went with us as well even though it was highly unusual for a soldier not yet finished with his weeks of basic training to get a pass. Clarence, however, had told the Army that his grandfather had died and that was true in as much as Reverend Gabson had been married to his grandmother these last five years. The fact that Clarence didn't see Reverend Gabson as his grandfather, but as his pastor, made no difference to Clarence. He just wanted to go home. Oliver went with us too.

By the time we arrived at Great Faith it was midmorning and the field of grass that served as the school playground was already dense with people. There were even folks standing down by the woods that loomed immediately beyond the three wooden-grey school buildings. As we drove onto the grounds we greeted people who had come from as far north as Pinewood Ridge, from as far west as the Little Rosa Lee, from as far south as Smellings Creek, and as far east as the town of Strawberry. Folks had sure turned out for this funeral. But that was to be expected. Reverend Gabson had been a well-known man.

Before Stacey could park the car, Little Man emerged from the crowd and came over. He didn't bother to say hello. He just grinned and announced: 'Y'all in trouble.'

'We just this minute came in from Jackson,' I retorted. 'So how could we be in trouble?'

Little Man let me off the hook. 'Not you, Cassie,' he said, then slipped his hands into his pants pockets and leaned down so that he could peer into the car. 'Rest of y'all are, though.'

Clarence, sitting soldier-handsome beside me, asked the question first. 'Well, what's the matter? What we done?'

'Yeah, that's what I want to know,' said Little Willie from the back seat, where he was squeezed in between Moe and Oliver. 'Don't keep us hanging, son!'

Little Man grinned. He seemed to be enjoying himself. Attired in a navy blue suit, which Stacey had bought him, he nonetheless was not looking very mournful.

'Clayton,' said Stacey, with that one word ordering him to get on with what he had to say.

One word was enough. Little Man turned and nodded toward the other side of the field, where the class buildings were set in a semi-circle against the forest edge. 'Sissy,' he said.

'Sissy?' echoed Clarence. 'My Sissy?'

'What other Sissy is there?' I asked as we all looked for her. At first I didn't see Sissy, for there were a lot of people milling about the grounds, all dressed up in their darkest Sunday best on this Saturday morning. Too many folks to see Sissy. But then, as Clarence pulled his long body from the car, I spied her sitting on the steps of the middle grades class building with a couple of other girls. She was barefooted, and her shoes were dangling from one hand as she talked. Though barefoot days were supposed to be past, that was making no difference to Sissy. I wasn't surprised. Sissy was the kind of girl who, when her shoes hurt, simply took them off. Sissy never did stand on protocol.

Clarence leaned against the top of the car. 'What 'bout Sissy?'

Little Man on the other side of the car didn't have the opportunity to answer, for at that moment Sissy, her shoes still dangling from her hand, got up from the steps and started toward the church. Then we all saw very clearly what the matter was. Even from this distance it was plain to see.

Sissy was pregnant.

'Oh, goodness,' I said, but for a moment nobody else said a word. None of us had seen Sissy since late October. We hadn't seen her at all through November, not even at Thanksgiving. Supposedly she had moved over to Smellings Creek to stay with another great-aunt.

Little Willie followed Clarence out of the car. 'You best own on up to it, son!' he admonished.

We all looked at Clarence.

'Yep!' Little Willie repeated with a good-natured slap to Clarence's back as Oliver, too, got out. 'Best own on up to it!'

Clarence, though, looked as if he wasn't about ready to own up to anything. He crossed his arms against the car and leaned his chin against them. Still staring across the field, he muttered, 'I ain't ready to be no daddy.'

'Evidently,' I said, 'time to be thinking about that is past.'

Clarence didn't say anything.

Little Man grinned again. 'Ma Batie's talking about taking a shotgun to somebody.'

I laughed. 'That'll be Clarence, then.' I was sure of that.

'Not 'cording to Sissy,' said Little Man.

Clarence pulled away from the car, and Little Willie exclaimed, 'Clayton Chester, what you mean, boy? Everybody knows Clarence been the only one courtin' Sissy all this time!'

'Can't help that. Sissy said maybe Clarence the father, then again, maybe not.'

The man who wasn't ready to be a daddy stood with his mouth agape and eyes wide, obviously as shocked by this bit of news as the rest of us.

Little Willie glanced at Clarence. 'Ah, now, come on,' he protested. 'Who she blamin', then? Know it can't be me!'

Little Man shrugged. 'She's not saying. Said it could be Clarence . . . or maybe one of y'all right here.'

Little Willie yelped out a cry of disbelief.

'Well, anyway, that lets me out,' said Oliver, lighting a cigarette. 'I ain't even seen the girl since August. 'Sides, I ain't never been 'round that girl hardly long enough to even shake her hand.'

'Well, obviously somebody has,' I observed, amused by the state the boys were in.

While Oliver and Little Willie debated who had been around Sissy, Christopher-John came over. Unlike Little Man, he said his hellos and asked how we were. Then he looked around at everybody, and knowing something was wrong, turned to Little Man. 'What's the matter? Clayton, you tell them 'bout Sissy?'

Little Man grinned. 'Just now.'

'Oh . . . told them 'bout Ma Batie and Miz Noble coming to talk to Mama and Papa 'bout Sissy?'

'What?' said Stacey.

'Yeah, they sure did,' Christopher-John went on. 'They been talking to everybody's folks. Oliver, they even talked to Cousin Sylvie and Cousin Hugh this morning.'

Now it was Willie's turn to laugh as Oliver groaned. Cousin Hugh and Cousin Sylvie had driven down from Jackson on Friday. Having grown up here in the community, they both had known Reverend Gabson well. 'Shoot! Gonna be all hell to pay now,' said Oliver.

'Not if you haven't been into something,' I smart-mouthed.

Oliver did not find that funny.

But that wasn't the last of Christopher-John and Little Man's bad news. 'Ma Batie and Miz Noble, they even talking 'bout meeting with y'all after the funeral to get this thing straightened out,' continued Christopher-John, and this time it wasn't only Oliver who groaned.

I looked around at Moe. 'You've been mighty quiet sitting back there. You got any secrets you want to tell?' I was having a high time teasing them all.

Moe smiled. 'It was mine, Cassie, I wouldn't be sitting here quiet.' I returned the smile, and the dimples deepened. But there was no smile deepening in Moe's eyes, and that bothered me. Moe had been quiet all the way down from Jackson. That could have been because he was tired and sleepy from working all night at the box factory, but I didn't think so. He had been quiet for some days now. Quiet was like Moe; this prolonged silence wasn't.

Stacey put the car in gear. 'I'm going to go park.'

Little Man and Christopher-John jumped in for the short ride. Stacey parked the Ford some distance from the many wagons and pickup trucks that dotted the grounds. He was taking no chances that somebody might accidentally hit the car. He stepped from the Ford, looked back at it, and frowned. Dust and insects marred the double coat of paint. Little Man frowned too. He didn't like to see the car dirty

67

any more than Stacey did. 'We can clean it up after the funeral,' he said.

'Don't bother,' Stacey replied. 'It'll just get messed up again on the drive back.'

'What time you leaving?'

'Midafternoon, I reckon. Want to give ourselves plenty of time to get back, seeing we got to work tonight. 'Sides that, I want to stop in Strawberry and see Mr Jamison. Want to pay off my note today.'

'Well, why don't you just pay him in Jackson?' suggested Christopher-John, and that made sense since Mr Jamison now had an office in Jackson. 'That way you won't have to stop in Strawberry and you can stay here a bit longer.'

Stacey shook his head. 'Don't like going to his sister's house in Jackson, and that's where his office is. Don't like going to that white neighbourhood. Rather stop at his office in Strawberry.'

Christopher-John looked at me. 'What about you, Cassie? You going to stay over and go back with Cousin Hugh and Cousin Sylvie tomorrow?'

'Can't. I've got a debate to prepare on President Roosevelt's New Deal. It's a big part of my history grade. Not only that, but I'm supposed to be meeting some students from my class this evening at the cafe to study for it.'

'Too bad,' he said.

'Yeah, I know.'

'Look, we best go on and see the folks,' said Stacey. 'Services'll be starting pretty soon now.'

'You all go on,' I said. 'I want to talk to Moe a minute.'

Stacey looked from me to Moe, nodded, and went on with Christopher-John and Little Man. As they left, Moe leaned against the car and smiled. 'What is it, Cassie?'

'Something's wrong.'

'Wrong? What you mean?'

'What I said. You've been mighty quiet – '

'You don't think me and Sissy – '

'I don't care about that.'

'Well, I ain't had nothing to do with her. She's Clarence's girl.'

'Didn't think you did.'

'Then what you asking, Cassie?'

'Like I said, something's wrong, and I know it. You been too quiet, not hardly even talking.'

'That ain't so.'

'This morning when you came off work, I was figuring something was wrong. Now I want to know what.'

'Cassie –'

'Don't you tell me it's nothing. I want to know.'

Moe sighed and looked away across the field.

I touched his arm. 'Moe?'

'There's Papa. Him and the younguns, they're most likely looking for me.' He watched them but didn't move to leave. He heaved a despondent sigh, pushed back his hat so that the brim just barely shadowed his forehead, and looked at me. 'I got fired last night, Cassie. I got fired.'

'Fired? What for?'

He turned as if to tell me, but then Mr Turner saw us and started our way with three of Moe's brothers. 'Look, don't say anything 'bout this, all right? Ain't the right time. Want to get another job first . . . a better job 'fore I tell my papa. Don't want him worrying.'

'All right.'

The dimples returned. 'Thanks,' he said as his father stretched out his arms to him.

I greeted Mr Turner and the Turner boys then, as the church bell began to ring summoning folks in for the funeral, made my way through the crowd to find Mama, Papa, and Big Ma. I found them standing by the truck with the boys, Cousin Hugh and Cousin Sylvie, and after taking the time to hug and kiss them in greeting, we all headed for the church to say our last good-byes to the Reverend Charles Gabson.

Reverend Gabson had always been a preacher of tumultuous hellfire and brimstone sermons that went on and on. Today all the ministers who had gathered were obviously attempting to pay adequate tribute to the reverend by preaching in the same long-winded fashion. The services seemed to go on forever. Finally we were dismissed from the church, and we followed the pallbearers up the trail that led to the graveyard. There, more words were spoken, and Reverend Charles Gabson was at last laid to rest.

Throughout the services there hadn't been many tears. Reverend Gabson had been dearly loved, but nobody much was crying about his passing on. He had lived a good many years, and the Lord had called him home; that was the way of life. Folks had mourned him for two days, including an all-night wake. Respects had been paid, and now life got on.

The day took on a festive air. Having come the distance, everybody now took the opportunity to visit. What with the miles between Pinewood Ridge and the Little Rosa Lee, Smellings Creek and the town of Strawberry, a lot of folks hadn't seen each other since the Revival in August, and most likely would not be gathering again in such numbers until the next Big Meeting. So folks told good-natured stories about Reverend Gabson, laid out bowls of food on the backs of wagons and truck aprons, laughed and joked and talked, and had themselves a good time.

Nobody left.

After we ate, the boys and I stood near the well listening to Clarence talk about life in the Army. He hadn't even mentioned Sissy. He told a story about his sergeant and how he had already gotten on his wrong side by questioning an order he had been given. His punishment had been spending one whole night digging holes, filling them, then digging them up again.

'Well, I know one thing,' said Little Willie, as Clarence laughed at his own story, 'Army sure ain't for me.'

'Will be, they call you,' predicted Clarence.

'They didn't call you,' I said. 'You in the Army because you want to be.'

'Well . . . they'd've called me sooner or later. Sergeant said they getting mighty serious 'bout that war over there in Europe. Said we ain't in it yet, but we gonna be.'

'Yeah,' Moe quietly agreed. 'What with all this talking war, I been thinking maybe I'll do like Clarence and go 'head and join up myself.'

I shot him an incredulous look. 'What? Boy, what are you talking about?'

Clarence laughed. 'He wanna get sharp like me! You like these uniforms, too, don't you, Moe?'

Moe shrugged. 'Be twenty-one my birthday come up, and

I'm gonna have to go register anyways. Was just giving thought to when I do, I'd just go 'head, join up, and get it over with.'

I questioned his sanity. 'Are you out of your mind? You may get more than that over with, we ever end up in a war.'

Moe looked at me but didn't say anything. Little Willie did, though. 'Ah, face it, Cassie. These here white folks want to get in a war, we ain't got nothing to say 'bout it. We get in that war over in Europe, we all gonna hafta go soldiering, that's just the way it is, we like it or not. Just the way it is . . .' He smiled, but the smile just backed up the seriousness of what he had said. Little Willie wasn't often serious with his joking ways, but there had been no joking in his words now, no laughter in his voice now, and I found that disturbing.

'Well, I don't see it that way,' I said.

'That's 'cause you don't want to see it.'

I cut Little Willie a look but let it be. Maybe he was right. Maybe I just didn't want to see it that way. Maybe that was because I didn't give too much thought to a war, despite the fact that accounts about the war in Europe were plastered across the newspapers each day and news about it seemed to be always on the radio. The notion of war to me was far removed. War was something happening in a place called Europe that had nothing much to do with us, nothing much to do with the folks of Great Faith, except for the fact that all the boys reaching twenty-one were having to register for military service, but I didn't worry about that. I didn't figure anybody close to me would ever have to go fight, so I preferred not to think about it. The thought was too foreign.

'Was thinking, I join up,' Moe went on, 'maybe I could even get to be an officer . . . maybe a pilot or something.'

At that, Little Willie let go a rip of a laugh. 'An of-fi-cer? Maaaan, don't you know they ain't going to let no Negro be no of-fi-cer? Coloured regiments got white officers, fool!'

'Well, anyway, I read 'bout some,' said Moe quietly. 'There ain't many, but there's some.'

'Read 'bout 'em in what comic books?' scoffed Little Willie.

71

Stacey, having listened in silence to all this, now pulled away from the well. 'Well, y'all just go ahead and join your Army, but I'm telling you now, they get in this war, they can just fight it without me. I got no reason to fight their war.'

Little Willie laughed again. 'Well, they can just fight it without me too, son, they be giving out any choices 'bout the thing!'

On a sudden Oliver gave Little Willie a nudge. "Ey, look-a-there,' he said as Jeanette Jones, Georgia Henderson, and Peaches McDonald passed by with some young men from Smellings Creek. Both Oliver and Little Willie smiled their hellos, but not one of those young ladies uttered a word. At the snub Oliver said, 'Willie! Peaches talk to you yet?'

'Naw, nothing except to tell me to go take my talk to Sissy.'

'Yeah, I been hearing that same thing from Georgia,' commiserated Oliver. 'What 'bout you, Stacey? Saw you over there trying to talk to Jeanette. Seen you ain't talked too long.'

Stacey conceded that. 'Told her I'd talk to her later.'

Little Willie laughed. 'After Miz Noble's meeting, huh?'

Stacey smiled, acknowledging that was so.

"Ey, Stacey!' yelled Little Man from the church steps. 'Grandma Batie and Miz Noble said they want to talk to y'all. Now, they say!'

Without a word Clarence moved from the well, but not toward the church. "Ey, Clarence, where you going, man?' Little Willie called after him.

'Not in that church, that's for sure.'

'Man, you the main one s'pose to be in there!'

'Way I figure,' said Clarence, 'maybe you the one s'pose to be in there.'

'What! Man, you gone crazy?'

'You said you gone out with her, 'round here behind my back!'

'Man, that wasn't nothin'! Only seen her one time when we come down, and that was in October – '

'One time was enough!'

'You crazy, man! 'Sides, what you care? You wasn't

seeing her no more. Said you was shed of her and gone off to the Army!'

'Yeah, and soon's I was gone, you done made yourself right at home with Sissy, and from the looks of things you done made yourself at home long 'fore October – '

Little Willie, fists clutched, stepped right up to six-foot-six Clarence. 'Man, I oughta knock you out!'

Stacey stepped in front of Willie and faced Clarence himself. 'Now, just hold on, you two. Clarence, you got no call to go blaming Willie here. I went over to talk to Sissy myself to see how she was doing.'

Clarence's face, so full of good nature just a few minutes ago, was now clouded in doubt and jealousy. 'Well, then . . . maybe it's you.'

Stacey fixed his eyes on Clarence. 'You know better'n that.'

Clarence scowled across at his friends and mumbled, 'Well, maybe it ain't you, Stacey. Maybe it ain't even Willie here. But one of y'all 'sides me been messin' with Sissy, and that's the truth of it! She already done said so!' He glowered accusingly at Moe and Oliver. 'Sissy got no reason to go lying on herself.'

Oliver took real offence at that. 'Don't know what kind of thinking Sissy's doing. Don't know her reasons for nothing, but don't you come looking at me to blame, Clarence! I don't know who Sissy been 'round, but it ain't been me! Ask me, the girl is an out and out lie, and a girl lie like that could be sleeping 'round with anybody – '

No sooner than Oliver got that out, Clarence started in for him. Stacey pushed him back. Moe stepped forward as well, put an arm around Clarence, and tried to calm him down. 'Look, Clarence,' Stacey said, 'it's not going to help for you to go fighting with Oliver or any of the rest of us.'

Clarence looked at Stacey and Moe and backed off.

Little Man again hollered out. 'Ma Batie and Miz Noble said y'all coming?'

Stacey glanced at him, then back at Clarence. 'You still not going in?'

'Naw.'

'All right, then, it's up to you. Best the rest of us go on and get this thing straightened out.'

Little Willie shot Clarence a hostile look. So did Oliver. Then the two of them went with Stacey. Clarence turned to walk away, but I caught his arm. 'Since you not going in the church, you going to go talk to Sissy?'

'Naw . . . what we got to talk about?'

'What you got to talk about? Boy –'

'She done told everybody that baby ain't mine. Seem like to me she done said it all!' With that he pulled away from me and walked off across the church grounds toward his family's wagon. I watched him go, not liking any of this. Stacey, Clarence, Little Willie, and Moe had been best friends since they had been in short pants, and Oliver had joined that friendship whenever he came down on visits from Jackson. They had gotten themselves into much of the same mischief together, and they had gone through a lot of the same grief as well. Now Sissy with her trouble-making accusations was causing them to argue and almost fight, and I didn't like that. I didn't like one bit what Sissy was doing, and I decided I was going to tell her about it, too, all about it, as soon as I caught up with her.

'Cassie?'

I turned. Moe was still standing there. 'Aren't you going in for the meeting?' I asked.

He glanced over his shoulder toward the church. 'Yeah . . . in a minute. Just wanted to talk to you first.'

'Yeah, I want to talk to you too. Want you to tell me how come you got fired.'

He looked away, across the field. 'Just couldn't get along with some of the other men down there.'

'What men?'

'White men,' he said, as if that explained the matter. 'Look Cassie, I just wanted to tell you why I been thinking on joining the Army. I been thinking on my future. You know I want to make something of myself, Cassie.'

'And you figuring on doing that in the Army?'

'Figure maybe I can get me some opportunity in the Army. Read about how the Army give schooling and training of folks join up. Figure I could get some of that schooling and training. Cassie, you know how it's been with me. You know how since Stacey and me quit school I been trying to figure out a way to get a good living and

74

maybe get a place and move my family off that land we been sharecropping all this time. You know that.'

'I know you've been talking about it long as I can recall.'

Moe nodded. 'Know I can't buy four hundred acres like y'all got. Can't buy near to that, but if I could just get myself a little place – maybe twenty-five, forty acres, just enough so my daddy can make a living off it 'stead of cropping all his life ... It's important for a man to have land, something of his own, and I want my daddy to have something.' His eyes fixed on mine. 'Y'all oughta know how it is, 'bout having something, 'cause y'all got something already. Y'all got land.'

I could understand his feeling about land; yet I said nothing. Moe looked at me as if I didn't really know a thing about how he was feeling; then he looked away and bit at his lower lip. 'For me to go and get my daddy that land, Cassie, I need me a good job, and I need me some opportunity. I was thinking maybe the Army could give me some opportunity. Like I said, I been reading 'bout programmes set up for training coloured pilots and coloured officers too. Maybe they won't train me in that, maybe I ain't got enough schooling for them to train me for something like that, but maybe I can learn me something else. I don't know 'xactly what, but I'm just figuring, if we get in that war, there's going to be a whole lot of opportunities for me to get some kind of training.'

'There'll be plenty of opportunities, all right,' I agreed. 'Opportunities for you to go get yourself killed.'

Moe didn't respond to that.

''Sides, Uncle Hammer fought in that last war, and he said about the only opportunity most of the coloured soldiers saw was unloading ships and cleaning spittoons.'

'But don't ya see, Cassie? Things are already opening up. Just look at Jackson. We could get hired on jobs coloured folks used to not be able to get, seeing that white folks are taking them new defence jobs they setting up 'cause-a that fighting overseas. White folks can make more money working in them defence jobs, and we can make more money working them jobs they leaving – '

'Somehow, that doesn't seem like a whole lot of opportunity to me – '

'More'n we had.'

'Yeah, well, you tell me something, Moe. We got all this opportunity opening up, how come you want to go and join the Army then? Stay in Jackson and get your opportunity.'

His lips teased into a smile. 'I join up, you'd miss me?'

'Course I'd miss you. Besides that, it doesn't make a lick of sense to me for coloured folks to be going way over to Europe somewhere fighting in somebody's war and getting killed. Coloured folks want to get killed so bad, they can stay right here in Mississippi and do that.'

Moe glanced at me, started to say something, but then seemed to think better of it. He headed toward the church, then stopped, came back to me, and put his hands on my shoulders. But before he could speak Little Willie hollered, "Ey, Moe! Son! Ain't ya heard? Miz Noble said she want every last jack one of us up here? You comin'?'

I laughed. 'You best go on before Miz Noble comes out and get to looking for you.'

Moe half smiled and reluctantly it seemed, let go of me. He turned, the half-smile still etched on his face, and headed for the church. As he walked away I saw Sissy cross from a truck and head for the road. She was still barefooted. I took one more look after Moe and ran after her. I planned on talking some sense to the girl. I caught up with her and she smiled widely and stopped. "Ey, Cassie,' she greeted me.

'Where you think you going?' I said.

Her answer was simple. 'Home.'

'Home? Girl, don't you think you best get yourself on up to that church and straighten out your mess?'

'Mess? What mess?'

'Girl – '

'I'm going home,' she repeated and continued on her way.

It was obvious, if I was going to talk to her, I had to walk with her, so I did, fussing all the while. 'Sissy, you know you ought to be ashamed of yourself!'

'Nothin' to be ashamed 'bout.'

'Don't you figure all of this is your fault? You got everybody in an uproar around here. These girls Stacey and them been courting, they're mad, families mad, the boys are mad – '

Sissy laughed. 'Won't be for long. I got Clarence paying some attention now.'

I looked at her suspiciously. 'Sissy, just what are you up to?'

'Getting my man.'

'Well, it seems like a mighty funny way to get him, you ask me.'

'Well, I'm not asking you, Cassie. I'm not asking anybody. I know what I'm doing.'

'You're crazy.'

She rendered me a smart grin and turned away. I grabbed hold of her wrist. 'Clarence is the daddy of that baby you're carrying, and you know it!'

She jerked away, but the grin remained. She was pretty sure of herself. 'You promise me you won't tell Clarence what I tell ya?'

'That's what you want.'

'Well, it couldn't be nobody else's baby but Clarence's. Wouldn't never let nobody else touch me.'

'Well, why didn't you just tell Clarence that in the first place and be done with the thing?'

'And have him grumbling the rest of his life 'bout me hooking him into marrying me? When he gone off into that Army, he told me he wasn't thinking 'bout no marrying, and I told him he couldn't think 'bout marrying me, then what we fooling 'round for? Told him there was other boys got marrying on their minds could be courting me. Clarence wanna marry me now, he gonna just hafta decide that for himself. I want him to come to me on his own 'cause he wants to and do right by me and this baby. He don't want me, I ain't gonna force him into nothin'.'

I had to laugh. 'Well, then, all I can say is I sure am glad I'm not in love. Makes a person stop thinking straight.'

She had to laugh herself. 'I suppose so.' Then she walked on, and I walked with her.

When we reached Sissy's house, we found Harris sitting in the battered Model T truck that for the most part was seldom out of the yard. Harris was forever tinkering with it, even though he wasn't allowed to drive it; there was no money to spare for gasoline. Today he wasn't working on the truck. He was just sitting there behind the steering wheel, the door wide open, his bad leg, the one that had been so severely broken, hanging out. It was wrapped only from the knee down, allowing him to bend it. He was staring straight ahead. His crutch lay on the ground.

"Ey, Harris,' I said.

"Ey,' he muttered.

'What you doing sitting in that truck, boy?' snapped Sissy. 'You been messin' with it again?'

'Naw.'

'You know Ma said she ain't wantin' you messin' with it!'

'Ain't messin', Sissy,' he said. 'Just sitting here.'

'Doin' what?'

'Just sittin'.'

'Well, that better be all you doing and not messing with that truck again. You know Ma said she don't want that bit of gas in it gettin' used up with you just startin' and stoppin' it in the yard.'

'Yeah, I know, I know,' he said sullenly. Then Harris got out of the truck, favouring his bad leg. Picking up his crutch, he said, 'Guess I'll be heading on back up to the church. You going back now, Cassie?'

'You go on. I got a few more words for Sissy.'

'You watch yourself, now, Harris,' instructed Sissy. 'Don't you get to talking too much to Clarence, you hear me? I'll take care of him.'

Harris pushed his hands into his pockets. 'I got nothin' to tell Clarence.'

'Well, just see that you don't. And stay off that leg so much!'

He looked at Sissy, at me, nodded, and limped on down the trail. Sissy sat on the porch steps. 'Now, what you got to say to me?'

'I want you to go talk to Clarence and stop making a fool of yourself.'

Sissy was quiet a moment, then she said: 'You just think you know it all, don't you, Cassie? Well, one day you gonna fall in love yourself, and then you'll see how it feels. You'll see how it is to be a fool too.'

'Not me,' I said with utmost certainty. 'Because if love makes you go around acting this way, I don't much want anything to do with it. Besides, I don't figure I could be as foolish about anybody the way you are about Clarence.'

'Oh, yeah, you could, Cassie. Right man come into your life, you will.'

'Right man like Clarence, huh?'

She shrugged. 'Our love's blessed, Cassie.'

'Well . . . I don't know 'bout all that – '

'It is. I feel my love for that boy from the roots of my hair to the tips of my toenails. Been feeling that way 'bout my Clarence since I first laid eyes on him.' She laughed again, then placed her hands on her stomach with an unsuppressed joy. 'Oh, Cassie, I'm so happy! Clarence and me and this here baby, we gonna be us a family. Some folks, they been talkin' 'bout me 'cause I'm this way and I ain't married, but it don't bother me none. Clarence, he the best thing ever come my way, and he's my man and I'm right proud to have his baby! Right proud! We gonna do just fine, soon's he learn that.' She looked so firm in that conviction, I almost believed it too. She squeezed my hand with her joy. 'Don't worry, Cassie, me and Clarence, we're gonna work out fine.'

'That is, if your grandma Batie doesn't catch up with Clarence first and blast him with a shotgun.'

Sissy's laughter rang across the yard like a bell. 'Ah, Ma's just talking! Ain't nothin' gonna spoil our happiness. Nothin' at all.'

'Well, I sure hope not,' I said and got up. 'Not as crazy as you are about that boy. Look here, you coming back up to church later?'

'What I got to come back up there for? Anybody wanna see me, they can just come down here. Don't worry. He'll come 'fore he leaves. He'll come.'

'All right, you believe that,' I said. 'S'pose I'll be seeing you come Christmas. We're going to be leaving after while.'

She patted her stomach. 'Christmas already here for me.'

'Well, then, I guess I'll be hoping Santa Claus'll bring you one more present.'

'He will,' she said with assurance. 'He will.'

I laughed, told her good-bye, and returned to the road. As I made my way back toward Great Faith a truck came barreling over the rise. I stepped to the side of the road to let it pass. The truck slowed. A few feet from me it stopped. Statler, Troy, and Leon Aames sat in the cab. Statler stepped from the driver's side. "Ey, Cassie,' he said as Leon and Troy also got out. 'You're looking mighty good there, Cassie Logan. Haven't seen you in a while.'

I didn't say anything. Statler came toward me. I tried to walk on. Grinning, Statler stepped in front of me and blocked my way. 'Looking that good, you gotta know something good.'

I still didn't say anything.

"Ey, what? Cat got your tongue? Ain't you hearing me talking to you, girl? I said, what you know good?'

I met his grey eyes, and against good sense my smart mouth got the better of me. 'Whatever I know good, I won't be sharing it with you.'

Statler's smile was slow, then he let go a howl; so did Leon and Troy. When they finished with their laughing, Statler grinned down appreciatively. 'You know, you're something, Cassie.'

The smile made me nervous. I was a fool to use a smart mouth. These were young white men standing here. They could take offence to my words or be encouraged by them. Either way, I couldn't win. It was obvious that Statler liked my sass, but that was doing me no good. I just wanted to get by and get back to church. Statler, though, was still standing in my way. 'Would you move, please?' I said. 'I need to get by.'

Again he laughed. 'You ain't scairt of nothin', are you, girl?' He drew nearer and whispered, 'Out here on this road all by yourself.'

He was wrong about that, about my not being scared. I was scared of him, all right, of all three of them. But the last thing I wanted was for them to know it. 'What? You expecting me to go running like Harris that night on the Rosa Lee?'

Statler paled and pulled back. I walked past him. I got as far as the back end of the truck before he came after me. 'Cassie, let me give you a ride.' He blocked my way again. 'Got something here you might like.'

'You've got nothing I want – '

'Yeah . . . but you got something I want . . .'

80

Leon and Troy again howled. I stepped away, ready to flee back to Sissy's. I didn't know if I could make it, though. I glanced over at the forest looming tall on either side of the road and wondered if I could make the leap across the gully in my Sunday pumps and make a shortcut run up to the church. But then I wondered, if it came to that, if I could outrun them. If I couldn't, the woods was the last place I needed to be. If I headed for Sissy's place, I figured they would just stop me again; however, they wouldn't be expecting me to jump the gully. I knew every foot of this land, but right now I felt cornered, and I was uncertain how to escape.

'Well, Cassie, what you say?' Statler grinned and moved even closer. I made up my mind. I got set to jump.

Papa stopped me.

'Cassie,' he said in a voice as quiet as black night. 'Cassie, come on, now, back to church.' He was standing at the top of the rise.

Startled, Statler turned. I quickly passed him and headed for the rise. As I walked away Statler called, 'Don't break it, now, Cassie!' He and Leon and Troy let out a contemptuous laugh. My eyes flashed, ready to retort; Papa shook his head. His eyes bore down on mine, and I said nothing. Then he looked past me, at Statler and Leon and Troy, and the laughter stopped. Nothing more was said. I reached the top of the rise. Papa placed his hand on my shoulder. 'You all right?'

'Yes, sir.'

'They ain't touched you none?'

'No, sir.'

He nodded. 'Good' was all he said before turning and walking with me down the rise toward the church.

'Papa, how'd you know they were messing with me?'

'My business to know,' he said. Then he looked at me. 'You know I don't like you walking these roads by yourself.'

'Well, I wasn't by myself at first. Just walked Sissy home – '

'Seen y'all go off. Been waiting for y'all to come back.'

'Wasn't gone that long.'

'Long 'nough to be back. You s'pose to be at church, not walking the roads.'

'Yes, sir,' I said, deciding not to dispute with Papa. As always, his words were soft-spoken. As always, they were words meant to be heard. I didn't figure now was the time to go arguing with him; I didn't figure I could win anyway.

'Seen Statler's truck go by and figured I best come on down this way and see what done happened to y'all. That Statler got himself one bad reputation 'bout forcing his attentions on coloured girls. That done happened more'n one time 'round here, and ain't been nothin' them girls' daddies could do 'bout it, you know that. Got no laws t' protect our girls from the likes of him, but I ain't gonna stand for him forcing his attentions on you. I ain't gonna stand for it.'

I nodded, understanding.

The forest ended; the land opened up, and Great Faith stood before us. Papa stopped, looked up at the church, then back at me. 'You know, sugar, being my only girl, I worry 'bout you, worry 'bout you a lot, maybe more'n I oughta –'

'Papa, I'm all right,' I assured him.

Papa smiled at my declaration. 'Ever since you was a baby girl, I could most times feel when you was in trouble, when you was hurting, needing me. Always wanted to protect all my children. Figured, though, maybe you might be needing protecting most.'

'Because I'm a girl?'

He conceded that. 'Fact is, guess I worry 'cause that's what papas do. Worry 'bout you on these roads by yourself. Worry 'bout you up in Jackson, so far from your mama and me. Worry 'bout you getting in trouble like Sissy, making a bad start in life.'

Oh, Papa, you've got no cause to worry about that. I'm not stupid like Sissy.'

Papa gave me a long look, and his voice grew even more quiet, compelling me to listen. 'There's a lotta things that can happen to you in this world, Cassie. That's how come your mama and me, we taught you like we done. Sometimes things happen, and there ain't no way to keep them from happening. Other times things happen 'cause we get to thinking we so smart nothing can go wrong. Don't get so smart, Daughter, you don't use your head.'

I met Papa's eyes and promised him that. 'No, sir, I won't.'

He nodded, then we crossed the field to the church. He went in the deacon's door at the back. I went around to the front of the church and there found Little Man and Christopher-John, along with two of Willie's younger brothers, with their ears pressed against the door. Harris stood at the bottom of the steps leaning against his crutch. They didn't hear me coming, and all of them jumped when I said: 'What y'all doing?'

Little Man scowled at me for startling them. 'Listening to Ma Batie and Miz Noble in there talking to Clarence and them.'

'Clarence is in there?' I said, surprised.

'Yeah, he – '

Little Man didn't get a chance to say more, as the door shot open and Clarence exploded from the church, knocking Little Man down the steps to the ground below. Paying Little Man no attention Clarence slipped on his sliver of a soldier's cap and stomped away. As Little Man got up and dusted himself off, Stacey and Willie came out. 'What happened?' I asked them.

Little Willie grinned. 'Nothing that should've gone on in church.'

'Well, what's got Clarence so mad?'

'Fool mad 'cause he think Sissy done made a fool of him.'

'He doesn't still think one of you – '

'Don't know what that boy think, he gone so addle minded,' declared Willie. He turned and cast an accusing look on Harris. 'Why don't you go do something 'bout this, boy? She your sister!'

Harris looked as if he'd been wrongly accused of some crime. 'What – what I'm gonna do? Y'all know Sissy – '

'Yeah, I know her, all right. Tell you one thing. She was my sister, I wouldn't let her go 'round tellin' tales like this! I'd put a stop to it!'

Harris shook his head weakly. 'I . . . I can't stop Sissy. Can't nobody stop Sissy. She . . . she too hardheaded.'

'Ah, Willie, leave him be,' ordered Stacey. 'Your quarrel's with Sissy, not Harris.'

'Quarrel's with the whole darn family, Sissy keep messin'!' retorted Willie.

Stacey glanced across the field at Jeanette, still talking to one of those Smellings Creek boys. 'Well, I'm finished with it. I've said my last word about the whole thing. I'm going to go talk to Jeanette before we head back.'

'Try to, you mean,' corrected Willie. Stacey just looked at him and went off. 'Yeah, well, you gonna be brave 'bout the thing,' Willie called after him, "spect I'll go 'head and try to talk to Peaches too!'

'Good luck,' I said as he, too, started off.

He went off grumbling. 'Gonna need it. That devilish Sissy and that fool Clarence, they just ruinin' my love life . . .'

'Well, I guess that's that,' said Little Man, inspecting his suit to make sure he had rid himself of all the dust.

'No, it's not,' I said.

Christopher-John gave me an odd glance. 'What you mean, Cassie?'

'I'm going to go talk to Clarence.'

Little Man cast me a suspicious look. 'Well, what you got to say?'

'Plenty,' I replied and crossed the field. True, none of this was my business, but I figured this thing had gone just about far enough, especially since I knew the truth. I caught up with Clarence, and I told him everything. I wasn't thinking about any promises to Sissy.

At first Clarence didn't know what to make of the news. 'But, then, why'd she say – '

'To make you mad. Get you jealous.'

'J-jealous?' Clarence stumbled over the word. 'What she wanna get me jealous for? Sissy know how I feel 'bout her!'

'Look here,' I said. 'I'm not supposed to be telling you any of this, so don't you go back and tell Sissy I told you. But she wanted you to be jealous so you'd come to your senses about how you feel about her. She knew you didn't want to get married.'

Clarence pouted. 'She got everybody laughing at me.'

I was about tired of him and Sissy too. 'Look here, just go talk to Sissy. She loves you, Lord only knows why. You know you got no right to deny your own child.'

Clarence thought again, then somewhat relented. 'Well . . . like I said, I ain't ready for no marrying now. Other girls, they have babies and they don't get married. Sissy can do that too.'

'Well, that's between you and Sissy. Least, though, you can do is talk to her.'

Clarence considered. 'Where she at?'

'She went home.'

He stood there indecisive.

'Now, you know you want to talk to her, so go on.'

Clarence sighed and looked up the road. 'Okay. Gotta tell my folks good-bye, then I'll go on and talk to this girl.' He started away. 'Tell Stacey to pick me up at her place, will ya?'

'Be happy to,' I replied, figuring I had just about resolved this whole mess. Sissy could just be mad at me if she wanted to.

It was late afternoon when Stacey, Moe, Willie, Oliver, and I said our good-byes to everybody, left Great Faith, and headed for Sissy's to pick up Clarence. As we neared the trail leading to Ma Batie's we saw Clarence and Sissy standing out on the road. We heard them too. Obviously, what with all the hollering going on, they hadn't made up. As we pulled alongside them Clarence turned to us. 'Y'all know what that old woman Ma Batie done? She took a shotgun to me!'

'What?' we said. Then we couldn't help ourselves. We laughed.

'Yeah! She coulda killed me!'

'Shoulda killed ya!' judged Sissy. 'What you doin' up here, anyway, Clarence Hopkins?'

'Just come to tell you to stop makin' a fool of yourself.'

'Me make a fool of myself? Negro, I wasn't the one hiding behind some tree up there 'fraid of a shotgun!'

Clarence cast a cautious glance up the trail toward the house. 'I know what you doin' 'round here, Missy. You think I don't know? You trying to get me to marry you, girl.'

'Now, just what would I want with you?'

'Don't play games with me! Cassie told me! Told me

85

everything you up to! Yeah, Cassie done told me all about it!'

Sissy's head turned like a rattler's.

'Oh, Lord,' I groaned and got out of the car. I was used to dealing with Sissy Mitchum, and I got myself ready for her.

'You done that, Cassie?' she hissed. 'You told him, knowin' all the while I ain't wanted him to know it?'

There was nothing I could do but admit the truth. It was out now. 'Yeah, I told it. Only thing was, Clarence wasn't supposed to tell you I told it.'

Clarence looked a bit chagrined. Sissy took note. 'Ain't Clarence's fault 'bout that. Fault's yours and the fault's mine, ain't it, now? I'da kept it to myself, then you wouldn't've known. You'da kept it to yourself, then he wouldn't've known.'

I didn't like the way this was going. Sissy was being too calm. 'Guess you got something there,' I admitted, feeling the contest of wills now between her and me.

She crossed her arms over her bulging stomach. 'You just can't stand it, can you, Cassie? To have another girl close to any of 'em?'

I studied her good. 'Girl, just what're you talking about?'

'Them boys. Can't stand it, can ya? You just had to go tell it and put yourself in good with Clarence, like you was closer to him than me. This here ain't been none of your business till you put yourself in it! It was all gonna work out, and I told you that – '

'Yeah, you told me that, all right!' I shot back. 'Meanwhile you were making such a mess around here you had everybody fighting – '

'Maybe so. But who're you to step into it?'

'Just trying to be your friend!'

'Well, maybe I don't need your kind of friend!'

''Ey, wait, now, Sissy!' interceded Clarence. 'Don't be gettin' on Cassie – '

Sissy turned like a tigress. 'And don't you be defendin' her! Not to me, you don't! Here I am carryin' this baby of yours, and you gonna take up for her 'stead of me? I'll kill you, boy!'

'Leastways you admitting now it's his,' I said. 'Got something set right out of all this mess.'

Suddenly, without warning, Sissy turned and lunged at me. I should have been expecting it, knowing Sissy as I did, but I suppose her condition caught me unprepared for the viciousness of her attack. I saw the flash in her eyes, then shielded my face with my arms before she could claw me. Clarence caught her and pulled her off. 'Now, Sissy,' he cried, 'you cut that out, girl!'

Sissy screamed to high heaven at the order. 'Now you protectin' her too! Well, I don't care! You don't mean nothin' to me!'

'Sissy! Calm down, girl!' He held her by the arms and tried to talk sense to her, but she wrenched away. She was a strong little thing. 'Tell it to Cassie!' she screamed. 'I don't wanna hear it! My ears closed to anything you got to say, Clarence! Oughta get me Ma's shotgun and take it to you my own self!'

I stepped forward. 'Ah, Sissy! You gone about as crazy as a loon – '

'Get 'way from me, Cassie Logan! I don't wanna talk to you!'

'Then I expect you don't much want to talk to nobody,' said Clarence. He let her go and walked back to the car.

Sissy's eyes went hot with rage. 'Don't you turn your back on me, Clarence Hopkins! You hear me? Don't you leave from here!'

Clarence didn't say anything. He held the door open for me. I sighed and got back in the car. Things weren't supposed to be turning out like this.

'Clarence!' Sissy screamed again.

'I'm sorry,' I said as Clarence got in beside me.

'You got no need,' he said. 'Let's go, Stacey.'

Stacey glanced over at Sissy. 'You sure you want to leave it like this, Clarence?'

'Yeah, I'm sure. The girl's crazy. Whole family's crazy.'

Stacey didn't say anything else. He started the car, and we went on, leaving Sissy behind still hollering after us.

'Look here, Stacey,' Clarence said, 'we get to Strawberry, I wanna stop a minute at the store, get me some BC head medicine.'

'All right. Have to stop in town myself to see Mr Jamison.'

'Good, then, 'cause that girl Sissy sure done give me one bad headache.'

I looked at him. 'Thought you had a headache before you left Jackson. Didn't you get rid of that thing?'

'Yeah, for a while. But it's back now, and that Sissy, she just done made it worse.'

'Yeah, well, I can understand that,' I said. 'She gave me one too.'

Incident in Strawberry

I had never much liked riding down the main street of Strawberry. I hadn't particularly liked it as a child, and I sure didn't now. Strawberry had always been a sad, desolate kind of place to me, and in the years since I'd first seen it nothing much had changed. Verandas still sagged in front of gloomy store buildings and raised wooden sidewalks still creaked and groaned. Wagons and pickups still lined the short strip of paved road that ran hurriedly through the town and away from it, and the spindly row of electrical lines that gave the town its claim to modernity still looked out of place. On Saturdays farm women wearing dresses cut from cotton flour sacks and farm men wearing denim populated the town, and a hound dog that looked to be as old as the town itself still slept wherever it pleased, in the middle of the road mainly, and folks just left him be and went around him.

That was Strawberry.

And then there were the old men. They were always sitting there on that bench in front of the Barnett Mercantile watching folks, reporting every move, just like some old police force. Like old grey sentinels from another era, they were always on the alert, reporting the latest comings, the latest goings, the slightest stray from the ordinary. It was December, yet they were sitting right there, and would be until the weather turned chill and damp and the dreaded days of winter swept this hot land, forcing them inside. Nothing much got past that bench that they didn't see, so we hardly could. We expected them to stare at us and wonder about our business, for they always did. They were staring now as Stacey parked in front of Mr Wade Jamison's office, across the street from the mercantile.

As we got out of the car Stacey frowned down at one of the tyres. 'What's the matter?' I asked.

'That left front tyre looks low.'

Little Willie came over. 'Lookin' more than low, hoss. Best put some air in it.'

'Been low too often,' said Stacey. 'Best to change it. Put on the spare.'

'Well, you go on see 'bout your business with Mr Jamison, man. We take care of it for you.'

'Thanks, Willie. The jack's in the back with the spare. But I tell you what. Take the car on down to Mr Dueeze's garage and see if you can't get this tyre here patched. Don't like to drive without a spare.'

'Don't worry 'bout a thing,' said Willie. 'It's already taken care of.'

Stacey gave Willie some money and the keys. 'I'll catch y'all up there.'

Willie started to take the driver's seat, but then Clarence said, 'Y'all wait on up a minute while I run in here and get me some BCs for my head. Be right back.'

'I'll go with you,' said Moe, and the two of them crossed the street to the mercantile. As they stepped onto the porch Statler Aames and his brothers came out of the store and Jeremy was with them. They looked at Clarence and Moe as they went in, then leaned against the store posts and began talking to the old men.

Stacey, who had been watching, turned and headed for Mr Jamison's office. As he reached the walkway Mr Jamison opened the door to his office and came out carrying a briefcase. He was a lean man, grey, in his sixties, and as usual when we saw him, he wore a suit and a hat. He noticed Stacey and gave a nod. 'Were you coming to see me?' he asked.

'Yes, sir, I was, but it looks like it's a bad time – '

'No matter. Glad you caught me. I was just on my way to Jackson.'

'We're on our way there too. It be better for you, I can come by your office in Jackson next week sometime. Wanted to make my final payment on the car.'

If Mr Jamison was surprised that Stacey was paying the car note off so quickly, he made no indication of it. He glanced over at the Ford, at Willie, Oliver, and me, spoke to us, then said, 'Car looks mighty good, Stacey. Mrs Jamison would be proud to see it.'

Stacey smiled, for those were fine words coming from Mr Jamison. 'Thank you. Course, it's not looking the best right now, what with all the dust from the trip down, but I'm right proud of it.'

Mr Jamison's eyes studied the Ford a few moments longer, then he looked back to Stacey. 'I take it you're all home for the funeral.'

'Yes, sir. Folks came from all over.'

'Well, Reverend Gabson ministered throughout the county. Wouldn't have expected any less. He was a respected man.'

'Yes, sir, that's a fact.'

Mr Jamison turned back to his office. 'You'll be needing a few legal papers now that you've got full ownership. Come on in and I'll write them for you.'

Stacey followed Mr Jamison back up the walkway and into the office. Little Willie, Oliver, and I waited by the Ford. Across the street the old grey men were watching us and so were Statler, Troy, and Leon Aames. I could feel Jeremy's eyes on us too. I knew they were all wondering about our business. I turned my back to them, leaned against the car, and looked the other way.

'Ah, there's that scound,' said Willie. 'Come on, we can go.'

He opened the car door. I turned around and saw Clarence coming out of the mercantile. Moe wasn't with him, but I didn't figure him to be far behind. I started to get into the car but then stopped as Statler hollered out to Clarence. "Ey, soldier boy!' he called. 'That uniform you got on making you forget your manners?'

Clarence was already at the steps. He turned, his face etched with surprise. 'S-suh?'

Statler now moved from his post toward Clarence. 'You walked right on past me twice now, boy, and ain't minded your manners neither time.'

Clarence stared at Statler as if not certain what he was talking about, but he apologized anyway. 'Well ... I'm sorry.'

'You sorry, then what your cap doing on your head, nigger, when I'm talking to ya?'

Immediately Clarence's hand went to his head and snatched off the cap.

'Niggers put on a uniform, make 'em get the big head. You got the big head, boy?'

'No, suh.'

'Well, why don't you just show me that, then?'

Clarence looked puzzled, not knowing what he meant. Leon and Troy sniggered at Clarence's confusion. 'Suh?'

'Come on over here, let me see your head. Want to see how big it is.' He motioned him over with a friendly gesture, as if inviting him to come sit down to tea. 'I said, step on over here!'

The old men on the bench laughed. Clarence looked at them, then slowly walked over to Statler and waited, his eyes questioning what was coming.

'Bend that head!' Statler ordered. Clarence obeyed. Statler walked around Clarence, his eyes on Clarence's head, giving it close inspection. Then he lifted his hand, balled it into a fist, and knocked on the back of Clarence's head as if he were knocking on somebody's door. He looked around at the others. 'Well, watcha think?'

Jeremy stood aside and said nothing. Leon and Troy laughed, then Troy knocked his knuckles against Clarence's head too. 'Well . . . it sure 'nough hard!' And then all the grey men and the Aames boys burst into raucous laughter. Clarence didn't react. He just stood stock-still.

'Well, what you think, Leon?' called Statler. 'Come on over here and see what you think 'bout this nigger, whether or not he got the hard head.'

Leon, though, objected. 'I ain't touchin' no nigger's greasy head.'

'Shoot, boy, don't mind that! Papa always told me it bring good luck to rub a nigger's head. Don't you know that, boy?'

Leon shrugged and gave it a try. Clarence clutched the flat cap in his hand. Jeremy looked on soberly, then turned and started off the porch. Statler called after him. ''Ey, Jeremy! You could do with some good luck, can't ya, now? Come on, give a feel.'

92

Jeremy glanced back. 'I gotta see 'bout my truck.'

'You rub this black nigger's head, you won't have to worry 'bout your truck. Maybe you'll come into a new one.'

Jeremy shook his head and went on down the street toward the Dueeze Garage. As he walked away one of the old grey men called Clarence over. When Clarence didn't move, Statler ordered, 'Go on 'round there, nigger! Just 'cause Mr Jeremy don't want no good luck don't mean Mr Bowater don't. Go on! Let Mr Bowater feel your head, boy!'

Clarence, his head bowed in humiliation, still didn't move. His eyes were downcast, looking at no one.

'You hear me, boy?' questioned Statler. 'You move when I speak to you!'

Clarence looked up. He was bigger than Statler. He was bigger than Leon and Troy. He could have taken any one of them on and whipped the mess out of him. But he couldn't whip the mess out of all three of them. He couldn't even whip the mess out of one of them and expect to sleep well tonight. He could never expect to hit a white man and sleep well.

'Don't you be eyeballing me, boy,' Statler warned, "cause we gonna get us some luck outa you. Now, go on, do like I say and get on there to Mr Bowater.'

I looked on, hoping Clarence would knock him flat; but I knew he could never do that.

'Watch yourself, son,' Little Willie murmured. 'Watch yourself.'

Clarence looked around, almost as if he had heard. I stepped forward, but Little Willie slipped his hand tightly over my wrist and stopped me. He knew as well as I did that there was nothing we could do. If we started something, *they* would finish it. We couldn't win, not against white folks. They did what they wanted, and there was no sense in starting up trouble just about a little ridicule. A little ridicule wasn't supposed to hurt. But it did. It sliced like a knife.

'Boy!' commanded Statler.

Clarence moved slowly toward the bench and Mr Bowater Jones. Just then Moe came out of the mercantile. As he stepped onto the porch he saw Clarence with his hat in his

93

hands and his head bent, and he said, 'Clarence . . . come on.'

'We got business with him,' said Statler Aames.

Moe glanced across the street at us, at me, then he turned back. 'Cl-Clarence?'

Statler Aames now turned his attention to Moe. 'Nigger, you hard of hearing? Ain't I just done said we got business with this boy?'

Moe seemed unable to speak. He opened his mouth, but no words came. Statler Aames started toward Moe now. Moe didn't move.

'Moe Turner! Clarence Hopkins!'

Statler stopped and looked across the street. Everybody looked. Standing on his office steps was Mr Wade Jamison. Stacey stood beside him.

'Clarence!' Mr Jamison said again. 'Would you come over, please? I'd like to see you. You too, Moe.'

Clarence, uncertain what to do, looked around at Statler, Leon and Troy, and the old grey men. Moe, keeping his eyes on Statler, moved slowly down the steps.

'Clarence! Moe! Now, please!'

At the second summons Clarence moved quickly and followed Moe into the street. Statler, Leon, Troy, and the others watched them go and didn't try to stop them. They didn't say a word. Mr Wade Jamison, after all, was a formidable figure and, despite everything, one of their own. In the past there had been those who had retaliated against Mr Jamison's liberal ways by burning out his office late one night, but he had survived. He seemed always to survive. Now they weren't about to go against him in broad daylight. If they did anything at all, it would be under the cover of darkness. That was their way.

Moe and Clarence went and spoke to Mr Jamison, then Clarence went back inside the office with Stacey. Mr Jamison remained standing on the porch. Moe came back to the car and said, 'Let's go on to the garage. Clarence and Stacey'll be down in a bit.'

Little Willie, Oliver, and I didn't question Moe. We just got into the Ford with Little Willie at the wheel and headed for the Dueeze Garage.

'That sure was a lowdown thing they did to Clarence,' I said as we drove down the street.

'Just be thankful they ain't done no more,' said Willie. ''Sides, nothin' to be done 'bout it, Cassie. They do what they want.'

'Still lowdown. Wish Clarence had knocked them out.'

'No, you don't,' said Moe and looked out the window. 'No, you don't.' I sighed and looked away.

The main street of Strawberry was only three blocks long. The Dueeze Garage at the other end was at the town's outskirts. Upon reaching the garage, the pavement ended, and just beyond the garage the forest sprang up. As we drove onto the lot, we saw the Simmses' pickup truck parked in front of the garage alongside Mr Dueeze's car and another truck. Jeremy was on the back of his truck, arranging a load. He glanced over but said nothing. Neither did we. We saw no one else. The doors to the garage were open, but no one was inside. 'Looks like we gonna hafta go on 'round back to get Mr Dueeze,' said Willie, parking the car at the far end of the lot, some distance from the pickups.

When we got out of the car, Oliver took the jack from the trunk and placed it in position. The hub cap was jammed in tight. Moe took out the crowbar and pried it off, then Oliver slipped off the tyre. It was then that Little Willie noticed that the spare looked as if it could use a patch job too. Taking the tyre that had just come off the Ford and the spare from the trunk, he and Oliver went around to the back of the garage to look for Mr Dueeze. Moe and I stayed by the car.

Moe, still holding the crowbar, walked around the car checking the other tyres. I started to lean against the car, then straightened and stared down the street toward town. I didn't believe what I saw. 'Can't be,' I said.

Moe glanced over. 'What is it?'

'That truck coming . . . isn't that Harris's old truck?'

Moe stared at the beat up vehicle coming our way and smiled. 'Sure looks enough like it.'

'Well, what's he doing here?'

As the truck drew closer we could see Harris at the wheel with Sissy beside him and Christopher-John and

Little Man riding in back. We left the Ford and walked toward the road. The old truck sputtered to a stop in front of us, and Sissy jumped out. 'Where's Clarence?' she demanded. 'Cassie – '

I left her to Moe and went around to the back. 'Christopher-John, Man, what y'all doing here? Papa and Mama know y'all in Strawberry?'

'Nope!' said Little Man, jumping down and brushing himself off.

'Well, what you doing here?'

'We were with Harris when Sissy got to hollering at him about coming into town to see about Clarence leaving her the way he did.' He grinned. 'Look like it was going to be too good to miss.'

'I imagine that punishment that'll be waiting for y'all won't be too good to miss either,' I pointed out. Little Man shrugged off the probability.

'I told him we ought not come,' complained Christopher-John as he, too, got down.

'Well, too late now,' I said.

They glanced over at Jeremy, who met their eyes and turned away without a word as he went on loading his truck. Then they noticed the Ford all jacked up and Little Man asked, 'What happened to the car?'

'Bad tyre,' I said. 'Oliver and Little Willie inside getting it and the spare fixed.'

'Oh,' they said and went over to inspect. Harris got out of the truck and hobbled over as well.

Sissy's voice rose impatiently. 'Y'all gonna tell me or not? Where Clarence at?'

'He's with Stacey,' said Moe.

'Well, where?'

'There, over at – ' Moe didn't finish. His eyes were on the road. Another truck was coming toward the garage.

'Oh, goodness,' I murmured. 'Statler Aames.'

But Sissy wasn't caring about Statler Aames at the moment. All she was concerned about right now was Clarence. 'Moe! Where is he?'

'Hush, girl,' I said as the truck turned into the garage lot and parked alongside the pickup next to Jeremy's. Over at the Ford, Harris's eyes grew big. He limped back toward us and his truck.

"Ey, Cousin!' exclaimed Statler, getting out with Leon and Troy. They walked toward Jeremy's truck. 'Uncle Charlie here?'

Jeremy picked up a feed bag and stacked it against the cab. 'Yeah, in back there. We gotta make a run up to Bogganville and take Mr George Goods a load. Been having a bit of trouble with this clutch, though. Had to get Mr Dueeze to take a look at it. Just hoping we don't have no more trouble with it 'fore we get back.'

'S-Sissy, c-come on,' hissed Harris, his eyes on Statler. 'Come on, let's get on 'way from here!'

'Not till I find out 'bout Clarence,' insisted Sissy stubbornly.

'B-but, Sissy – '

Statler turned and looked at us, and Harris froze. 'What you need, Jeremy, to keep this here truck running is some good luck,' said Statler. 'Like I told ya, maybe what you need to do is knock on a few heads here!' He squinted at Moe, as if trying to place him. Then he smiled in full recognition. 'Ain't you the boy messed with our getting ourselves some luck with that soldier boy?'

Moe didn't answer.

Statler came toward us. There was a look of mock uncertainty in his eyes. He stopped in front of Moe and studied him some more. 'Yeah,' he said, as if now certain. 'Yeah, you the one. Well, now, seeing you the one done stopped us from getting all our good luck before, seem like to me you need to do something 'bout that. Don't you figure that's only right?'

Moe's jaw slackened, and he looked at me. His grip tightened on the crowbar.

'Unh-unh, boy! Don't you be looking at Cassie when I'm talking to ya! You owe me some luck, and I'm planning on getting it. Get that hat off!' he ordered, but he gave Moe no time to react before he knocked the hat off himself.

Moe gazed at him with a fierce look.

'Nigger, don't you eyeball me! Now, you pick it up!'

Moe didn't move.

'Nigger, I said pick up that hat!'

The stiffness went out of Moe, and he bent to obey. At that moment Troy moved in close and goosed him, and Leon knocked on his head. Moe jumped back without retrieving the hat.

Leon laughed. 'He got the hard head, too, Stat. You the one figure rubbing a nigger's head bring good luck, come rub his.'

Statler grinned. 'Yeah, you must got a powerful lotta luck in you, boy, you courtin' a gal like Cassie Logan here. Put that head on down, boy, let me get a good feel at it. Who knows?' he said, reaching for Moe's head. 'Maybe I get lucky with Cassie myself – '

Suddenly the anger in Moe burst forth like a thunderstorm. He knocked Statler's arm away with the tyre iron, then smashed it full force into Statler's side.

'What the – ' screamed Statler as he fell to his knees.

'Nigger, you gone mad?' cried Leon as Statler held his side in shock. 'What done got into you?'

'Y'all get holda him!' ordered Statler. 'Y'all get hold of him now!'

Leon and Troy moved cautiously toward Moe as the rest of us just stood there stunned, watching. 'Now, boy, put that iron down 'fore you get into more trouble,' warned Troy. 'You put it down right now!' Moe stepped back, holding tightly to the crowbar.

'I said, get hold of him!' hollered Statler, and both Leon and Troy rushed at Moe, who swung the crowbar as hard as he could. As Troy came at him Moe laid the crowbar upside his head. Leon came at him, and he smashed the crowbar into his chest. Both brothers went down.

It was all over in a matter of seconds.

Troy, his head bleeding, lay prone on the ground. So did Leon. Statler knelt, holding his side, staring icily at Moe but was unable to rise. Moe, as if in a dream, stood frozen, gazing at Statler and his brothers, as if he had had no part in what had just happened. The rest of us stood frozen too. Then we heard shouting and came back to ourselves. Someone was coming.

Moe looked around wildly and threw down the bloody crowbar. Then he turned to Harris, who had already gotten into his truck. Moe took a step toward Harris, but Harris hollered: 'Naw, naw, they get me! Like that night on the Rosa Lee! Like that night on the Rosa Lee!' Then he rammed the gas pedal and tore away, up the road, out of the town, leaving Moe and Sissy, too, behind.

'Harris!' called Sissy. 'Harris, come back here!' But Harris didn't stop.

Moe turned frantically, searching for a place to hide. But there was no place. There was no escaping in the Ford; it had no tyre. There was no place to run either. Then Moe saw Jeremy standing on his truck, staring down at him. Jeremy had seen the whole thing. A moment passed, and their eyes remained fixed on each other. Then, without a word being spoken, a decision was made. Jeremy nodded and motioned Moe onto the truck. Moe glanced around, his eyes meeting mine, then quickly climbed on. Statler, Leon, and Troy, lying on the ground, did not see. Leon and Troy were both out; Statler, looking dazed, faced away from Jeremy's truck. Jeremy threw the tarpaulin over Moe and jumped down just as Mr J. D. Dueeze and his wife came running from the garage with Mr Charlie Simms. Oliver and Little Willie came running too.

'Lord! Lord have mercy!' screamed Mrs Dueeze. 'Lord have mercy! What happened here?'

Mr Simms took one look at us standing there and accused us. 'Y'all dirty, filthy niggers! I'll see y'all hung for this!'

'Naw, Pa, ya wrong!' cried Jeremy, hurrying over to see about Leon. 'They ain't done nothin'! They ain't touched 'em!'

'Then, who done it?' hollered Mr Simms as Mr Dueeze and his wife knelt to help the fallen Aames boys. 'Jeremy, who done this?'

Jeremy didn't answer. He rolled Leon over, and hoarsely whispered his name. 'Leon . . . Leon . . .'

Mr Simms jerked Jeremy up. 'Boy, you hear me talkin' to ya? You answer me!'

Jeremy looked blankly at his father. 'Coloured boy . . .'

'What coloured boy? Where the nigger at?'

'Moe . . . It was Moe Turner . . .'

'One nigger done this?' questioned his father, as if not believing.

'Yes, sir, Pa ... He ... he had a crowbar. That one yonder, on the ground.'

Mr Dueeze picked it up, recoiling at the sight of the blood. 'Lordy,' he said. 'Lord . . .'

Mr Simms swore an oath. 'Lowdown filthy animals! This here what happen we give 'em too free a rein. This what happen!'

Mrs Dueeze looked up from where she was kneeling beside Troy. 'Would y'all leave that be for now and help me see to these boys here? We need to get them some help!'

Jeremy slipped from his father's grasp and knelt beside Statler. 'Stat ... Stat, you all right?'

Statler looked at him and closed his eyes.

'Lord, these boys is hurt bad,' said Mrs Dueeze. 'Hurt real bad. Troy, he's bleeding something awful 'round the head.' She looked around, searching for help. Her eyes settled on two little coloured boys who were running up to see what was going on. 'Henry!' she cried. 'You run get Doctor Cranston for me! Run quick, now! Homer, jump in that truck there and lay on that horn! Get some folks up here to help us!' The two boys quickly obeyed. Little Homer jumped into Statler's truck and began honking wildly. Little Henry took off down the street screaming to high heaven.

Mr Simms looked down, aghast, at his kin, at all the blood, and started in questioning Jeremy again. 'Where that nigger gone off to?'

Jeremy slowly raised his head and looked at his father. 'It ... it happened so fast, Pa. I ... I was on the truck finishin' the loadin' ... heard all the commotion.' He glanced over at his truck, and my heart, already beating hard and fast, began to race. 'Seen Moe swinging that crowbar – '

'Well, where'd he go off to, boy?' asked Mr Dueeze. 'You gotta seen.'

Jeremy looked over at us. I felt my heart would burst. 'He ... just gone off ... down the road ...'

Mr Simms studied Jeremy through narrow, dangerous eyes. 'You seen all this, why ain't you helped? What your cousins doin' bleeding on the ground and you ain't got a mark on ya?'

Jeremy whitened. 'It ... it happened so fast. Wasn't time – '

'Wasn't time for you to stop that nigger from gettin' away either?'

'I ... he took off so fast, Pa, and I ... I wanted to see to my cousins. I'd've gone after Moe, but I figured he wouldn't get far on foot and – '

Statler groaned, then supporting his weight with one arm, he sat up and called weakly, 'Uncle Charlie ... Uncle Charlie ...'

Mr Simms hurried over and knelt beside him. 'What is it, son?'

'That nigger ... Harris Mitchum was here. He was driving a truck.'

At that, Sissy's eyes went wild. 'Naw, Harris, he left here by hisself – '

I caught her arm and dug my nails in before she could say more. In silence I looked at her, warning her to keep hers.

Mr Simms kept his eyes on Statler. 'What happened, son?'

'Couldn't see exactly, Uncle Charlie. Felt dizzy. But Moe, that nigger done this, he gone. What 'bout Harris? He gone too?'

'He ain't here.'

'Then, Moe, he gone with him, then.'

'Don't you worry, now, boy. Just lie on back. We'll get him, I promise you that. We'll get both them niggers.'

'Naw!' cried Sissy. 'No, not my brother!' But Mr Simms paid her no attention as he and Mr Dueeze jumped into Mr Dueeze's car and took off down the road after Harris. People from the town came running toward the garage. Even the old grey men had left their bench and were heading to see what all the commotion was about. The boys, Sissy, and I moved away from the trucks and huddled together at the far end of the lot beside the Ford. There we told Little Willie and Oliver what had happened. We also told them where Moe was. They looked at us in disbelief. We said little else as we stayed to ourselves and kept watch on the truck.

Soon we saw Stacey and Clarence coming up the street. They passed the townspeople and came over, surprised to see Christopher-John, Little Man, and Sissy with us. 'Sissy, girl, what you doing here?' demanded Clarence first thing.

Stacey said, 'What happened?'

We told them.

'Where's Moe now?' asked Stacey.

I nodded toward Jeremy's truck. 'There.'

Stacey gazed past the crowd of people to where Jeremy was standing beside his truck conferring with Sheriff Hank Dobbs and Deputy Haynes. 'He know?'

'He knows, all right. He told his daddy it was Moe hit his cousins.'

'Jeremy did that?' Stacey asked, sounding surprised that he would, and I found that surprising after what had happened on the Rosa Lee.

'He just about had to tell him since his daddy saw all of us and figured we had something to do with it. Besides, Statler told his uncle about Moe anyway. Jeremy told him Moe ran off down the road.'

'What I wanna know,' said Willie, 'is how the devil we going to get Moe outa here? All these people 'round, and here he is, sitting right in the middle of them. How do we get him out, man?'

'What I wanna know is what 'bout Harris?' cried Sissy. 'These folks think he done helped Moe get away?'

'We worry 'bout Harris soon's we finish worryin' 'bout Moe,' said Willie.

'Maybe you worry 'bout Moe first, but Harris, he my brother, and he my first worry!'

'Hush up, Sissy!' said Clarence. 'Hush up and just take it easy. Give us a minute to study this out.'

Sissy cut her eyes at Clarence, folded her arms across her chest, and turned angrily away. Clarence looked back to Stacey, waiting for his solution to the matter. 'Well, Stacey, what you think?'

I spoke before Stacey could answer. 'Mr Jamison's still in town, isn't he?'

'Far's I know,' Stacey replied. 'Said he had to go home to get his sister 'fore he heads for Jackson.'

'Well, why don't we go get him? Maybe he could help us.'

'No,' Stacey said quickly. 'No, we best take care of this ourselves for now anyways. Best not bring him into it.'

I looked at him and agreed. I understood his thinking, but that didn't solve our problem. 'Well, what'll we do then?'

Stacey looked again at the truck and was thoughtful for some time. Finally he said, 'We'll get Jeremy to take him out.'

'Jeremy!' Willie exclaimed. 'Man, you crazy. . .'

'You gotta be crazy, Cuz!' objected Oliver. 'That's his kin Moe done near to killed!'

'You think I forgot that?'

Oliver shook his head in disbelief.

'You really think he'd do it?' I said.

'I can ask.'

I, too, shook my head. 'I don't think you ought to.'

'No other way, Cassie. Don't see any other way.'

'Well, where could he take him?'

'Jackson. He could take him to Jackson.'

'All the way to Jackson after what he did to Harris?' I wasn't ready to trust Jeremy that far.

'All I can do is ask.'

'You're crazy,' Oliver muttered again.

Christopher-John moved in closer. 'Stacey, maybe we oughta all just go back home and talk to Mama and Papa – '

'No time,' said Stacey.

'But – '

Stacey held up his hand, warning us into silence. The sheriff and his deputy were on their way over. They were stopped by one of the old grey men. Jeremy was now alone at the truck.

'Well, if you're going to talk to him, you best go talk to him now,' I said.

Stacey nodded, glanced around at us, and started toward Jeremy. I tagged along with him, for I was hoping I could talk to Moe. As we approached the truck I could feel Jeremy watching us with eyes that were nervous and frightened and looked about to weep.

'Heard what you done,' Stacey said softly when we stood beside him.

Jeremy glanced around nervously. There was no one near. 'Ain't done nothing.'

'Need to ask you to do something else.'

Jeremy looked at him.

'Need for you to take Moe on to Jackson.'

Jeremy's lips parted, and for a moment he said nothing. Then he said: 'You know what you asking me? They find Moe in my truck, I'm already in a powerful lot of trouble. I don't even know how Moe's gonna get outa the truck without my Pa seeing. I already done took a awful chance – '

'I know. But they find Moe, you know what they'll do.'

Jeremy glanced over at the sheriff and shook his head. 'You askin' something awful hard of me, Stacey.'

'I know that.'

'I . . . I just can't. My pa and me, we s'pose to be going to Bogganville – '

''Ey, you, boy!' called the deputy. 'You, boy, Stacey! Sheriff Dobbs said he wanna talk to you and your sister! Come on!'

We glanced at Jeremy, then moved slowly away. I wanted to whisper to Moe, hunched down like some cornered animal under the tarpaulin, but there was no time. Stacey and I turned and made our way through the crowd back to the Ford where Sheriff Dobbs was now busy talking to another one of the old men from the mercantile. The boys and Sissy stood nearby. After several minutes Sheriff Dobbs finally addressed us. 'Understand Moe Turner was the one gone crazy 'round here,' he said. 'Hear he came in with y'all. Heard y'all was with him when he took that crowbar to these boys.'

'Well, I didn't see it,' said Stacey. 'I just came up from Mr Jamison's office.'

'He tellin' the truth on that, all right,' said one of the grey men. 'That boy done all this devilment, and the rest of the nigras, they got in that car and come down this way. Other boy here and that soldier boy gone in with Mr Jamison.'

The sheriff turned to the rest of us. 'Well, y'all seen where Moe gone?'

We all said he had just run down the road.

The sheriff looked at us as if he knew we were lying, then he started in questioning Stacey again. 'What y'all doing in town anyway? Heard y'all was working in Jackson.'

'Came down for Reverend Gabson's funeral. On our way back to Jackson now.'

The sheriff grunted.

'Fact . . . we're supposed to be back at work come evening. Like to get going, that be all right with you.'

Sheriff Dobbs showed little interest about that. Statler Aames hollered for him, and he said, 'Y'all wait right here.' He left us and went over to where all three of the Aameses still lay on the ground being tended by the doctor, Mrs Dueeze, and some other town folks. The sheriff leaned over Statler. 'Yeah, what is it, Stat?'

'That boy Moe, y'all catch him yet?'

'Not yet, but we will. Don't worry none 'bout that.'

Statler's eyes left the sheriff, and his look was wild. 'Where's my cousin? Where's Jeremy? Jeremy!'

Jeremy was still leaning against the rear of his pickup. At the call he straightened, and his ashen face grew even whiter. The sheriff motioned him over. 'Come on, Jeremy! Come on here. Keep this boy from straining hisself hollering so.'

Jeremy glanced back at the tarpaulin and went over. 'What – what is it, Stat?'

'You seen what that nigger done to me, ain't ya? Ya seen it! Just gone crazy all of a sudden and hauled off and hit me and my brothers. Well, I ain't gonna stand for it! Ain't gonna stand for no nigger doin' me thataway! I ain't gonna stand for it, ya hear? Wherever that nigger is, he's mine! He can run, but he can't hide!'

Jeremy nodded.

'You keep an eye out, now.'

'I'll do that,' said Jeremy, then stood back watching as Statler, Leon, and Troy were lifted onto the back of a truck. As the truck rolled down the street toward the doctor's office, Mr Simms and Mr Dueeze returned.

'See y'all ain't found him,' said Sheriff Dobbs.

'Naw, but we will,' said Mr Simms. 'We will. I ain't gonna rest 'til we get him.'

'Well, we gettin' ready to go lookin' now. Got plenty of men lined up.'

Charlie Simms nodded, then turned to Jeremy. 'I'm gonna stay on here and help look for that nigger,' he said. 'We find him, we gonna learn him better'n t' raise his hand to a white man. Now, you get that load on up to Bogganville. It's late and they 'spectin' it.'

'Yes, sir, Pa.'

'You tell George Goods and Joe Hanley what done happened here. Tell them to keep they eyes open for any new niggers showin' up 'round there.'

Jeremy nodded and turned toward the truck.

'You keep watch on that oil, now, Jeremy. See that engine don't burn up!'

'Yes, sir, Pa.' He reached the truck, opened the door, and looked back. His eyes rested on us, but I couldn't read them. He said nothing. He just got into the truck and drove away, north toward Bogganville.

'Stacey!' said Sheriff Dobbs. 'I'm gonna let y'all go on, but I'm gonna be keepin' an eye on y'all. I see this car of y'all's back this way, y'all gonna have a whole lotta explainin' to do, ya hear me, now?'

'Yes, sir, we hear.'

'Just so's I know y'all don't get addle minded on down the road and decide y'all smarter'n me, I'm gonna send some men down to follow y'all out and block that road off. Y'all decide to double back, ain't gonna do no good. Y'all just gonna end up spending jail time 'long with Moe. Y'all understand me, now?'

Stacey answered for us all. 'We just want to get back to Jackson.'

'All right, then.' He turned and called to a group of men some feet away. 'Mr Boudein! You and Mr Josias there and your boys, y'all mind following this Logan boy on out and keepin' watch on that road awhile? I'll send somebody to spell y'all later on.'

Mr Boudein gave a nod, and the sheriff said to us, 'All right, y'all go on.'

'Yes, sir . . . soon's we get our tyre on.'

The sheriff looked at the jacked up car, nodded, and turned back to the crowd.

As Little Willie and Oliver put on the still-soft spare tyre, Sissy said, 'Shoulda told 'em 'bout Jeremy.'

'Can't,' Stacey said. 'Can't tell them about Jeremy.'

'But they think Harris – '

'Please, Sissy, they don't get Harris, keep it to yourself.'

'Naw, naw, I ain't! Not after what him and them others done to sweet Harris! Maybe y'all done forgot, but I ain't forgot that night on the Rosa Lee! Ain't 'bout to forget it!'

Clarence grabbed her by the shoulders. 'Sissy, you listen to me, girl! This here ain't got to do with Jeremy! It got to do with Moe! Ya hear me? Ya hear me, Sissy?'

'Ah, get away from me!' she said, pushing him back. Then she turned angrily and walked off and stood by the road. Clarence didn't go after her.

'Look,' said Stacey to Christopher-John and Little Man, his voice low and urgent, 'don't tell *anybody* but Mama, Papa, and Big Ma about Jeremy and how Moe got away. Less folks know about that the better.'

'But what we s'pose to tell Mr Turner?' asked Christopher-John.

'Papa'll know what to tell him.'

Christopher-John nodded, then glanced to the road. 'You . . . you think Jeremy gonna get Moe to Jackson?'

Oliver, stooped by the tyre, straightened. 'Ask me, he probably circle right on back to home and hand Moe over to some folks with a rope!'

Christopher-John frowned, uncertain. 'I . . . I don't think so.'

'Watch my words,' said Oliver. 'He get hisself in a tight enough spot, he will.'

'Hey!' Sheriff Dobbs yelled from the Boudein car. 'Ain't y'all got that tyre on yet? Thought y'all wanted to get on back to Jackson so fast. What y'all still standin' there for?'

Little Willie slapped the cap on the tyre. Stacey glanced over as he unhooked the jack. 'We're going now,' he said. The sheriff looked away. Stacey looked back at Christopher-John and Little Man. 'Y'all go on over to Mr John Rankin's place, see if he can't take y'all home. Now, you'll be all right?'

'Yeah, we'll be fine,' Little Man assured him.

'Yeah, don't worry none 'bout us,' said Christopher-John.

'Remember what I said, now.'

Both boys nodded. 'We will . . .'

107

'Look,' said Clarence, glancing to the road and Sissy standing there, her arms folded across her chest staring up the road the way Harris had gone, 'y'all see to Sissy getting home, will ya? Don't let her give ya no trouble. Spite what she might wanna do, y'all just make sure ya take her on home when y'all go.'

'Sure we will,' said Little Man.

'We take care of her,' Christopher-John promised him. 'All of us, we be fine. Don't y'all worry none. Y'all better go.'

Stacey embraced each of them. 'Y'all take care.'

'Y'all do the same,' they returned.

I hugged them as well. I hugged them tight and got into the car. Little Willie and Oliver got in too. Clarence took one last look at Sissy and followed. Stacey started the Ford, and we left Strawberry. Mr Boudein and the other men trailed us. I looked back for a last glimpse of the town. Christopher-John, Little Man, and Sissy were still there, watching us. The street curved, and I looked straight ahead to the rusty, dirt road that we would travel to Jackson.

Oliver leaned forward. 'You really trust him?'

Stacey turned slightly. 'What?'

'That white boy, Jeremy Simms. You actually believe he's going to take Moe to Jackson?'

Stacey met Oliver's eyes in the rearview mirror and sighed. 'Trusted him before. Figure I got no choice but to trust him now.'

Oliver settled back and said nothing else. Stacey said nothing else either. Yes, we had trusted Jeremy before all right, but now that seemed so long ago. All we could do was hope that we could trust him still.

Escape From Jackson

When we got to Jackson, we went straight to Lynch Street and the cafe. We hoped to find Moe waiting there, but he wasn't. With Cousin Hugh and Cousin Sylvie still at Great Faith and not expected back until late Sunday, Oliver's older sister, Jessie, and her husband, Jasper, were running the cafe; they said they hadn't seen Moe. No one else had either. We went to the house, checked there and down the street at Mrs Stalnaker's, where Little Willie and Moe roomed. We called a few places we thought Moe might have gone, then returned to the cafe and waited.

'Now, that scound left from Strawberry 'fore we did,' said Little Willie, sipping at a cup of coffee. 'Should've done been here by now. Where is that boy?'

Oliver shook his head. 'Maybe they got him. Maybe they caught up with him.' He looked around at Stacey. 'Or maybe that white boy Jeremy Simms changed his mind and let his daddy have him.'

'You think that?' I asked Stacey.

Stacey, who had for some time been staring into his cup, raised his head and looked at me. 'Don't think anything yet, Cassie.'

'Well, what we going to do?' asked Willie.

Stacey was thoughtful, then he looked at Willie. 'Going to sit here and wait for Moe. He doesn't come in soon, though, I figure to go out looking for him.'

'Where?' I questioned. 'I know he got fired from the box factory.'

He looked at me as if he hadn't expected me to know.

I shrugged. 'Moe told me.'

Little Willie checked his watch. 'You know, Stace, we got

less than an hour to get to work ourselves, we don't wanna be late.'

'Well, I'm not going to work. Least not till I know about Moe. We can't find him here in Jackson, we'll have to call down to Strawberry, or go home, see what happened to him.'

Little Willie nodded sober agreement. 'Course, now, we might just hafta kiss that ole job good-bye then, we don't show up. Know they got rid of that Allen boy just last week for not showing up.'

'Well, I'm about ready to be finished with it anyway,' said Stacey.

'Yeah, me too,' agreed Willie, 'especially if we can finally get on with the trucking company.'

'Anybody got any more BC?' asked Clarence, who had been sitting quietly in the booth, his head leaned against the back of the wooden seat. 'My head is killing me.'

I turned. 'Boy, you took a whole pack of those things already.'

'Yeah, I know. But seem like I just can't get rid of this here headache. That Sissy and all that mess in Strawberry done got me so worked up, can't make it go away.'

Oliver motioned toward the back of the cafe. 'There's a sofa in that back room there. Maybe you better stretch out.'

'Don't need to stretch out. Just need something for my head, then I be ready to take on the world.'

'Uh-huh,' I said, and got up. 'I'll see if maybe Jessie has some in the kitchen.'

'Thanks, Cassie.'

'Least I can do, seeing you about to become a daddy.'

Little Willie laughed. 'Yeah, that's right, Cassie! Take care of this man!'

I got two packs of BCs from Jessie and a glass of water, then returned to the table. As I sat down a man and a woman came in and I took note of them. The woman was striking, fashionably dressed in a bold Irish-green suit, and wore a dart of a green hat on her upswept hairdo. She looked out of place in the neighbourhood cafe. I only got a glimpse of the man, whose back was to me, his eyes on the woman in green. I hadn't seen either one of them in the cafe before. Oliver, who was at the cash register, hurried

110

over and shook the man's hand, then personally found them a table.

'Cassie, you gonna let me have my medicine?'

'What?' I said, turning back to Clarence. 'Oh, yeah.' I gave the medicine to him, and he quickly ripped open one of the packages and took out a sliver of wrapped powder. Putting the wrapping to his mouth, he threw back his head and downed the white dust. I grimaced. 'Boy, how can you sit there and take that stuff without water?'

He made a face at the taste. 'Ain't so bad. Done tasted worse.'

Stacey slapped the table and got up. 'I'm going looking for Moe.'

'Well, I'll be going with you, then,' said Willie, standing too.

Oliver came over. 'Y'all leaving now?'

'Figure it's time,' said Stacey.

Clarence and Oliver decided to go as well. So did I. Stacey, however, wouldn't hear of it. He said I needed to stay and study with the students I was supposed to be meeting for my upcoming debate. 'But they're not even here yet,' I pointed out.

'They'll come. That grade's important so you just wait for them. Besides, maybe Moe'll come here, so you'll be here if he comes. We won't be long.'

I decided not to protest further. They left, and I went off to the kitchen to let Jessie know I was going to be studying in the back room. 'Anybody comes in looking for me, tell them I'm back there, will you?' Jessie, who was busy frying a batch of hamburgers, grunted that she would. I pushed the kitchen door open, then turned back to Jessie. 'It's getting pretty crowded out there. You need me to help out? I can, you know.'

'No, you go on study, sugar. Jasper and me, we can handle things.'

'All right, but you need me, you call me, now.'

'Don't worry, I will,' she assured me as she turned her burgers.

I went back through the cafe and down a short hallway to the storage room. Officially the storage room was supposed to be Cousin Hugh's office, but he didn't spend much time in it. Neither did Cousin Sylvie. They were always too busy in the cafe or the barber or beauty shop. The room was cluttered with boxes and crates, but it also had an old sofa, and I found it a comfortable place to study. In fact, I was here more than just about anybody else.

I pulled three of my books from a shelf and sat down. Two of the books were library books I had gotten to prepare for the upcoming debate. The third book was my own and had nothing to do with FDR and the New Deal. It was titled *The Law: Case Histories of a Free Society*, and it was what I called my lawyer book because Mr Wade Jamison had given it to me. Though it was my favourite book, I put it aside for the time being and opened up one of the other books, and tried to concentrate on the debate. My mind, though, wasn't on the debate at the moment. It kept slipping back to Moe and what had happened in Strawberry. Finally I decided I couldn't be worrying about the New Deal right now, and I put the book aside, picked up *The Law: Case Histories of a Free Society*, turned to where I had last left off, and began to read. Soon I was engrossed in the reading. The book was filled with court cases, and it gave me great satisfaction to read a case, then try to figure out what the decision would be before the decision was disclosed. To me reading a case was like reading through a puzzle. Though I knew there was nothing in these cases that could help Moe out of his mess, they were much more satisfying to me than reading about FDR and the New Deal.

As I read I kicked off my pumps, curled my legs onto the couch, and got comfortable. No sooner than I did, someone knocked on the door, and I looked up, scowling at the interruption, wondering who could be knocking, for most folks just came right on in since the room wasn't considered a private place. 'Door's not locked!' I called irritably, my mind on my case.

The door then swung open, and a man stood in the shadowed doorway. He wore a finely cut grey suit and held a grey hat in his hand. He was smiling. 'You're obviously not Jasper,' he said. 'I was told he was back here.'

'Well, he's not.'

'I can see that.' He looked around the room at all the

112

clutter. 'Not unless he's stuffed himself into one of these many boxes in here. If you should see him, would you please tell him Solomon Bradley was looking for him?' He turned to leave; then he stepped out of the shadows into the room and came toward me. Now I knew who he was. He was the man who had come into the cafe with the women in green. 'Excuse me, but what's that you're reading?' He extended his hand before I could tell him. 'May I?'

I gave him the book.

He read the title: *'The Law: Case Histories of a Free Society*. What college do you go to?'

'Hope to be in college next year, but right now I'm in high school.'

'So this is what they're reading in high school these days?' There was a twist of a tease in his voice.

'That's not a high school book.'

'You don't say.' He glanced from the book to me, as if he expected me to explain what I was doing with it. But I gave no explanation, and he asked for none. 'I've got to say, this is pretty difficult reading for a high school student.'

I looked at the book, having never thought that myself. 'You think so?'

'Believe me, it is. It's pretty difficult reading for a college student. I've read it.'

I stirred with new interest. 'No kidding, you have?'

'Constitutional law.'

'What?'

'That's the law school course I had to read it in.' He sat on a wooden crate near me, leaned forward, an elbow on each knee, and began to thumb through the book.

'You're a lawyer?'

He kept his eyes on the book. 'I didn't say that.'

'But you were studying the law?'

He was reading now and took several moments before answering. 'Uh-huh,' he finally said and pursed his lips, seemingly absorbed in the book. Then he looked at me and flashed a smile. I found myself staring. He was a very attractive man, this Solomon Bradley. He looked to be in his mid-twenties and had an intriguing face. What struck me particularly were his eyes. They were dark, flecked with hazel, and perhaps it was that oddity in them, the sense of light emanating from them, that gave his face such appeal and made me keep my eyes on him longer than I should have. 'Plessy versus Ferguson.'

I was so struck by his eyes that he startled me when he spoke. 'What?'

'That's a case. Have you read it?'

'That's the one where the Supreme Court said that separate but equal was all right. It said segregation was constitutional.'

He smiled as if he hadn't expected me to know. 'I'm impressed. Very impressed. Thing is, though, we might be separate, but we're certainly not equal, at least not under the law.' He looked off to nowhere in particular, as if his mind was fixed on something else, and nodded. Then he looked again at the book.

As he studied it I studied him. The man was beginning to fascinate me. 'Did you finish law school?'

'Yes.'

'Well, if you finished law school,' I said, 'then why aren't you a lawyer?'

'You're making an assumption. I didn't say I wasn't.'

'But you said – '

'What I said was, I didn't say I was. Never make assumptions. That can be a dangerous thing.'

'Well, are you or aren't you?'

He turned another page and read it before he replied. 'I figure you have to practise the law to be a lawyer.'

'And you don't? Why not?'

He closed the book, looked directly at me, and held my eyes. 'I spent time in jail once and that had somewhat of a disturbing effect on me. After that, I didn't have much respect for the law.'

I was silent.

'Aren't you going to ask me why? Why I was in jail?'

'No.'

'Why not? You haven't been bashful about asking anything else so far.'

'Well, I figure jail time is kind of personal, you know. Maybe you wouldn't want to talk about it.'

'Oh. I see.'

114

I looked straight into those hazel-flecked eyes. 'Would you? Would you want to talk about it?'

He laughed good-naturedly but didn't answer. 'Where did you get a book like this, anyway?'

'A lawyer gave it to me.'

'You planning on becoming a lawyer?'

I hesitated. 'No . . . I just like reading up on the law.'

'That sounds to me almost as if the idea has crossed your mind.' I didn't say anything. 'You should think about it. Especially since you don't seem to mind asking direct questions.'

'You didn't answer my last one.'

'And you're persistent too. No, I wouldn't want to talk about it, not today, thank you.' He cupped his chin in his left hand and studied me. 'You know, law's a tough business. You'd have to be determined.'

'I know. Thing is, even if I studied law, I couldn't do it here. There's no law school in Mississippi for coloured. I checked.'

'The Gaines case. Are you familiar with it?'

'No.'

'Well, back in '36 a Negro by the name of Lloyd Gaines applied for admission to the law school at the University of Missouri and was rejected. He went to court about it, and the case went all the way to the Supreme Court. The Supreme Court said that it was the duty of the state of Missouri to provide education to all its citizens and to provide it within the state, not ship them off and pay tuition for them in another state. There's hope in that, I'd say. Perhaps the same thing could be done if you want to study law.'

I stared at him, wondering if this knowledgeable man knew anything about Mississippi. He half smiled. 'What is it?'

'You expect me to go applying to the University of Mississippi?'

He laughed, a deeply resonant kind of laugh. 'You say that as if you think I'm a bit crazed.'

'Not for me to say. But Missouri's one thing, Mississippi's another, and Mississippi is definitely *not* Missouri. A body'd have to be crazy to try something like that here.'

115

'An outspoken woman. I like that.' He was still smiling. 'Well, if you're not up to taking on the state of Mississippi quite yet, you can always apply to the state to fund your law school education somewhere else. As I said, the state's supposed to do that, at least, for those fields of study that aren't open to you here, and that's still in effect despite the Supreme Court ruling.' He paused and grinned. 'Course, the hitch is that they seldom do. They decide what Negroes should be studying, and what they usually decide Negroes should be studying are those fields Negroes can already study here in the state.'

I shrugged. 'Well, I'm not going to worry about that now. First thing I've got to do is get to college. I'll worry about the law later.'

'If you do study the law, it'll take a long time, and marriage could get in the way.'

'No, it won't. I don't plan to get married until I've finished my schooling. Body had to take care of some man and a whole bunch of children, she wouldn't ever have time for school.'

Again he laughed. 'Well, don't be so sure about marriage, young lady. Some young man could possibly come along and change your mind.'

'No, I wouldn't let that happen,' I said, sure of that. 'Getting all involved with some boy takes up too much time, and I can't afford it.'

'So what do you do, to keep boys from being a distraction?'

'Well, I really haven't had a problem so far.'

'You mean you haven't been in love so far.'

I wasn't quite sure how I should react to that; but it was true. 'Guess not.'

He seemed amused by my honesty. 'Tell me,' he said, 'just what do the young men have to say about all this? I mean, after all, it must be pretty rough on the fellas at your school.'

'How's that?'

'Because you're a very pretty girl, and you deserve to be courted.' He flashed that wonderful smile again, stood, and gave me back my book.

'Did marriage get in your way?'

116

'Marriage?'

'Aren't you married?'

'No.'

'I thought you were . . .'

'As I said, it's not good for a lawyer, making assumptions.'

'. . . to that woman in green out there.'

'Woman in green?' He seemed puzzled, then he laughed. 'Are you a Dashiell Hammett fan?'

'Dashiell who?'

'Dashiell Hammett. He wrote a book called *Red Harvest*, first chapter titled "A Woman in Green and a Man in Grey". Your comment seemed appropriate.'

'Especially since you're wearing grey.'

'You're right. But what about Sherlock Holmes? Are you familiar with him?'

'He's a writer too?'

Solomon Bradley pushed his suit coat back in a smooth, liquid movement and slid his hands into his pants pockets. 'You don't go to films much, do you? Or listen to the radio?' He gave me no time to answer. 'Write this down,' he dictated. 'Sir Arthur Conan Doyle, comma, creator of Sherlock Holmes, comma, one of the world's greatest minds, period. *Case Histories of a Free Society* might be fine for bright young ladies boning up to become lawyers, but, believe me, Sherlock Holmes can be a lot more fun.'

We heard footsteps in the hallway, and Jasper came in. 'Eh, Solomon Bradley! Heard you was here!' He vigorously shook Solomon's hand. 'What brings you into town?'

'Just on my way back from New Orleans. Thought I'd stop in and get some of that fine cooking you folks are always serving up.'

'You gonna be here long? You know we got that place right upstairs. Stay overnight. We can fix you up a bed.'

'Thanks, Jasper, but I've got to get back tonight. I've got to work tomorrow.'

Jasper laughed. 'Shoot, man, I had your money, I sure wouldn't be worrying about getting back to work!'

Solomon smiled. 'Wish I had the money you seem to think I do.'

117

'That your fine-looking woman all dressed in green sitting out there?'

'She's with me.'

'Well, let me fix y'all up some food to take with you, since Jessie said y'all done already ate. Hope everything was all right.'

'Fine as always.'

'Good.' Jasper grinned, looking pleased. 'Look, you come on out here and have some coffee with me. I'll go on and tell Jessie to fix up some chicken and some pie for y'all to take.' With that he slapped Solomon's shoulder and went out.

Solomon Bradley walked slowly to the door. At the doorway he turned and looked back at me. 'I liked talking to you,' he said.

I laughed. 'You sound kind of surprised.'

His smile widened. 'Well, frankly, I guess I am. It's not every day I meet a high school student reading *Case Histories of a Free Society*.' Those hazel-flecked eyes studied me once more. 'What's your name, by the way?'

'Cassie. Cassie Logan.'

'Well, Cassie Logan, maybe we'll talk again sometime.'

'I hope so.'

'And don't forget to check up on Sherlock Holmes. And Dashiell Hammett.'

'I won't,' I promised.

Still smiling, he left, passing Stacey and Little Willie on his way out. Stacey looked after him. 'Who was that?'

'Man looking for Jasper. You find Moe?'

'No. We just came back to check and see if you'd heard from him.'

'Not yet.'

Stacey turned back to the door. 'Well, there's a couple more places we want to check.'

I got up. 'I'm going with you. I can't study.'

This time Stacey didn't object. All he said was 'What about those students coming to study with you?'

'I'll catch them later.'

I grabbed my coat, and we went back into the cafe. The man Solomon Bradley and the woman in green were no longer at their table. Oliver was again seated at the cash register. Clarence sat alone in the booth, holding his head with his hands. 'Y'all going back looking?' asked Oliver.

'S'pose we better,' said Willie, 'we gonna catch up with that boy. What 'bout you?'

Oliver looked around the room. 'Crowd's picking up, and both Jessie and Jasper pretty busy. Best stay here. Look, Stacey, what if Moe show up while you gone? What you want me to tell him?'

'Just tell him to stay here. We'll be back soon.' He turned to Clarence. 'You going?'

'Naw, y'all go without me this time. I'll just wait here with Oliver.'

Stacey looked at him with concern, nodded, and we left the cafe. We walked down the street and got into the Ford. Just as Stacey started to pull from the curb a truck came alongside and cut him off. It was Jeremy. He drove on and parked. We hurried from the Ford to meet him. 'Where's Moe?' Stacey asked as soon as we reached the truck.

The tarpaulin moved in back, and Moe stood up.

'Man, get down from there!' ordered Little Willie, relieved to see him.

'Are you all right?' I asked, reaching for Moe as he got down.

'Yeah.'

'You sure?' said Stacey.

Moe nodded. I studied him to see if he was telling the truth. 'Well, what took y'all so long? We've been worried to death about you!'

'Had to stop in Bogganville. Jeremy had that load to deliver for his pa.'

'And that took all this time?'

Moe glanced at Jeremy, who said, 'Truck broke down right outside Bogganville. Took us awhile to get it fixed.'

'You didn't have any trouble, though,' said Stacey. 'I mean, you didn't get stopped?'

Jeremy, still sitting behind the wheel, met his eyes. 'Naw, we ain't got stopped.'

'Good, then,' said Willie, ''cause we was beginnin' to imagine all sorts of things.' He slapped Moe's shoulder. 'We was worried 'bout you, son!'

Jeremy shifted gears. 'Well, I guess I best be getting on back.'

'Wait,' said Moe. He leaned into the cab. 'I thank you for what you done. Couldn't't've made it without you.'

'It's all right. Hope you don't have no more trouble.'

'You figure you going to have trouble explaining to your pa about the time and all?' said Stacey.

Jeremy shrugged. 'Figure to just tell him the truth . . . truck broke down.'

'Well . . . hope all this doesn't cause you trouble.' He hesitated. 'We thank you for what you did, bringing Moe to Jackson, I mean. You didn't have to agree to bring him.'

Jeremy's pale eyes met Stacey's. 'Yeah, I did. 'Sides, you'd've thought different, you never would've asked me.' He glanced away and was momentarily silent. 'You know, Stacey,' he said, looking at the street, 'back that night Harris got hurt, you told me I'd asked something hard of you to believe I ain't meant Harris – none of y'all – no harm. I know y'all ain't never forgot that night. Ain't never forgive me for it neither. I figured I owed y'all. Now maybe the debt's paid. Maybe we's even.' He looked back at Stacey, his eyes strangely empty. Stacey kept his silence, stepped back from the truck, and Jeremy drove away. We watched, saying nothing, until the red taillights dimmed into the blackness; then Willie, still looking down the street, said, 'So what do we do now?'

For several moments, none of us answered Willie. Finally, Stacey turned, glanced at him, then looked at Moe. 'Moe, I don't figure you can stay in Jackson. You got to get out. Only way. They know it was you hit the Aameses, and they know you live here. Won't be long before they come checking.'

Moe sighed. 'Yeah, guess you right.'

'Figure you best leave tonight.'

Moe didn't say anything. He looked at me, then at Stacey, and turned away. Stacey watched him, then asked Willie, 'How much money you got?'

Little Willie dug into his pocket. 'Not much, man. Paid Miz Stalnaker for my room last night, then give most of the resta my pay to my folks. How 'bout you?'

Stacey shook his head. 'Paid off the car. Just held out enough to get by on for the week.'

'I got a little money,' I said. 'Cousin Hugh and Cousin Sylvie paid me yesterday.'

Moe looked around. 'How come y'all figuring money?'

'Got to figure money,' said Stacey, 'we going to get you a ticket.'

'Ticket?'

'Yeah. Like I said, Moe, you gotta get out. We got to get you on a train or a bus outa here tonight – '

'Train's better,' advised Willie. 'More room to move quick, you hafta – '

'But where'll he go?' I said.

Stacey considered. 'Chicago. He can go to Uncle Hammer.'

'Stacey, we gotta talk 'bout this,' said Moe. 'I can't just go way off north to Chicago and leave my papa and my family like this. I just can't do that!'

'You gotta do it, Moe. You don't, these folks down here, they'll get you, then what your family going to do?'

Moe spoke quietly. 'We ain't got the money. I ain't got the money. I done what Willie done. Done give my last money to my pa.'

'Don't matter. We get the money somewhere. Cassie has some, and I'll ask Oliver. Maybe he can let us have the money from the cafe – '

'No – '

'Cousin Hugh and Cousin Sylvie, they won't mind. They'd want you to have it.'

'No – '

'It can be a loan.'

'Yeah,' advocated Willie, ''cause you gotta get outa here, man!'

Moe took a few steps away, stopped, then turned to face us again. 'I wanna see Mr Jamison.'

That was the last thing we expected him to say.

'You crazy?' yelped Willie.

'Wanna see Mr Jamison. Wanna talk to him, see what he got to say 'bout all this.'

'What in the world for?' I cried, not seeing the first sense in such a thing. I knew Mr Jamison was a fair man. I knew

121

he had more than one time proven himself to be a fair man. But I didn't figure there was anything he could do, and if there was nothing he could do, there was no sense in talking to him.

'My papa's here, Cassie. My whole family. I ain't wanting to run, not come back. Mr Jamison, him being a lawyer, maybe he can tell me what's best – '

'Boy, we already know that!'

'Got no choice, Moe,' said Willie urgently. 'You gotta run, man. They catch up with you, you could be swinging from a tree, and there won't be no questionin' that, one of them Aames boys die.'

Moe glanced from Willie to Stacey. 'I leave from here, I be running the rest of my life. Can't never come back – '

'Better that,' I said, 'then never being able to leave at all.'

Moe looked at me, then said to Stacey, 'Just take me over to talk to him, will ya? I gotta know if there's another way.'

'There's not.'

'I'm asking ya.'

'You wrong. There's no other way – '

'Then I be the one that pay. Can't leave knowing I ain't tried.'

Stacey stared at Moe as if he would like to have just knocked him out and put him on that train. 'All right, I'll take you to see him. But you got to promise me something, Moe.'

'What's that?'

'Things don't work out with Mr Jamison, you going to get on that train and leave.'

'Won't be nothing much else I can do.'

Stacey and I went back inside the cafe to tell Oliver that Moe had arrived and that we were headed for Mr Jamison's. 'Check the train schedules, will you?' Stacey asked him. 'I figure we'll have to head on there afterward. We'll pick up some of Moe's things from Mrs Stalnaker's, then we'll go.' He looked around. 'Where's Clarence?'

'Lying down in back. Want me to get him?'

'Naw, let him rest,' said Stacey.

Oliver followed us out and greeted Moe, hidden in the shadows beyond the corners of the cafe. Then, as he moved back toward the door, he said: 'I'll see y'all back here in another hour or so.'

The rest of us got into the Ford and headed for Mr Jamison's widowed sister's house, where Mr Jamison resided when practising law in Jackson. Because Stacey and I had been there once before when Stacey had made a payment on his car, we knew what to expect. Houses were huge and set back on deep lawns that were lush and meticulously mowed. Folks that lived on that plush street seemed civil enough; still they had stared curiously that time we had come, for coloured folks, except for domestics, were a rarity and not welcomed in white neighbourhoods. I was not looking forward to going there again.

When we reached the house, Stacey turned off the engine, then looked back at Moe. 'Why don't you wait here?' he said. 'I'll go in and talk to Mr Jamison.'

'I'll go with you,' I volunteered.

'Maybe I best go in myself,' said Moe.

'I don't think that's such a good idea,' I said. 'The law, it's a funny thing, Moe, and Mr Jamison being a lawyer and all, he might have to tell somebody about seeing you.'

Stacey agreed. 'Best you stay here.'

'Yeah, y'all go on,' instructed Little Willie. 'I'll keep the boy company. And hurry back, will ya?' He glanced nervously at the street. 'Don't want to be sitting up here too long.'

Moe said nothing further. He seemed tired of arguing. Stacey and I got out of the car, passed by the front door, and walked up the darkened drive to a side door and rang the bell. A few moments passed, then we heard footsteps. The door swung open, and a woman, grey haired and middle-aged, stared out at us, a curious look on her face. 'Yes?' she said.

'We ... we're here to see Mr Jamison,' said Stacey. 'Name's Logan. Stacey and Cassie Logan.'

'David Logan's children?'

'Yes, ma'am.'

She peered out and studied us closely. 'Oh, yes, I remember your father. Come in. I'll tell my brother you're here.'

She pushed the screen door open, and we stepped inside. Leading us down a softly lit hallway, she ushered us into a comfortable room with deep-set sofas and a fire burning brightly in the hearth. Mr Jamison, standing behind a huge desk, was talking on the telephone. He looked over as we entered. He didn't seem surprised to see us. He motioned us to sit down, then continued his conversation. His sister left the room. We continued to stand. When Mr Jamison hung up, he said, 'Am I correct in assuming you've come about Moe?'

'You heard, then?' said Stacey.

Mr Jamison nodded. 'Yes.'

'Well, we were wondering ... what's the best thing for him to do?'

'Assuming he happens to show up here?'

'Yes, sir ... assuming that.'

He motioned again for us to sit, and this time we did. He sat across from us. 'Well, I'd say that'll partly depend on how the Aames boys fare, and at this point it looks as if Troy might not make it. He was hurt pretty bad.'

'But what if he pulls through? What if they all pull through?'

'If Moe's in custody, he'll still most likely have to go to jail.'

I leaned toward him. 'Even though it was Statler and them that started it all? Mr Jamison, you know Moe. You know how hard he works. He minds his own business and doesn't go out looking for trouble. He was thinking on joining the Army, was figuring on trying to get to be an officer or maybe get some pilot training or something like that. He always figured to make something of himself. But today Statler Aames and them, they were teasing at him, like they teased at Clarence, and he had that crowbar, and he just hauled off and hit them with it. He shouldn't've done it – he knows that – but they pushed him into it. Now he's trying to do the right thing. He doesn't want to run. He – ' Nothing in Mr Jamison's face changed; yet I knew I had slipped and said too much. From what I had said, Mr Jamison had to know that we had seen Moe since the incident in Strawberry. I glanced at Stacey, but it was too late to correct myself now, so I just went on. 'He was figuring that maybe if Statler Aames and them were all

124

right and seeing this here's Jackson, not back down in Strawberry, maybe things wouldn't go so bad for him.'

Mr Jamison considered. 'Even if Moe were to go to the Jackson police, he'd still have to stand trial in Strawberry.'

I sighed. 'Then he's got no chance.'

Mr Jamison's lawyer eyes studied me. 'I know you're interested in the law, Cassie. I'm sure you already know that the law can sometimes be a tough thing. As a lawyer I often find that giving advice can be a tough thing too. What I'm telling you and Stacey now is some legal advice mixed with a good measure of common sense. If you're asking me strictly about the law concerning Moe's situation, I have to tell you what the law says. Any man who raises his hand against another man and injures him must be held accountable. If you're asking what Moe should do, then I feel obliged to tell you that the law is an imperfect piece of machinery and not blind to colour, not here in Mississippi. The law here is bound by race. No matter what Moe's defence, his being a Negro will affect what happens to him. Yes, he could go to the police, but as the law stands and as Mississippi justice stands, he would go to prison.'

'What if . . . Could you help him?'

'I could defend him, if that's what you mean.'

'Well, what . . . what about if he goes north?'

Stacey moved uneasily and cast me a harsh look. Mr Jamison took note and was silent for some moments. He seemed to be pondering his answer. 'Most likely he'd be better off,' he finally said.

He had spoken the truth, and Stacey and I both knew it. There was nothing further to discuss. We started to get up. Mr Jamison stopped us. 'My secretary said that they're still searching for Moe around Strawberry, but they're thinking he might be out of the county by now.'

I tried to keep from looking at Stacey. I tried to keep that same lawyer face Mr Jamison showed when he knew a secret and wasn't about to tell.

'There's been some speculation on how he might have gotten out and who might have helped him. Either someone took him without knowing the trouble Moe was in, or someone knew the trouble but took him anyway. The sheriff has even suggested that Moe could have gotten a

125

ride with someone headed for Jackson ... such as myself – '

I leaned forward. 'Mr Jamison, they don't think you – '

Mr Jamison smiled thinly. 'No, Cassie. My sister and another lady accompanied me back to Jackson, and there's no questioning the word of those two fine ladies. Statler, though, thinks it was Harris Mitchum who helped Moe get away. In fact, some men have already been to Harris's grandmother's place looking for him – '

'They get him?' I asked, my lawyer poker face gone.

'No. He wasn't there.'

I was relieved, and I didn't care if Mr Jamison knew it.

Stacey stood, and I got up too. 'We thank you, Mr Jamison,' he said, 'for taking the time to talk to us.'

Mr Jamison shook Stacey's hand. 'You have any more questions, you come back.'

'Yes, sir, we'll do that. We're obliged.'

Mr Jamison waved away any obligation with a slight motion of his hand and saw us out. He walked us down the front hallway to the front door. Stacey glanced out into the night. 'Maybe ... maybe, Mr Jamison, it be best we leave the way we come.'

'Nonsense,' said Mr Jamison and turned on the porch light as if he had no fear of eyes watching in the night, seeing coloured folks walking out his front door. 'Watch your step, now.'

We said good-bye and returned to the car. Moe and Little Willie didn't ask any questions, and Stacey and I said nothing until we were out of that neighbourhood. Just being there made us nervous. Once we were back on the main street, we told Moe everything Mr Jamison had said. Moe's first thoughts were of Harris. 'They ... they think it was Harris helped me, then he in 'bout much trouble as I am.'

'They haven't caught up with him yet,' I said. 'Maybe they won't.'

'And what 'bout Jeremy?' said Moe. 'What if they find out it was him, and he faces trouble after what he done for me?' None of us answered. 'Maybe ... maybe I oughta think of going back.'

I turned all the way around in my seat so I could look

straight at him. 'Are you crazy? Boy, you can't go back there!'

'May be the only way to keep Harris outa trouble. Jeremy too.'

'Make sense, man!' admonished Little Willie. 'Shuckies, Harris'll be all right! They ain't got him, and no doubt he hid good by now. And as for Jeremy, that's his family, man! He one of 'em! They ain't gonna hurt him!'

'But – '

'Moe.' Stacey was looking at him in the rearview mirror. 'Forget it, Moe. You're not going back.'

Moe said nothing and looked out into the night. Stacey drove on. A block from Rose Street a lanky figure stepped into the street and waved us down. It was Oliver, and Clarence was with him.

Stacey rolled down the window. 'What is it?'

'Man, the police, they been up to Miz Stalnaker's,' said Clarence. 'Best not go up there.'

'Yeah,' continued Oliver. 'Got a call from Miz Stalnaker, and she said don't bring Moe there. Seem that Strawberry sheriff called up here about Moe.'

'Well, then, we'll just take Moe right on to the train,' said Willie.

'Wouldn't advise it. Miz Stalnaker said they know he's here, they know he'll wanna get out. Said they could be keeping an eye on both the train and the bus station.'

Little Willie, sitting directly behind Stacey, leaned forward. 'Well, what we gonna do, Stace?'

Stacey glanced at the silent Moe, then checked the street. 'This here's no place to talk. Let's go back to the cafe.'

'Yeah, you right,' Oliver agreed as he and Clarence moved away. 'See y'all there.'

When we got to the cafe, Stacey looked around cautiously, then parked several buildings down. Oliver and Clarence passed us, parked as well, and we all got out. We met, shielded by the night and the broken streetlight overhead.

'So,' said Oliver, 'what we doing?'

'If the police are watching the train and the bus station,' said Stacey, 'then I figure the best thing to do is to drive Moe out myself.'

Moe spoke for the first time since we had learned about the police. 'No, Stacey, I won't let you do that.'

'No other way. I'll drive you to Memphis, and you can get a train from there to Chicago and Uncle Hammer. Once you in Chicago, you don't have to worry. They'll have a hard time getting you there.'

'Look, it's me in trouble, and I got no right bringing y'all in it. You got any idea what'll happen if we get picked up? You'll be going to jail too! No, sir! I'm not gonna let ya do it!'

Stacey turned back to the Ford.

Moe grabbed his arm. 'Stacey, you hearing me?'

'Well, what you going to do, then?' Stacey asked him. 'Stay here and let them take you back? You want to go to jail? Man, what's the matter with you? You want to end up like T.J.?' After those words, Stacey looked around fiercely as Moe released his arm, then was silent. We all were silent at the mention of T. J. Avery. All of us except Oliver had known T.J. well. All of us except Oliver had grown up with him and had witnessed the day he had been taken off to prison at the age of fourteen for, supposedly, killing a white man.

Finally, Moe broke the silence. Slowly shaking his head, he sighed and said, 'No . . . no, that's not what I want.'

'Then you going to have to go.'

Little Willie looked anxiously across the street, where a car had slowed. 'Well, looka here, we can't be standing up here all night jawing 'bout the thing.' The car drove on, and he looked back at Moe. 'We gotta move!'

'I just can't have y'all in trouble on my account. Y'all done risked enough as it is.'

'Seem to me,' said Stacey, 'I've been in trouble on your account before, and you been there, too, on account of me, so don't fight me on this, Moe. We got no time to fight.'

I hooked my arm with Moe's. 'Well, whatever y'all finally decide to do, I'm going with you.'

'Ah, naw, Cassie,' said Stacey. 'Naw, you're not. Papa and Mama would skin me alive, I took you with me and anything happened – '

'But you're going – '

'Look, Cassie, I get into trouble, I got only me to worry

about. You be with me, I'm going to have to worry about you too.'

'You don't have to worry about me. I can take care of myself. Besides, if I'm with you, it might make things easier.'

'She got a point,' said Oliver. 'If police start looking, they won't be looking for a girl travelling with Moe.'

Stacey was still against it.

'Ah, man,' said Willie, 'you know you ain't gonna get no peace 'less you let her go. We all watch out for her, 'cause we goin' too.'

'Yeah, that's a fact,' said Clarence.

'Well, I thank y'all,' I said snidely. 'I'll watch out for y'all as well.'

Stacey looked at me as he had often done in past years when we were younger and I had insisted upon tagging along with him; it was not a look of brotherly love. 'What about that debate of yours?'

'I don't think that's so all-fired important right now, do you?' I took hold of his arm. 'Stacey, I care about Moe much as you do. Let me go. Please.'

Maybe it was the fact that I seldom pleaded with him about anything. Maybe it was just that he was understanding how I felt about Moe. In any case, he gave in. 'I don't want you giving me a hard time, you hear?'

'What I'm going to give you a hard time about?'

'Just mind my words.'

I agreed to that, just to get the thing settled.

Little Willie slapped his hands together, ready to go. 'Good, then! Let's get on outa here!' Both he and Clarence turned for the car.

'Wait a minute, Clarence,' Stacey said. 'What about your pass?'

'Shoot! Got till tomorrow night, six P.M. for that. Plenty of time to get to Memphis and back and still take a bus down to Camp Shelby. Ain't 'bout to miss seein' Memphis!'

'Thought you had the headache so bad,' I reminded him. 'You up to this ride?'

Clarence shrugged. 'Ain't so bad right now. 'Sides, ride might do me good.'

'Yeah.' Little Willie laughed. 'Maybe it'll get your mind off that girl Sissy and becomin' a daddy.'

'Don't you start up again with me, Willie.'

Little Willie just slapped Clarence's back and kept on laughing. He loved teasing Clarence.

'Look here, Stace,' said Oliver, 'don't think I'll be going with y'all, 'less you figure you need me. Jasper ain't been feeling too well tonight, and Jessie pretty much having to run the cafe by herself. All these people here, I best stay on and help her out.'

'Yeah, all right. We'll be fine. Need to borrow some money from you, though, for Moe's ticket and for gas, too, if you can spare it.'

'Yeah, sure. Can probably get forty or fifty bucks, what with what I got in my pocket. That be enough?'

'Yeah, that'll be fine.'

Oliver returned to the cafe to get the money. When he came back, he gave the money to Stacey, then pulled a small notebook from his coat pocket. 'Look here, y'all get to Memphis and you run into any trouble, look up Solomon Bradley – '

'Solomon Bradley?' I said.

'Yeah. He was in here this evening. Gone now, though. He's a lawyer up in Memphis.'

'He actually practises the law?'

Oliver seemed puzzled by my interest. 'Among other things. You meet him?'

I nodded. 'How did you all come to know him?'

'He drives down to New Orleans a lot and he just stopped by one day to get something to eat. Met him then.'

'Oh,' I said as Stacey looked curiously at me.

Oliver went on. 'Wrote down his address. He's a good man to know. Y'all run into any trouble, y'all get in touch with him. Most likely he can help.'

Stacey took the paper. 'Thanks,' he said.

'You know how to get to the train station once you get to Memphis?' asked Oliver, who knew Memphis well. 'There's more'n one you know. One y'all wanna go to is Central Station.'

'It's downtown?'

'Yeah ... let me draw you a map.' Oliver quickly

sketched out the directions on the notepad. When he finished, he gave Stacey the pad. 'Shouldn't have any problems, but you do, you can always ask somebody.'

Stacey nodded, then went to the driver's side of the car and opened the door. 'Ought to be back tomorrow morning or early afternoon sometime.'

'Yeah, all right . . . if that white boy Jeremy Simms or that Mr Jamison ain't done sold y'all out and told the police about Moe 'fore then.'

Stacey glanced once more at the distrustful Oliver and got in. Oliver shook Moe's hand. 'Moe, you take care, hear? Things gonna work out.'

Moe nodded. 'Thank ya, Oliver. That money, I'll pay you back every cent.'

'Yeah, I know you will. Don't worry 'bout it. You just make it to Chicago, ya hear? Tell Cousin Hammer I said hello. Hope to see him down here come Christmas.'

'I'll do that.' Then Clarence got in the back seat, and so did Little Willie. I slid in beside Stacey, and Moe sat next to me. We were set to go.

Suddenly Oliver said, 'Wait a minute, wait a minute!' and ran back into the cafe. We didn't know what had gotten into him. His return took more than a minute, but when he came back out, he was carrying a large bag. 'Got shoeboxes of food for you there, Moe. Fried chicken and corn bread and some sweet potato pie. You'll be needing it on that train. Got 'nough for the rest of y'all too, y'all get hungry.'

Moe smiled his thanks and took the bag.

'See you tomorrow sometime,' said Stacey and started the car.

'Yeah,' said Oliver. 'Yeah . . .' He slapped the roof in farewell and stepped back.

Then we were on our way, leaving Oliver behind, a solitary figure in front of the cafe. We left Lynch and headed out State Street into the blackness of the Mississippi night. A few minutes later we were on the road to Memphis.

The Road to Memphis

All around us the world lay black. Only the headlights of
the Ford cut a swath of brilliance across the night. Earlier
a few cars had passed us going toward Jackson, and several
huge trucks travelling north had closed in behind us, then
sped on. But no other vehicles were now on the highway.
There were no lights along the roadside either. For a while
after we left Jackson we had seen lights flickering in
roadside houses and in little towns still awake as we passed
through. Now the towns were asleep, and all lights were
out; we seemed alone in the world. Once Stacey stopped the
car, and all the boys got out and walked off to the woods. I
didn't go with them. I didn't like the thought of squatting
out in the night over things I couldn't see. I told them I'd
just wait.

'Won't be any toilets we can use between here and
Memphis,' Stacey told me.

'Said I'd wait.'

'All right, suit yourself.'

As we made our way through the hill country the smell
of skunk and other wild things seeped like a gaseous stink
into the car. Little Willie complained about the smell for a
while, then fell off to sleep. Clarence, too, slept. Moe and I
remained awake, and, of course, Stacey was at the wheel,
but none of us said anything much. I suppose we were all
too caught up in our own thoughts for talking. The day had
moved so fast and the night even faster. There was a lot to
think about. I thought about all that had happened in
Strawberry. I thought about the once important debate,
the once important grade I needed to get, and realized how
unimportant they seemed now. I thought about Solomon

Bradley, too, and wondered if we would see him in Memphis. I hoped so.

Since there was no radio in the car, there was no distant voice to soothe the night or the ride. Stacey fixed his eyes on the road; Moe stared out the side window into the blackness of the night. I shivered and pulled my coat close. The heater was barely working, and I was cold. Stacey glanced over at me and pushed the heater up to full blast, but it didn't make much difference.

'Right about now I'm wishing this car had a better heater,' he said.

'No more than I,' I replied.

He smiled, then glanced at the gas gauge. He had filled the tank in Jackson, so there was plenty of gas. But I knew something about the car was bothering him. 'What is it?' I said.

'I don't know. Car's not running quite right. Think I need to stop at a station somewhere and check under the hood.'

'You figure we can find something open this time of night?'

'I recall, there's a truck stop along here somewhere. We'll stop there.'

The silence settled in again. The night passed on. Finally we saw lights in the distance. It was the truck stop. In addition to the gas station, there was a small store and a cafe. Several huge trucks were parked on the lot. Stacey drove the Ford in and stopped alongside one of the gas pump isles.

Little Willie stirred in back. "Ey, son, we in Memphis?"

'Does this look like Memphis?' I said, glancing back at him. Little Willie looked out. 'Could be. 'Member, I ain't never been there.'

'Got a ways yet 'fore Memphis, Willie,' Stacey informed him and opened the door.

Little Willie and I followed him out. Clarence didn't waken, and Moe refused to leave the car. 'Could be police here,' he said.

I looked around. 'Don't see any police cars.'

'Figure it's best I stay here.'

'Well, suit yourself, then.'

Stacey, Little Willie, and I stood by the car and waited.

After a few minutes the station attendant came from the store. Stacey asked him to fill the tank. The attendant was a sandy-haired man, middle-aged with a cherublike face and a mind to talk. As he slipped the nozzle into the tank he looked around, his cheeks red under the lights that flooded the station, and observed: 'Don't see many of y'all travelling the road this late at night. Where 'bouts y'all headed?'

I cut my eyes to Stacey, wondering how he was going to answer. He stood there straight-faced and lied. 'Nashville,' he said without a blink.

'Nashville? That a fact? Y'all know folks up there? Always figure a place just ain't right somehow less'n you know folks.'

I waited for Stacey's reply to this. If we had kin in Nashville, I wanted to know about it too. But the man went on cheerfully, not giving Stacey a chance to speak. 'Been to Nashville once, and it was all right. Nothing like Memphis, though. Always preferred Memphis myself. Body can have a fine time in that town.'

'Well, maybe we'll get lucky enough to get there one day.'

'Y'all do that, 'cause I know y'all'll like it. I ain't heard a nigra yet been there say they ain't liked that place. It's got all those kind of doings your folks enjoy so much. Got a lotta dancing and good-time music places, so's I hear. That Beale Street, I hear, is really a jumping place with all you people there.'

Stacey's eyes hardened. White folks were always doing that, assuming they knew what we all liked or didn't like, what we all were like or weren't like. Stacey changed the conversation. 'I'm having a bit of trouble with my car. Seems to be running a bit rough. Had trouble with the engine missing before. Be obliged if you could check it for me.'

'Just give me a minute and I'll give it a look.'

Little Willie glanced over at the store. 'Suh, that store there open?'

'Yep, sure is. Y'all go on in. My wife and boy's in there. Got some nice sweet potato pies and some pecan pies, too, y'all might wanna buy if y'all gonna be on the road all night. They're fine, too, mighty fine. I oughta know. They keeps ten pounds too heavy on me.' He laughed generously at that. 'Ole nigger woman – Aunt Hannah Mays – cooks up those pies for us twice a week. Can't hardly keep 'em in the place, folks love 'em so.'

'Sounds good,' said Willie. 'Maybe we'll give 'em a try.' Little Willie offered the attendant a pleasant grin, then as he turned his back to him he made a face only Stacey and I could see before asking us, 'Y'all going in?'

'I'll stay with the car,' Stacey said. 'I need to get it checked out.' He glanced at the attendant. 'Want to see what he thinks might be wrong with it.'

'While you talking to him,' I said, 'ask him if they got coloured restrooms.'

Stacey again glanced at the attendant, then, taking my arm, pulled me several feet from the car. 'Course they don't have them!' he hissed.

'Well, see if they got something – '

'Now, Cassie, you know good and well we're not going to find a gasoline station that's going to let us use their toilets.'

'Well, ask him anyway. He call himself being so friendly, maybe he can tell us where we can find one.'

'No need to even ask, Cassie, especially not this time of night. We get out from here, I'll find a place to pull over.'

'Boy, I told you I'm not going squatting out somewhere in the middle of the night in a whole bunch of bushes! Anything could be crawling out there! You don't ask him, I'll ask him myself!'

Stacey's look was scowling. 'Thought you promised to mind my words.'

'Yeah, well . . . that was before I had to face stooping down over some bushes in the middle of the night. Won't hurt to ask.'

Stacey sighed in exasperation, then went back to the attendant. 'Excuse me, sir,' he said, 'but I'd like to know if you have a restroom my sister here could use.'

The man's cheerful countenance didn't change. 'Like I said, don't see many nigras travelling this road after dark. Truth of the matter is, don't see many of y'all doing much distance during the day, neither, those of you got cars.

Now, these was daylight hours, I'd tell y'all to look for Aunt Hannah's place. She live just right down the road a piece. But seeing it's way over past midnight, I know Aunt Hannah ain't gonna wanna break her sleep this time-a night to show strangers her outhouse. That ole gal'd have my head, I sent y'all down waking her up.' He laughed. 'Best I can do for y'all is to advise ya to make y'allselves welcome to the woods and bush we got 'round here. Got plenty of that!'

'Yeah, we saw,' I muttered.

Stacey cast me a chastising glance. The attendant came around to the front of the car. 'Looks like your left front tyre's a bit low there,' he said. 'I'll get that for ya after I take a look under your hood.'

'I thank you,' said Stacey.

The attendant checked the water and oil and whatever else was under the hood, then pulled back with some bad news. 'That fan belt of y'all's is looking pretty worn through. It break on you, the car's gonna run hot and damage the engine. Could mean big trouble, y'all goin' all the way to Nashville.'

Stacey leaned down and took a look for himself. His frown told me the attendant was right.

'Now I got a fan belt here, I can go on and put on for ya.'

'How much would that be?' Stacey was sounding cautious. I knew he was thinking about the money.

'Gonna hafta check that.' Leaving the hood up, the attendant stepped back, admiring the car. 'Fine-looking Ford. What year is it?'

'Thirty-eight.'

'Well, it sure looks good. New paint job?'

'Just a good polishing.'

The man nodded. 'Got a real nice shine, all right. Can just 'bout use it for a mirror.' He grinned, then walked back toward the pump. 'I'll see how your gas doing here, then I'll go check on that fan belt for ya.' As he pulled out the nozzle, another car pulled up on the other side of the gas isle. Two couples were in the car. The driver and another man stepped out, and the attendant, after hanging up the pump, crossed over to them. 'Yes, sirs!' he said. 'What can I do for y'all? Can I fill it up?'

'As much as it'll take,' said the driver, turning and looking south down the road. 'Can you tell me 'bout how far we are from New Orleans from here?'

The attendant said he had been to New Orleans himself, just as he had told us he'd been to Memphis, and was soon deep into conversation with his new customer. While the men talked the women got out of the car, said something to the attendant, who turned and pointed to the corner of the store building, where a restroom sign hung from a low lamppost. I watched as the women walked over, turned the corner at the lamppost, and disappeared. I started to mention the sign to Stacey but then saw his frown and didn't bother. He was looking at the fan belt and I could tell he was worrying about it. For several minutes he waited for the attendant to return, but the attendant was busy with his white customers now, too busy to pay us further attention. We had to wait. Stacey knew that as well as I did. That was the way of things. Soon, though, Stacey grew impatient. 'We're losing time,' he said.

'Well, why don't we go on in the store, man?' Little Willie suggested. 'The man'll fix the belt in another minute here. Meantime we can get ourselves a couple of Aunt Hannah's sweet potato pies!'

'You go on. I'll wait for him and put some air in this tyre while I do.'

'Okay, then. You coming, Cassie?'

'Be there in a minute,' I said, my eyes on that restroom sign.

Little Willie went over to Moe's window. ''Ey, Moe! Come on, get out the car and stretch your legs a bit, man. Figure it'll be all right.'

Moe glanced at the car on the other side of the isle. Then he looked around the stop and saw only trucks. There were no police cars. Evidently figuring he could take the chance, he got out of the car and went with Little Willie. As they walked off, Stacey reached for the air hose. The attendant looked over. 'I said I'd get that!' he snapped, sounding vexed that Stacey was going to put the air in the tyre himself. Stacey left the hose alone. Finally the attendant came back. He took the air hose from its hook, stooped down to the left front tyre, and began pressing air into it. 'There. That oughta do it.' He stood again.

Stacey studied the tyre. 'Still looks kind of low to me.'

The attendant looked at the tyre. 'No, it's enough,' he said, as if his decision closed the matter. He wiped his hands on a dirty rag and looked at the pump. 'That'll be one-sixty for your gas.'

Stacey took out his wallet. 'I like to keep my air pressure in those front tyres at thirty-five pounds, and doesn't look to be thirty-five.'

The attendant gave Stacey a sharp look but took the money. 'It's enough,' he declared all-knowingly, then turned and headed for the store. 'Y'all wait here. I'll bring your change. Also get that fan belt for ya.'

'Well, I guess he told you,' I said.

Stacey didn't comment. He was looking at his tyres. He walked around the car, studying each one. 'They're too low,' he decided. Then, as the two men headed for New Orleans also went into the store Stacey, with a cautious glance after them, took the air hose, stooped down to the left front tyre, and put more air in. While he was stooped there two more cars pulled into the station. One, a Chevrolet, pulled to the other side of the isle and stopped. The other, a Hudson, pulled behind the Ford. Several young men were in each of the cars. Most of them went into the cafe, but the drivers remained. The driver of the Hudson stuck his head out, saw Stacey, and shouted at him. "Ey, boy! That your car?'

Stacey didn't even look up. He kept on putting air in the tyre.

"Ey, boy, you hear me talkin' to you?'

Stacey now looked around. The man at the wheel was a ruddy-looking sort, young and big boned with a faint moustache. The driver of the other car stepped out. 'Having trouble over there, Orley?'

'Don't 'spect so,' said the man called Orley. 'Just got me a nigger hard of hearing here. Either that or he got a hard head, one. That what you got, boy? You got yourself a hard head? Yeah, I'm talking to you! You see any other hard-headed niggers squatting there? One thing I can't stand is a hardheaded nigger. Now, I said, is that your car?'

138

Stacey nodded slowly.

'Then move it, then!'

'I'm waiting on the gas station man.'

'Well, you can do your waiting yonder, 'side them bushes.'

Stacey turned again to the tyre. 'Gas station man told me to wait here.'

'You back-lippin' me, boy? I'm telling you to move on out the way. Now, you gonna do like I say, or I'm gonna hafta get out this car and see that you do?'

Stacey stood and went around the front of the Ford to the other side. There he stooped to press air into the right front tyre. The driver of the Chevrolet stepped onto the isle and eyed the Ford. 'Pretty nice car you got here, boy,' he commented. 'Oughta see it close, Orley. This boy's taken mighty fine care of it. Got it all shined up and everything, not a scratch on it.' He stepped down and walked around the Ford, inspecting it closely. 'You sure this your car, boy? Don't see too many niggers got cars all fixed up and looking new like this. Got a shine on it you can see yourself in. Orley! Come on over and take a look!'

'I come over, I'm gonna do more'n look!' replied the driver of the Hudson as he stepped out and leaned against the open door. 'Now, I said move that car. You hear me, boy?'

Stacey eyed him coldly and stood up. 'Cassie,' he said, keeping his eyes on the man, 'move the car.' He handed me the keys.

'Naw, boy! I told *you* to move it.'

Stacey stared at the man, then took the keys back. He slammed down the hood and went around the car to the driver's side. 'Get in,' he told me. I obeyed, and he slid in beside me.

'There, now, that's a good nigger!' commended the man standing on the isle.

'Still hardheaded, you ask me,' said Orley. 'Niggers get a bit of a machine under they butt, and they start to feeling they can back-talk a white man whenever they get a mind. Well, I don't stand for that.'

'Good whippin' usually fixes a smart mouth,' advised the other man.

'Yeah . . . I been thinking on that.'

139

Stacey started the car and drove to the edge of the lot. I glanced uneasily back at the men. 'Don't you think we ought to be leaving from here?'

Stacey watched as the Hudson pulled forward, taking our spot beside the gas tank. 'We got to get that fan belt fixed first. It won't last till Memphis. I'm going to go check and see how much longer it'll be 'fore the man can get to it.'

'I'll stay here.'

He glanced at Clarence, still asleep in back. 'All right, but they come over here messing again, wake Clarence and try not to aggravate them. We don't need a mess with them tonight.'

'Don't I know.'

He tossed the keys to me. 'Move it if you have to.' Then he got out, and I slid under the wheel. I put the keys back in the ignition, ready to move, then leaned my arms upon the wheel and watched the men. One of them hollered at Stacey as he went into the store, then both of them laughed. They grew quiet as the two women returned from the restroom at the side of the store building. I glanced over at the restroom door, dimly lit by a low-voltage bulb hanging outside, and noticed that the door had been left slightly ajar. Inside, the room was dark. I felt sorely tempted to go over there, for that side of the building could not be seen from the gas isle, and no one was near the restrooms. Besides, it was a long way to Memphis still and no toilet for me but bush and forest.

I made up my mind.

I took the keys, slipped them into my purse, and got out of the car. Glancing over at the men by the gas pumps, I crossed to the side of the building. At the corner I stopped and looked back again. No one had noticed me. I saw the station attendant and the men headed to New Orleans come back to the isle and I quickly turned down the muddy path for the open door. When I reached it, I stopped again, for there was a sign on the door, a sign that said: WHITE LADIES ONLY. There was a second door and a second sign too. It said: WHITE GENTLEMEN ONLY. I knew perfectly well what the signs meant. I knew perfectly well that I should walk right on past and go down behind the bushes at the

140

end of the path, but it made no sense to me that I had to go stooping behind a bush when there was a perfectly good toilet right behind the door. I knew perfectly well the kind of trouble I'd be in if I disobeyed the signs. I knew perfectly well that I would be breaking the law if I did. Still, as I stood there facing those signs I felt such an anger, such a hostility, such a need to defy them that I couldn't just walk right on past. Again I looked around. Again I saw no one, and with my heart racing I placed my hand on the door and pushed it fully open.

'What do you think you're doing?'

I jumped back, as if touching the door had seared my hand. I turned quickly and saw that one of the women had come back. She glanced at the open door, then stared at me, waiting on an answer. I was too scared to give her one.

When I said nothing, the woman abruptly turned on black leather pumps and went back to the corner of the building. 'Sam! Sam, come here!' she called. 'And bring that gas station man with you!'

All I could think to do was run. I backed away, but she turned and made me stop. She pointed a finger straight at me and ordered, 'You just stay right there!'

'Please . . .' I pleaded. 'Please . . .'

'Nora, what is it?' asked the woman's escort as he and the other man bound for New Orleans came hurrying over with the attendant right behind him.

The woman turned an accusing finger my way. 'That nigger there, she was using the restroom.'

The man in the suit looked at the gas station attendant. 'What kind of place you running here, letting coloured gals use white ladies' restrooms?'

The attendant looked apologetically at the couple, then moved over to me. 'Now, ain't I told you we ain't had toilets for y'all? Y'all wanna pee, y'all best find y'allselves some weeds and do your business.'

'Th-that's what I was doing . . . looking for some bush – '

'Up here?' he questioned. 'Here I try and treat y'all niggers decent, give you good service and make y'all welcome, and this here how ya do. Go sneaking 'round trying to use white ladies' restrooms!' He acted as if I had

141

personally insulted him. "Round here putting your black butt where white ladies got t' sit. Oughta call the sheriff and have him take you down to that jail. Maybe then you learn what happen you go breakin' the law!'

'But I – I didn't go in. I didn't!' I looked frantically at the woman. She met my eyes, and I believe she felt my fear. Her lips parted, and she looked at the attendant. 'I . . . I don't think that's necessary.'

'Well, I sure do it, ma'am. I don't want y'all to get the wrong idea 'bout our place here. We runs a good place – '

'Just leave her be,' said the woman and turned.

'Nora, sweetheart?' called her escort.

The woman walked away, leaving me in the hands of the men.

'I sure do apologize to you folks for this,' said the attendant. 'It won't be happening again.' Then he turned back to me. 'You, gal, you be thankful to these good folks I don't have your black butt put in jail. Now, you get them other niggers, and y'all get on outa my place, and don't let me catch y'all back here again. I do, I'll have all of y'all throw'd in jail. Now, get! Get fast 'fore I change my mind!'

I hurried past him and up the muddy path. I glanced back and was so scared, I began to run, and that was a mistake, for I slipped and fell. My stockings ripped, and my knees skinned back. My purse hit the ground, popped open, and everything spilled out. The attendant stalked over. 'Nigger, I said get!' he shouted.

I scrambled to my knees and tried to gather my things.

'Now!'

'But – but my purse – '

The attendant squashed the purse under his foot, then he kicked at me with his other foot, like somebody with no heart would kick a dog. His shoe struck me sharply, but that's not what wounded me. It was my pride that suffered. I was stunned by the humiliation. 'Leave it and get!' he cried.

I saw the car keys through blurry eyes, grabbed them, and leaving everything else, I jumped up and ran for the Ford. But then I saw that Orley, the man from the Hudson, and the rest of the riders were gathered there now. They had surrounded the car. I saw no sign of Clarence.

'I got me a good mind to show that nigger – ' expounded Orley to his listeners, and I didn't wait to hear more. I turned and ran to the store.

'Cassie, what – ' said Stacey as I dashed in.

I grabbed his arm and pulled him aside, away from the storekeeper and her son. 'Those men from the Hudson, they're over there by the car, and Clarence, I think he's still inside sleeping. They're talking about getting you!'

Stacey looked at me hard. He looked at the torn stockings, at the muddy coat, and grabbed my arm. 'What happened to you? They touch you?'

'No ... I wasn't even at the car. I ... I went down to check out those bushes that man was talking about, and I ... I fell on the path. Saw those men by the car when I came back.'

He stared at me, as if not wholly believing me. I didn't like lying to him, but I knew I could not tell him the truth, not if we were going to get away from here. I was afraid of what he would do if he knew the truth.

Moe hurried over. 'What's wrong? Cassie, what happened to you?'

'I'm all right.'

Stacey glanced out the window, then called to Willie, who was standing at the counter with two pies in his possession. 'Willie! Come on! We're going!'

Little Willie looked around. 'What 'bout the fan belt, man?'

'Can't worry 'bout that now. We've got to go.'

Little Willie started to protest, but then he saw me and minded Stacey's tone. He nodded, got his change, and we left the store.

The men saw us coming. One of them still standing by the pump hollered, "Ey, Orley! Feel like a little cooooon hunt t'night?'

'Could be the right time,' replied Orley. 'Been seein' plenty of them low smellin' things 'round.'

We crossed to the car. One of the men stood in front of the car, another leaned against the hood, and Orley blocked the driver's door. We stopped. Stacey studied Orley, studied the other men, then looked back at Orley and said, 'Excuse us, please, we'd like to get in.'

Orley just looked at him and stayed where he was. 'Nigger, where you get this car?'

There was a moment of silence before Stacey answered. 'Bought it.'

'Where a nigger like you get money t' buy a car, that's what I wanna know.'

Stacey's jaw set, and he said nothing.

'You answer me!'

'Worked for it.'

'You sure it's yours?'

'I'm sure. Now, I'd be much obliged if you'd move so we can go.'

Orley gave Stacey a long, silent stare.

Stacey stared back.

Orley moved.

Stacey opened the door and ordered me in. I slid quickly inside, then glanced back down the path in front of the restrooms and wondered about my purse. I hated leaving that purse. It had been my favourite, and more important than that, all my money for Moe was in it.

Moe went around to the other side of the car, and Little Willie opened the back door and woke Clarence. Clarence sat up sleepily. 'What?' he said, then he saw the men. 'What – what's going on?'

'Not now,' Willie said as he got in.

Stacey started the car. The man leaning against the hood still remained. Another of the men moved in front of the car. 'You ain't gonna just let these niggers go like this, are ya, Orley?' he asked. 'Thought we was gonna do us some huntin'.'

Orley seemed to be studying on the matter.

Stacey gave him no time to announce his decision. He accelerated and the car moved forward. The man in front of the car jumped like a scared rabbit and leapt out of the way. The man leaning against the hood fell away, too, and yelled an obscenity. Stacey flattened his foot to the gas, and we sped away, off the lot and down the highway.

Stacey checked the rearview mirror. Little Willie let out a long, slow whistle at our escape. I looked back. 'You expecting them to follow?' I asked Stacey.

He hesitated. 'Don't know.'

All of us kept watch of the road. It remained black, except for the ghostlike grey cut by the Ford's headlights into the night. After several minutes Little Willie said, 'Take it easy, children, take it easy. Them peckerwoods ain't giving us no mind.'

No sooner than he had said that, lights appeared behind us.

'Course, now, I could be wrong,' he added. He stared uneasily out the back window. 'Guess they headed same way's us.'

'Yeah,' I agreed, 'looks that way.'

Stacey checked the mirror, keeping track of the lights. I fixed my eyes on the road ahead, not needing to see the lights to know they were there or to know the evil they could bring. For an eternity, it seemed, the car rolled on. For an eternity, it seemed, the lights followed right behind. Stacey sped on, but the lights began to gain. Finally Stacey said, 'I'm turning off up here.'

'They'll just follow,' I said.

'Not if I turn off the lights.'

'Boy, you crazy? You can't turn off the lights!' But Stacey paid no attention to my words as he pressed his foot flat to the floor and told us to hang on. We left the highway and swept onto a dirt road. The lights followed. Dust billowed out behind us, and rocks smacked hard against the car's underbelly. A hill shot up before us. Stacey took it and on the downward side turned off the lights and leaned forward. 'Look for a road! Look for a road!' he cried. We found one a few seconds later, and Stacey took the car in. He held tight to the new road several hundred feet before pulling the car off into a stand of trees. We stopped abruptly as the car hit something hard and low on the ground, ran over it with a jolt, and died. Then we sat. Waiting. We all knew what could happen if those cars were following and those men found us.

I was scared. I knew Stacey, Little Willie, Clarence, and Moe were scared too. We had all known this kind of fear before. But for Stacey and me that had been years before, and Papa and Uncle Hammer and Mr Morrison had been there to protect us, to protect us all. Their strength had made things all right, had made us feel safe. But they weren't here now to give that strength. Now we were on our own.

After some time Clarence broke the silence. 'Stacey, just how long we gonna be sitting here?' he said.

Little Willie gave Stacey no time to respond. 'Be sitting here all night, we hafta!' he answered in sharp reply.

The car again grew quiet, and we continued to wait, but the night was long and seemed to have no end. Finally Stacey reached under his seat and pulled something out. I couldn't see what he held in his hand, but then he opened the car door, and the moonlight pouring in made it very clear. He was holding a gun.

I grabbed his wrist. 'What you doing with that?'

'Going to walk up to that highway and see if those cars are there.'

I held tighter. 'Not with that gun, you're not. What're you doing with that thing anyway?'

'Always carry it.'

'Since when?'

'Look, Cassie, Uncle Hammer always ride with a gun.'

'Well, you're not Uncle Hammer!'

He jerked his wrist from me. 'You rather I go up there without a gun?'

'Rather you not go at all.'

'Well, I'm not going to sit out here all night afraid of something maybe's not even there.'

'And if it is?'

He looked out into the night's blackness. 'They don't see us, then I guess we play possum.'

'And they do?'

Stacey looked back. 'Leastways we've got the gun,' he said and got out. The other doors to the Ford opened, and Moe, Little Willie, and Clarence stepped out. 'Y'all best stay case there's trouble,' he said.

'You figure there's not trouble waiting for you?' asked Moe.

'I'll do better alone,' he said and headed for the road.

I got out, too, and called after him as softly as the night would permit. 'You be careful! You hear me, now?'

'I'll be okay, Cassie,' he said, then moved off into the night. Soon we could no longer see him. I walked around the car and leaned heavily against it. Little Willie put his arm around me, but for once he had nothing to say. Moe and Clarence were silent as well. It seemed forever, the time Stacey was gone. Finally he came back; he said he had seen nothing.

'How far up you walk?' questioned Little Willie, his voice not quite sounding like himself. 'Maybe you ain't gone up far 'nough.'

Stacey's look was sharp in the moonlight. 'Went up a spell both ways, back the way we came and up the road too. They there, they well hidden.'

'Maybe that's what they is. Maybe they is well hidden, and you just ain't seen 'em.'

'You wanna go take a look, then?' Stacey shot back at Little Willie. He slapped the gun into Willie's hand. 'Here! Take this thing and go on and you look for yourself!'

Little Willie was silent, his head bowed as he looked at the gun in his hand, then he handed it back to Stacey. 'Man, I don't want this thing. You say they ain't there, then they ain't there. Ain't no more to say 'bout it.' He sounded more like himself now.

Stacey took the gun and started around to the other side of the car. I followed after him. 'Stacey,' I whispered, 'you think they ever were out there? You think they followed us at all?'

Stacey was a long time silent. Then he looked toward the highway. 'They weren't out there, Cassie, it doesn't really matter now, does it?'

'I figure it does. I figure you think that way too.'

He just looked at me and said nothing.

Little Willie slapped the hood of the car and walked around to the other side. 'Ah, hell,' he said, opening the back door. 'Let's get outa here and get on up to Memphis.'

'Yeah,' said Moe, 'I think it's time.'

I questioned leaving right now. 'Don't you think we ought to wait here a spell and make sure those men aren't out there?' I was still scared, and I wasn't too proud to let them know it either. 'Maybe we ought to just wait here till morning, when we can see something.'

'Well, I don't even know if the car'll start,' said Stacey, getting in. 'We hit something, and I don't know how bad it is.' He slid the key into the ignition, but nothing happened. 'Damn!'

I looked at him, feeling his anger and his frustration in a word I had seldom heard him use before.

He got back out, and flashlight in hand, he took a look under the hood. The rest of us joined in the inspection, though I didn't know what the devil I was looking for. Finally I said, 'What is it?'

'The fan belt's completely shot now, and some wires got knocked loose. One of them's the distributor cap wire. I can fix the wires but not the fan belt.'

'Then we stay here, huh?' I asked, feeling some relief.

Stacey slammed down the hood. 'Looks like there's nothing else we can do. Might's well try getting ourselves some sleep.'

Moe walked off. 'I'm not feeling sleepy. I'll just stay out here awhile and keep watch.'

'Then I'll just keep you company there, hoss,' volunteered Little Willie with a yawn. 'Rather not get caught out in the middle of these here wood's sleeping.'

Stacey decided he didn't want to sleep either. They were all being very manly, but I knew they were scared, just like I was. Stacey turned to me. 'Cassie, why don't you go 'head and sleep? You can stretch out in back of the car awhile.' He took my arm and walked to the rear of the car with me and spoke quietly. 'Look, you want to go before you lie down, I'll go on out with you, help you find a spot and keep watch.'

I considered his offer, then decided I would just wait until daylight. It was near that already. 'That's all right. I'll just wait.'

He looked at me with suspicion, then took hold of my shoulders. 'You sure nothing happened to you back at that gas station?'

'I'm sure,' I said, grateful that he hadn't noticed I didn't have my purse. 'I'm okay.'

He stared at me, as if not quite feeling settled about the thing, then he dropped his arms to his side, let me be, and walked back to the others.

As I settled down on the backseat Clarence opened another pack of BC powder, threw back his head, and let the powder slide down. A few minutes later he got onto the front seat on the driver's side, heaved his long body over, and leaned his head against the opposite door.

"Ey, hoss!' Little Willie hissed at him. 'Don't tell me you going off to sleep again, man! Not after all that sleepin' you been doing ever since we left Jackson.'

'Just wanna rest myself a minute,' Clarence answered. 'See if I can't get my head to ease up. I'll be on out to keep watch after while.'

'You pitiful, boy, you know that? Pitiful!'

I leaned forward and tapped Clarence's shoulder. 'You all right?'

'Yeah,' he sighed. 'Yeah . . .'

I let him be and tried to sleep. But sleep for me didn't come. Clarence, though, seemed to be having no trouble sleeping; he was soon snoring. I listened to his snoring and tried to get myself warm. For some reason now, as I lay there alone on that backseat, my knees pulled toward my stomach, my arms wrapped against my chest, I couldn't stop shaking. My stomach felt queasy, and I kept having to swallow away the saliva that kept filling my mouth. I pulled my legs tighter to my chest, gripped them, and tried to make the queasiness go away. I tried not to think on what had happened at the gas station. I tried not to dwell on the fear; I tried not to dwell on the men.

Instead I thought of good things. I thought of home, of Mama and Papa and Big Ma, of Christopher-John and Little Man. I saw myself sitting by a crackling red and blue fire, smelling the pine burn and listening to a soft winter's rain. I thought of a dark winter's morning, sitting down to breakfast with the family all around, and enjoying the warm smells of Big Ma's biscuits, just baked, and sausages that had been cured in the fall, and of dipping into huge mounds of fried grits and scrambled eggs and pear preserves. I thought of all that and fixed my mind on it. I wished the fear away.

I saw myself lying on that thick feather mattress next to Big Ma. I heard her snoring and rolled toward her, feeling secure. I thought of the mule, Jack, and his steady pace when I rode him. I thought of Lady, our golden mare, and how her sleek body felt as I raced her across the pasture, the wind slapping in my face. I saw myself down by the Caroline. I saw the forest, tall and green, shading my walk along the trail to the pond, and I thought of the Little Rosa Lee and saw myself with a fishing pole in my hand and my bare feet skimming the water on a hot summer's day. I only allowed myself to think of good things, and those good things comforted me.

But the good thoughts wouldn't stay. I couldn't make them stay. The warm bed and Big Ma's snoring faded in the reality of the black, cold night. The Caroline and the Little Rosa Lee grew cold and froze. The warm smells of breakfast were overcome by the stink of the wild. The swift ride atop Lady, the wind against my face, was now a terror. I was falling. My stockings were ripping. I was in the mud, and angry, foul-talking men were kicking at me. I felt the humiliation and the fear again, and they were more than I could bear.

I screamed.

Clarence sat straight up and looked back. 'Cassie?'

I had fallen asleep, but there was no time to tell him that, for the queasiness had been real. I dashed from the car and tried to make it beyond the clearing to the trees and the brush. 'Cassie!' Stacey called after me. 'Cassie, what's wrong?'

'I feel sick on the stomach,' I managed to cry out, and kept on running into the blackness, trying to find some shelter to take my fear. I looked for a spot to crouch in the darkness, found some bushes, fell to my knees and threw up. I couldn't stop retching. Stacey came after me, but I sent him away. When the vomiting was finally over, I remained there behind the bushes for some while, feeling weak, feeling so far from home and alone in this wild, even with the boys so near. On my knees, the vomit all over my once beautiful clothes, I broke down and cried.

When I returned to the car, both the back and front doors were open and Moe was sitting on the front seat facing the open door, his feet planted on the running board, and he was looking toward the woods. Clarence, Little Willie, and Stacey stood beside the car.

Moe got out as I approached. 'You all right?' he asked.

'Yeah, I'm fine. Just got an upset stomach, that's all.'

'Thought you had more'n that,' said Clarence. 'That screaming scared the daylights outa me, girl.'

'I was screaming because of a dream.'

Stacey came over and cupped my shoulder. 'You sure you okay?' He was being very tender with me. I knew he had to be worried and was no doubt regretting his decision to let me come along.

I nodded.

Little Willie, too, looked concerned. "Ey, Cassie, why don't you get on back inside? Lie down on that back seat. Moe, you sit on back there with her. Any of the rest of us wanna sleep, we can get in front.'

I didn't argue with that. I got in, so did Moe. I stretched out, as much as I could, my head on Moe's lap, my legs pulled again to my stomach, and tried to keep from throwing up anymore.

'You comfortable?' Moe asked softly, leaning down, his hand gently upon my head.

'Comfortable as I'm going to get, I reckon.'

I saw his smile, then closed my eyes.

When I awoke, I was alone in the car. As I moved there was an awful stinging in my knees, and it took me a few moments to realize where I was. I sat up slowly. The sun was barely up, rising timidly over a ridge of pines and white oaks. We were in a small clearing that looked to have been purposely hacked out of a brooding forest. All around the clearing, except for the trail that led back to the highway, there was nothing but pine and oak and brush. I squinted out at the sun, then noticed the boys standing quietly off to one side, staring at the car, and I got out.

'Yeah, man, you can fix it!' said Little Willie. 'Why, shuckies! Ain't that bad!'

'What's not so bad?' I asked.

"Ey, Cassie!'

'How you feel?' asked Stacey.

'Don't feel like throwing up, but I don't know if that's saying a whole lot. What's wrong?'

'The car,' said Willie. 'Just telling Stacey here, it can be fixed.'

'Don't want it fixed.' Stacey was adamant.

'What you mean, you don't want it fixed?' I countered, figuring they were talking about the fan belt. There was no choice about fixing that. 'We've got to get a new fan belt so we can get out of here.'

Moe's eyes met mine. 'It's not the fan belt we're talking 'bout, Cassie. Take a look at the car.'

I looked from him to Stacey and turned. It was then that I saw the ring that gouged the car. The beautiful, wine-coloured finish was now marred by a deep, ugly scratch that ringed the car and festered like a sore under the rising sun. I glanced at Stacey, and what had been fear in me now was pure rage. This is what those men had done to my brother's fine new car. 'Those men at the gas station, they did this.'

'Good guess,' said Willie.

'They did it when I left the car. They did it when I was gone and Clarence was sleeping. I should've stayed there.'

'Best you weren't there,' said Moe. "Sides, none of this would've happened we hadn't been on the road in the first place.'

'What y'all doing laying blame on yourselves for?' asked Little Willie. 'Y'all don't hear Stacey laying no blame!'

'Good,' said Clarence. "Cause I was sitting right up in that car all the time myself and ain't heard nothing.'

'Yeah, sleeping!' admonished Little Willie. 'What's the matter with you, anyway, boy? 'Round here sleeping all the time?'

Clarence shrugged. 'Sorry, Stace. I shoulda heard 'em. Don't know what's the matter with me. Maybe it's this here BC I been taking . . .'

'Like Willie said, I'm not laying blame. Leastways to nobody here.'

I studied the car closely. 'Maybe . . . maybe like Willie said, you can fix it, Stacey. You can't fix it, maybe you can find somebody – '

'Said I don't want it fixed, Cassie! I don't want to fix it, and I don't want anybody else to fix it either!' He stepped away. 'We get in this war and I have to go fight, this here car can just remind me 'bout what all Mississippi done for me. I go to fight, I don't want to forget I'll probably be shooting at the wrong white folks.' With that said he abruptly turned and started for the road.

'Where you going now?' I called.

'Up to see if maybe I can't find something open so we can get that fan belt and get out of here. There ought to be a town not far from here.'

'Well, I'll be walking on with you, then,' decided Little Willie. 'Maybe we'll even meet up with Aunt Hannah Mays and get some more of them pies of hers. Them pies are good!'

'You going too?' I asked Moe as he started after them.

'Just as far as the road. Need to stretch my legs.'

I watched them walk off, then I took off for the bushes. When I got back, Clarence was stretched out again, this time on the backseat of the car. I stuck my head inside. 'That headache still bothering you? Don't you feel any better?'

He gave me a dull look. 'Can't seem to get rid of it, Cassie.'

'You got any more BCs?'

'Took my last one in the night.' He was speaking softly, as if it pained him to talk. I spoke softly too.

'Anything I can do for you?'

'Naw,' he said and closed his eyes.

I slid into the front seat, curled my legs under me, then turned to face him. 'You know, Clarence, I've been thinking about Sissy.'

'I been thinking 'bout her, too, for all the good that's doing,' he confided, his eyes still closed, his voice still soft. 'She ain't nothing but a misery.'

'Now, you know that's not so,' I contested. 'That child's crazy about you.'

Clarence grunted.

'I've been thinking I shouldn't've told you what I did about Sissy. I've been thinking maybe I shouldn't've broken my promise to her, especially since you went right back and told her I told you – '

'Sorry 'bout that, Cassie.'

'Found out you can't be trusted with anything.'

'Look who's talking.'

'Yeah, well ... forget all that. Time for you to be thinking about making things up to Sissy.'

He opened his eyes now. 'Ah, Cassie, come on, now! Said I'm through with that girl, and I mean that thing!'

'You through with that baby too? Tell me you haven't been thinking about that child. Tell me you haven't been thinking about how much you care about Sissy.'

'You worrying me, Cassie.' His eyes closed again, and he was quiet for some time. I didn't bother him. I just stared at him until he had to look at me again. 'Cassie, look,' he said, raising his arm behind his head and resting against it, 'even if I was in a mind to make it up to Sissy, she won't listen.'

'You talk, she will. She just wants you to *make* her listen. Why you think she came all the way to Strawberry to talk to you?'

'Well, don't matter no way. I ain't likely to get me a pass to go home again till Christmas. She be stubborn as a mule by then.'

'Don't you know how to write?'

He stared at me as if the thought were foreign to him. 'What?'

'Write her, Clarence!'

'Lord, Cassie, my head is splitting. . .'

'Well, maybe writing Sissy'll take your mind off your head.'

'Don't have no paper.'

'I can fix that,' I said and opened the glove compartment. As I rummaged through it I found a brush and comb as well as a black ribbon and pulled them out. I found a note pad and a pencil and gave them to Clarence. 'It doesn't have to be a long letter now, just a few words telling her how you feel about her and the baby. You can mail it in Memphis.'

Clarence looked at the paper. 'I ain't much on writin' letters, Cassie. I can't half spell.'

'Don't you ever write Sissy from that base?'

He looked at me with a shamefaced grin.

I let him have it. 'Boy, you ought to be ashamed of yourself! Here this girl just crazy to death about you – don't ask me why! Talking about your love is blessed and

154

all that kind of thing, and about how proud she is to be carrying your baby, and here you haven't even been writing that child all these weeks you've been away. Can't even find a few words to tell her on a piece of paper not much bigger than a postage stamp, and then you got the nerve to be calling yourself mad because Sissy was trying to keep her pride and not force you into anything! Negro, I'd let you go!'

'Well, that's what Sissy done.'

'Well, maybe she was right, then.' Clarence studied the blank note pad and didn't say anything. I watched him, then, disgusted with the whole mess, got out of the car. 'Well, I'm through with it. You write the letter or not, it's up to you. I just know one thing. I sure am glad I'm not in love.'

Clarence glanced up as if to speak, but there wasn't anything else I wanted to hear from him. I took the comb and brush, left the car, and went over and sat on a stump. I undid my hair, combed it out and brushed it, then tied it back with the ribbon. As I finished I saw Moe coming and went to meet him. 'See anybody on the road?'

'Couple of cars passed, that's all,' he said.

I folded my arms across my chest and shivered. 'Well, I'm hoping it won't take too long for Stacey and Willie to get back here. I don't feel none too comfortable in this place.'

'You cold?'

'I'm okay. Kind of hungry, though.'

'Well, what 'bout some of that food Oliver packed? Or maybe some of them store-bought pies? Willie said they was mighty good.'

I cocked my head toward two stumps. 'We can sit there and eat. Be like a picnic.'

'All right. You go 'head and sit down. I'll get the food.'

I gave Moe the comb and brush to take back, and he went to the car. Soon he returned, carrying one of Oliver's bags in his hands. 'What was Clarence doing?' I asked as he settled beside me.

'Sleeping.'

'Already? Again?'

Moe shrugged and served the food. We each took a chunk

155

of pie and a piece of chicken. We ate hungrily, then split a third piece of pie and a chicken breast. As I finished off my first bite of this second helping, I studied Moe. He hadn't said much of anything since we had started eating. 'Moe? You all right?' I asked after a while. 'You been so quiet.'

Moe took another bite of pie, swallowed, then looked at me. 'I near to killed them boys, Cassie. How can I be all right?' I waited for him to tell me. He looked at me and away again. His shoulders bent as he settled an elbow on each knee and stared out at the glade. The slice of pie seemed forgotten in his hand. 'I don't know what come over me, Cassie, to go hit Statler and Leon and Troy like that. I been through a lot worse with these white folks down here, and I know how they are. I wasn't 'tending to hit nobody, hurt nobody. Maybe I should've stood what Statler done. Remember that time Josie Wallace spat right in my face? Didn't use a crowbar then.'

'Maybe you should've.'

'You know . . . one of them boys could be dead. Maybe I killed one of 'em.' He looked at me, his eyes full of hurt and pain. 'Cassie . . . Cassie, what if any of them boys die? What if any of them already dead? I could be a murderer and not even know it. Maybe . . . maybe I done took a life, Cassie . . .'

I searched for words to comfort him. 'Well . . . you were talking about becoming a soldier. You'd've been killing folks you were in a war.'

He shook his head. 'Not the same thing. Not the same . . .'

'In a way . . . it is . . .'

'I can't go back, Cassie, I can't never go back.'

'Maybe one day.'

He seemed not to hear me. 'I know I shouldn't've done it, but it's just that I figure no man got a right to be laying his hands on another man that way and laughing at him about it. Just don't figure nobody got that right, and then Statler said what he done 'bout you. Well . . . a man don't like to hear that kinda talk 'bout his womenfolks.'

I smiled. *His womenfolks?* I teased. 'Since when did I become one of your *womenfolks?*'

156

He ventured a look at me. 'Guess you think I'm a fool, huh?'

'Now, what would I be thinking that for, Moe? I'm glad you hit them.'

He shrugged and looked at the ground. 'I was so scared, Cassie. All that time Statler was talking to me I was so scared . . . then he knocked me on the head like that. Like I wasn't nothing. Like I wasn't no man at all! Right in front of you too! I – I ain't wanted you to think me less'n a man, Cassie. Couldn't've stood it, for you to think that.'

'I wouldn't've thought that,' I said quietly. I wanted to tell him about what had happened at the gas station so he would know that I understood, I mean, that I really understood. But I knew that, like Stacey, if he knew, if any of them knew what had happened to me and they went back, they could possibly be killed or imprisoned, so I did not tell him. Instead all I said was 'I know what you feeling, Moe. I do. Really.'

He shook his head. 'How could ya?' He was silent for a long time. He ate the rest of his pie. I ate mine too. When he was finished, he spoke again, 'I'm kinda glad I'm on my way to Chicago, Cassie. Ain't glad 'bout how come, but ya know how sometimes a body talks and talks 'bout doing a thing but can't make up his mind to go 'head? How sometimes your mind just gotta get made up for ya? Well, that's what's happened with me. I can get me a good job there in Chicago – '

'Job? Thought you were going in the Army so fast.'

'Don't figure I can now. Army get to checking on me, they'll send me back.'

'Well, anyway, maybe some good'll be coming out of all this.'

'Guess you right.' He smiled. 'Chicago. Be making plenty of money up there. Maybe I'll even find myself two jobs. Maybe I'll get to making so much money I can send you something back for your schooling.'

'How come you always worrying so much about me?' I questioned. 'Like I told you before, you get yourself some money, you best be seeing to your own schooling.'

'Yeah . . . I know you told me that. But you going places, Cassie, and I wanna help you – anyway I can.' He looked away shyly; then suddenly he turned back, leaned over, and kissed me, flat on my mouth. It was a quick kiss, a mere brush of his lips against mine, but it surprised me. Moe had never kissed me before.

'What you do that for?' I asked, as if it were a puzzle I was trying to solve. I didn't feel uncomfortable about the kiss. I just wanted to understand it.

He shrugged. 'Oh, I don't know. Just got moved to do it, I s'pose. What?' he asked, his eyes smiling. 'Am I crazy?'

'You're the one said it.'

'Yeah,' he admitted with a laugh. 'Yeah ... guess so. That's what some folks keep telling me, anyway: I'm crazy.' He looked away from me. 'Cassie ... Cassie, there's something I been wanting to ask you –'

He didn't get the chance. Two white men carrying shotguns emerged abruptly from the forest and came toward us. We got up from the stumps. The men eyed us, then the older of them said good day and asked what we were doing there. Being quicker with my mouth than Moe, I answered. 'Had car trouble.'

The man glanced over at the Ford. 'That car yonder?'

'Yes, sir.'

The man looked at Moe. 'That your car, boy?'

Moe cleared his throat. 'No, sir.'

'Whose is it, then?'

'This here girl's brother's.'

'Well, where he at?'

Moe again cleared his throat. 'Gone to see if maybe he couldn't find a place where he can buy us a fan belt for it. Fan belt on it's shot.'

'Ain't gonna find no place 'round here open on a Sunday mornin' 'less'n he go back a ways to that highway truck-stop. That where he gone?'

'Fraid I don't know,' answered Moe. 'He just took off walking.'

The man squinted, then went over to the car and walked slowly around it. He saw Clarence sleeping in back and stopped. 'What y'all doin' this far off the road?'

Moe hesitated; I didn't. 'Pulled in here to sleep.'

'This far off the road?'

'Yes, sir. Couldn't park on the highway and didn't want to park on that road leading in. Just wanted to sleep. But

158

then when we woke up and tried to get this car started, it just wouldn't start. Found that fan belt busted.'

The man grunted, seeming to think that tale plausible, and walked to the front of the Ford. 'Let me see that fan belt ya talkin' 'bout.'

'Her brother, he took it with him,' said Moe.

'Well, let me see under here anyway.' He gave the hood a slap.

Moe and I looked at each other, then Moe went over and put up the hood. The man stooped down to look. After a few moments he straightened. 'My boy here and me, we maybe have what ya need. Y'all goin' a spell, it won't last ya long, but it oughta do ya till ya get to a city. Can pick another one up there.' He motioned to Moe. 'You, boy, come on with us. Keep us a lotta old parts up at the house. You can find what you need, you can have it.'

Moe glanced at me, then back at the man. 'Thank you kindly, sir, but we don't wanna cause you no trouble – '

'Ain't no trouble,' said the man, then he turned and started back into the woods with his son.

'I best go with them,' Moe told me.

'Are you crazy?' I hissed. 'You can't go with them!'

'I gotta, Cassie, else they be wonderin' why – '

'Let them wonder – '

'Look, Cassie, they might just have what we need, and could be Stacey and Little Willie won't be finding a fan belt in that town. They don't, then what do we do?'

The man stopped and looked back. "Ey, boy! You comin'?"

Moe nodded and moved off. I caught his arm. 'I'm going to wake Clarence so we can go with you.'

'No! Y'all wait here for Stacey.'

'But, Moe – '

'Got no time, Cassie,' he said and pulled away. 'Got no time.' As he turned I saw his fear. I think he saw mine, too, but he left me anyway.

I returned to the car, figuring to wake Clarence; but I didn't. There was nothing that Clarence could do except go after Moe, and maybe that would just make things worse. Maybe all three of us should have gone with the men, and just left a note for Stacey and Little Willie, but the men might have wondered about that too. Anyway, the decision

159

was made. Moe was gone. I leaned against a tree and waited. I felt all alone.

Finally Stacey and Little Willie returned. 'What's the matter?' Stacey asked when I ran to meet them. He glanced around the glade. 'Where's Moe and Clarence?'

I told them.

'That fool, he done what?' exclaimed Willie.

'How long ago Moe leave?' asked Stacey.

'About an hour. Think we ought to try and find him?'

'You got any idea where to look?'

'Just know which way they went,' I said, pointing to the east.

Stacey stared out at the forest and heaved a heavy sigh.

'Well, anyway,' said Little Willie, 'look on the bright side. Leastways maybe he'll come back with the fan belt we need.'

'You didn't get one?'

'Couldn't find any place open.' Stacey took a few steps, then stopped and gazed out at the trees.

'Moe don't bring one back,' said Willie, 'we gonna hafta wait here till morning, or one of us gonna hafta hitch to Memphis and get the thing. Man we met said that'd be the closest place we can find something open on a Sunday.'

'Moe doesn't get back,' I said, 'I don't suppose it much matters about the fan belt.'

Stacey noted my pessimism with a glance. Little Willie looked at me, too, and shook his head. Then we heard someone coming on the forest trail. We waited, hoping it would be Moe. It was. He stepped grinning from the forest, holding the much needed fan belt in his hand. As he held it up for us all to see, I ran to him and gave him a hug, fussing all the while. 'Don't you be coming out here grinning!' I warned. 'We've been worried to death about you!'

Moe grinned down at me, and his eyes danced.

'See you got the fan belt,' said Little Willie.

'Yeah . . . yeah, I did.'

Stacey took the fan belt and looked it over. 'Any trouble?'

Moe said no. 'Gone back up to those men's place, and like the man said, they had a lotta old parts and things. They told me to just go ahead and look for what I needed. Took me awhile, but I found it.'

'How much you have to pay?'

'Not a thing. They said I could have it.'

'Well, that was nice of them,' Stacey admitted and looked somewhat apprehensively to the woods again.

'Yeah, nice, all right, but how come?' said Willie. Moe and I didn't say anything, for we understood their suspicions. It most times paid to be suspicious of white folks, even in good deeds.

Stacey glanced around, expecting the men to come back. 'We'd best get this fan belt on and get out of here.'

'Yeah, I can sure enough agree with that, son,' said Willie. 'Them scounds could come back and maybe not be so nice. Could be they – '

There was a sudden scream. We turned back toward the car and saw Clarence bursting from it, his hands to his head and hollering like a madman.

'Clarence!' cried Little Willie, sounding a bit exasperated with him. 'What the devil the matter with you, boy, carrying on like some fool – '

Clarence fell to his knees and screamed again. Then he lowered his head and began pounding it against the ground.

We ran to him.

Stacey knelt beside him. 'Clarence! Clarence! What is it?'

Clarence didn't answer. He continued to beat his head against the ground, and Stacey and Moe tried to hold him. Clarence thrashed his arms about and would not be stilled. 'Oh, Lordy, Lordy!' he screamed. 'It's killing me! It's killing me! Oh Lordy, it's killing me!'

I knelt in front of him and tried to pull his hands from his head. 'Clarence?'

Little Willie looked on irritably. 'What's the matter with you, hoss? You doing all this carrying on like this 'bout a little ole headache? Thought you called yourself a soldier!'

Clarence was crying openly now, his body writhing on the ground.

'Damn, man!' Willie snapped. 'What kind of headache you got? Where's that BC powder?'

'I think he took them all,' I said.

'Then we oughta try and find him some more, then,' said unsympathetic Little Willie. 'Keep him from carrying on so.'

Moe shook his head. 'Won't be anything open, seeing its Sunday – '

'Besides,' said Stacey, 'I'm thinking BCs won't do much good now. Looks like something more than a headache wrong with him.'

Suddenly Clarence wrenched away from us, leapt up again, hands to his head, and ran across the glade faster than I had thought would have been possible with all his pain. We ran after him. Screaming, he dashed deeper into the woods. We followed, but we couldn't catch him. He was running like a madman. Finally he tripped and fell down a rocky slope, and we found him sprawled out flat and unconscious with a bloody gash along the side of his head.

'He out like a light!' exclaimed Willie.

I knelt on raw knees beside Clarence, then looked frantically up at Stacey. 'We've got to get him some help. Stacey, we've got to get him some help!'

'But where can we go?' said Moe, looking and sounding bewildered. 'We don't know anybody – '

'Hospital,' decided Stacey. 'We'll have to try and find a hospital.'

'A hospital!' exclaimed Willie, staring at Stacey as if he had lost his mind. 'Man, you gone mad? You think we gonna find a hospital take coloured folks way out here?'

Stacey ignored him. 'Help me get him up.'

Little Willie ranted on. 'White folks ain't gonna let Clarence in no hospital!'

'He got on a uniform,' retorted Stacey. 'They ought to allow him something!'

Willie shook his head. 'You crazy man!'

'Just help us get him in the car, will ya?'

Little Willie grumbled on as he helped Moe and Stacey carry Clarence back. They put him inside the car, and I tried to stop the bleeding by wrapping his head with the boys' pocket handkerchiefs. As I sat with Clarence, his head slumped on my shoulder, Stacey, Moe, and Little Willie got the fan belt on and reconnected the loose wires. Then Stacey started the car. There was an awful grinding sound to the engine, but at least the car could move. We left the glade and headed north again.

The nearest town looked much like the town of Strawberry, sad and red and desolate-looking on this Sunday morning. As we rode slowly over the main road we saw a coloured boy of around fourteen or so and asked about a hospital. The boy frowned, then muttered the word as if he had never heard it spoken before. 'Hospital?'

'That's right,' said Stacey.

'We ain't got us no hospital.'

'Nothing at all? What about a doctor?'

The boy studied on the matter. 'Ain't got us no doctor neither.'

'What about the white folks? They got one?'

'Yeah . . .'

'Well, where can I find him?'

He shrugged. 'Maybe at they hospital – '

'And where's that?' asked Stacey, his patience giving way.

The boy shook his head. 'Y'all can't go there – '

'Yeah, we know. Where is it?'

The boy pointed straight ahead, eyeing us, though, as if we all belonged at the state mental institution. Stacey thanked the boy and drove on. When we reached the hospital, we got Clarence out of the car and to an entrance. A nurse stopped us there. 'Y'all can't come in here,' she said. A few feet away a coloured cleaning woman was mopping the hallway floor. She stopped her mopping and stared at us much as the boy had done.

Stacey glanced at Clarence, whom he and Moe were holding upright between them. 'We know . . . but this fella here, he's a soldier, and he's sick something awful. Something's wrong with his head. He was having some terrible headaches, and then he fell, hit his head, and knocked himself out.'

The woman looked at the blood seeping through the handkerchiefs. 'Well, I'm sorry . . . but y'all can't bring him in here. We don't treat nigras here.'

'Well, what're we supposed to do? You've got no coloured hospital.'

The woman looked flustered. 'Well, y'all'll have to go on

163

to Memphis or back to Jackson, where they can take care of y'all.'

'But we can't make it that far! He's hurt bad! Can't you – '

'Nurse!' A man in white was coming down the hall. 'What's going on here?'

The nurse turned to him, waited until he reached her, then looked at us as if we were the cause of some personal embarrassment to her. She seemed chagrined to have to explain the connection. 'They . . . they want to bring that boy there in here for treatment, Doctor McClurg. I told them – '

'Yes,' said the doctor, cutting her off and sparing her from mouthing any further embarrassment. He set cold eyes on us. 'Y'all niggers know ya'll got no business here.'

Clarence began to moan again; he was coming to.

'Now, y'all get from here!'

'But his head – ' said Stacey.

'Now!'

Stacey started to say something else, but then the cleaning woman, standing behind the folks in white, shook her head in a warning, and Stacey said no more. After all, it was their hospital, like it was their laws that said they didn't have to admit coloured folks to it, and we couldn't fight them on it. They ruled the hospitals like they ruled everything else.

We took Clarence back to the car. As Stacey started the motor the cleaning woman came running out, waving for us to stop. 'Y'all come on with me,' she said in a hoarse kind of whisper. 'Just drive this car on 'round to the back. There be three doors there. Y'all stop at the first one. I meet y'all!' Then she darted back into the hospital entrance and disappeared.

'Well, what we supposed to make of that?' I wondered.

'Guess we best find out,' said Stacey. He drove to the back of the hospital and stopped at the first door, as the woman had instructed. We waited several minutes before the woman appeared. When she did, she glanced out cautiously, then hurried to the car and peered inside. 'Seen y'all inside there talkin' to that ole Doctor McClurg. Like talkin' t' a wall! What's the matter wit' the boy?'

164

'You know medicine?' I questioned.

'Knows somebody who do.' She studied Clarence. 'What y'all done for him?'

'He's been taking BC powder since yesterday,' Stacey said. 'This morning he ran out, but wasn't anything open to get him any.'

'BC powder, huh? Y'all wait here a minute. I'll get ya some.' Then she ran back inside the hospital. She was gone only a few minutes. When she returned, she pulled a thin tissue of paper from her apron. 'Give him this,' she said.

We just looked at the tissue. We didn't know anything about this powder.

'Well, give it to him! It's BC!'

Stacey took the powder from her and handed it back to Moe.

The woman shook her head, watching to see if Moe would give it to Clarence. 'Y'all sho got a nerve, I give ya that. But y'all crazy to come here. They don't 'low no Negroes in this hospital. Y'all oughta know that! Now, y'all wanna help this boy, take him on up to Ma Dessie's place. She 'bout the nearest thing we got to a doctor. Y'all take him up there, maybe she can help him.'

'How we find her?' asked Stacey.

The woman gave directions. 'Tell her Tesda done told y'all to come on up.'

'We're much obliged,' Stacey said and pulled off.

Ma Dessie's place was on the northern outskirts of the town. The roadway leading to the place was an overgrown wagon trail, and the house at the end of the trail could hardly be called little more than a shack. Barefooted youngsters, some bare bottomed, too, played in the yard, despite the chill. The woman we figured to be Ma Dessie sat rocking on the porch watching them. An old man sat on the steps. As we entered the clearing the children scattered. Some ran to the protection of the old woman; the others just stood aside staring. After all, we were strangers here.

Stacey got out. 'Day, ma'am,' he said, touching his hand to his hat. 'Sir. How y'all doing?'

'We be fine,' said the woman, returning the cordialities folks always exchanged.

'We looking for Ma Dessie.'

The old woman gave a slow nod. 'That be me.'

'Well, we just came up from Jackson, and we got us a friend sick in the car. Lady name of Tesda down at the hospital said bring him here. Said maybe you could help him.'

'What's the matter with him?'

Stacey explained.

The old woman squinted, studying Stacey. She studied us in the car as well, then got up. 'Y'all bring him on in here,' she said.

We did as she ordered. The boys got Clarence into the darkened squalor of the house and laid him on a corn-husk mattress. The old woman then looked him over. Sitting on the side of the bed, she reminded me of Big Ma the way she checked his eyes and his mouth and felt his head with her hands. Then she questioned Clarence. 'Tell me what ya feeling, child.'

'Like something . . . something growing in my head. Oh, Lordy, Lordy, something growing in my head!'

'Touch the pain. Show me where it at.'

Clarence gripped the left side of his head. 'Oh, Lordy!'

The woman watched Clarence for several moments as he writhed under the pain, then she nodded as if having made a decision about something and got up. She went over to a table in the darkened corner of the room and pulled two tin cans down from a shelf. She poured powders from the cans into a dish and mixed them together. She took the powder the woman Tesda had sent and mixed it in. Then she took part of the preparation, put it in a glass, poured in water, and stirred. She took the glass to Clarence and told him to drink it. 'It's powerful more stronger than them BCs. Lord willin', it gonna ease yo' pain some,' she said.

Clarence gulped it down and lay back.

'Y'all go on out now,' said the woman Ma Dessie.

'What about Clarence?' asked Stacey.

Ma Dessie looked down at Clarence; there was a frown on her face. 'He be all right for now. Just let him rest.'

'But those headaches – ' I said.

'Lord willin', they gonna ease up. But I done seen the headache bad like this befo'e. Sometimes they eases on up

166

and don't come back, then again sometimes they just goes on and on, jus' bein' the miseries.' She had kept her eyes on Clarence as she talked; now she suddenly turned. 'Y'all younguns hungry?'

'No, ma'am, we're fine,' said Stacey.

'Got some corn hoecakes jus' come out the stove. Mustard greens there in the pot. Maylene!'

We were surprised to hear her holler out, but almost as soon as she did a pretty girl of thirteen or so appeared at the back door. 'Yeah, Ma?' she said.

'Get them tin plates from yonder, rinse 'em out good, then you take that messa greens and that corn bread out to the porch and serve these folks.'

Stacey looked around at all the wide-eyed children standing barefoot on the dirt floor and thanked her for her hospitality but told her we weren't hungry.

'Y'all been travellin' all the way up from Jackson, y'all ain't had no dinner. We got plenty. Now, y'all go on outside, let this boy rest. I calls y'all when he wakes.'

Clarence was already asleep. Whatever she had given him was powerful stuff. At least for the moment the pain was gone. I looked at Stacey. He nodded, not wanting to insult her, and went out with Moe and Little Willie. I asked Ma Dessie if I could have some water to wash up. She looked at my muddy coat, my torn stockings, the dried vomit, but didn't ask questions.

'There's a pan out on the back porch. Bucket of water too. Ya help yourself t' it.'

'Thank you, ma'am,' I said and went as far as the door, then turned to give her some explanation. 'I fell too.'

She nodded, as if explanations were unnecessary. 'That happens, sho do.' Then she turned back to her powders, and I went out.

I washed up as best I could. Maylene brought me a towel, but it was sour smelling, and there was no soap. I put the towel aside, splashed water on my face, and tried to clean my hands. Then I checked my knees. They looked a mess. Each of the stockings had ripped open right at the knee, and blood was caked on both my knees and the stockings. Scabs had already begun to form, and I worried about the encrusted dirt. I had badly skinned my knees before, and I was fearful of infection. I thought about taking off the stockings, but with the heater hardly working in the car I needed something on my legs, even the stockings as torn as they were. I looked at the sour towel Maylene had brought me, but I didn't use it. Instead I wet the bottom of my slip, which was still clean, and gently dabbed at the sores. My knees smarted. I managed to get a little of the dirt off, then left my knees alone.

There was little I could do about the rest of me. I threw out the water and went around the house to the front porch. The old man who had been sitting on the steps was no longer there. I sat down beside the boys just as the girl Maylene brought out the food – the pot of collards and the corn bread. She also brought water for the boys to wash their hands, then she gave us each a tin plate and told us to dip out a portion. There was no meat. 'Y'all go 'head,' said the girl as the children looked on. 'We eats later.'

Stacey hesitated. It was bad manners to refuse what was offered, but there were so many children who had to be fed from that pot. 'Why don't y'all come join us?' he said.

One of the children stepped forward, but the girl pulled him back. 'No, suh, y'all go 'head. We eats later. There's plenty, now. Help y'allselves.'

Stacey started to object again, but Maylene insisted, and rather than offend, Stacey dipped out a spoonful of the greens onto the corn bread. He nodded his thanks, and the girl, holding the pot, offered us each a portion. When she had passed around the pot one time, she set it on the porch, then she and all the children stood around to watch us eat.

Stacey commended her on the meal. 'It's mighty fine,' he announced after one bite, and we all concurred, though the food was somewhat greasy to me.

The girl smiled widely, pleased by the praise, and offered us more. We declined with thanks, and she accepted that. We finished our eating, the girl collected our plates, then we waited.

Little Willie leaned back in his chair. 'How long that boy gonna sleep?' he asked impatiently.

Stacey stared out into the broom-swept yard. 'Don't know. That stuff she gave him sure knocked him out.'

'Hope it knocked out that headache too,' I said.

Stacey got up and left the porch. He went over to the car and put up the hood. I followed him down. 'What you doing?'

'Figure while we waiting I might as well try and see what's wrong with this car. Whatever we hit going off into those woods got the engine not running right.'

'You worried maybe the car won't get us to Memphis?'

'Lord, sure hope it gets us there,' said Willie, coming down the steps with Moe, 'or we sure are in trouble. Last thing we wanna do is go get stuck in this here town. Reminds me too much of Strawberry!'

Stacey glanced at Willie as if he had read his mind, then he bent under the hood. After some time he pulled off his jacket and slid under the car. When he pulled out from under it, he was frowning. 'Looks like the oil pan's busted. It's leaking oil. Transmission could be damaged too.'

'Is that bad?' I asked, dusting off his back.

'Couldn't get much worse,' said Moe despondently, and I knew he was blaming himself for the condition of the car, as he was for everything else that had happened. 'It's not fixed, it'll damage the engine bad.'

I glanced from him to Stacey. 'Well, what do we do about it?' Stacey looked at me, then put down the hood. 'Pray this Ford gets us to Memphis, Cassie . . . pray hard.'

I didn't like the sound of that, but there was no time for praying now as Ma Dessie hollered from the porch. 'Y'all can come on in now! That boy's awake!'

We hurried into the house. Clarence was lying quietly, his eyes closed, a clean rag now around his head. As we gathered by the bed he opened his eyes slightly and tried to smile.

'How you feeling?' we all asked.

'Lot better'n I was feelin' little bit ago, that's for sure.'

I took his hand. 'Boy, you had us scared.'

'Had myself scared, Cassie. Still got the headache but not like before. It's just a regular kind of headache now. Long as I be right still, don't feel it too much.'

'We can't stay here all day, now,' chided Little Willie. 'You say you feeling better there, Clarence, then get on up from there, hoss, so's we can get on to Memphis! You be all right now.'

Clarence sat up, grimaced with pain, and lay back down. 'Starts up again bad when I sit up.'

'Need to rest,' said Ma Dessie.

'Well, we can't leave him here,' said Stacey.

'Y'all comin' back this way?'

'Yes, ma'am, figure to be back through a bit later today sometime but – '

'Then y'all can leave him on here. We take care of him. Me and this girl Maylene, we don't mind tendin' him.'

Stacey consulted Clarence. 'What you want to do?'

'Figure these folks don't mind, maybe it be best I stay on, let this headache ease up.'

'We get to Memphis, maybe we can find you a doctor.'

'Lord, I move and get that headache back, don't think I could make it to Memphis. I'm feeling a sight better now, and much as I wanna see Memphis, I figure I rest up here, maybe get me another dose of medicine, then I be all fixed up time y'all get back.'

Stacey glanced at Ma Dessie, then looked again at Clarence. 'I don't like leaving you.'

'Oh, I be all right. Y'all gotta get Moe to Memphis. Get him to Memphis on that train to Mr Hammer, that's the main thing. So don't y'all worry none 'bout me! Only thing I'm worried 'bout is getting back to that base on time. I don't make it back there, I'm gonna be in a whole lotta trouble that ole sergeant get holda me.'

Stacey looked around at Little Willie and Moe. 'Maybe one of us better stay with him – '

'Well, it won't be me,' said Little Willie. 'I want to see Memphis!'

Stacey frowned. 'Well, one of us ought to – '

'Naw! Y'all go on and see to Moe!' insisted Clarence. 'I mean it, man! I'm all right! Y'all go on!' He motioned Stacey closer and said in a softer voice, 'That Maylene's sure a pretty girl, ain't she? Can't ask for no prettier nurse'n that. Y'all here, y'all just be in the way.'

Stacey smiled appreciatively and patted Clarence's shoulder.

I bent over Clarence and whispered, 'You best be putting your mind on Sissy and forget about this child Maylene.'

'Cassie's right, hoss,' said Willie, taking Stacey's place

by the bed as Stacey went to talk to Ma Dessie. 'Don't go getting too friendly with your nurse, now, 'cause look like to me Ma Dessie there, she take a shotgun to you quick as Ma Batie.'

Clarence managed another smile.

'Look here,' said Moe, taking Clarence's hand, 'you take care of yourself, now, Clarence.'

'You the one. Don't let the white folks get ya, Moe.'

Moe nodded. 'Gonna try my best not to.'

'Let us know how ya doing, now . . . and tell Mr Hammer maybe I be comin' up to Chicago I get outa this uniform.'

'Yeah, I'll do that.'

Stacey finished his words with Ma Dessie and turned once more to Clarence. 'You sure you'll be all right?'

'Stop worryin' over me like some ole mother hen. Told ya, Stacey, go on and get Moe to Memphis.' His speaking was laboured, soft as a whisper. We didn't want to leave him.

'All right, we'll go on,' Stacey conceded, 'but we'll be back soon as we can.'

'Y'all don't get back soon, I'm gonna go 'head and take the bus, now. Don't worry. I can make it back on my own just fine.'

'You take care of that headache, now,' said Stacey.

I gave his hand a gentle squeeze, then started to pull away, but Clarence kept hold.

'Cassie . . . I got that letter started.'

'Yeah?'

'Yeah. Gonna mail it I get back to Jackson. Don't let me forget it, now. I get to feeling a bit better here, I'm gonna finish it.'

'Then get to feeling better quick.'

'What letter y'all talking about?' asked Willie.

'Letter to Sissy,' I said.

Little Willie grinned. 'Letter, huh? Man, you keep messin' 'round here, Sissy gonna hook you yet, boy!'

'Yeah . . .' Clarence murmured. 'Yeah . . . but maybe that ain't so bad.' He managed a weak smile and a slight wave of his hand.

We said good-bye one more time, then went out. Ma Dessie, the girl Maylene, and all those wide-eyed, barefoot children followed us out to the car. Stacey tried to give Ma Dessie some money for all their trouble, but Ma Dessie wouldn't take it. 'I was a stranger, but ya took me in. That's what the good book say, and I don't recollect nowhere it sayin' nothin' 'bout no money.'

'Well, we sure do thank you,' said Stacey.

Ma Dessie waved off any gratitude. 'We take care of him. Don't y'all worry 'bout him none.'

Again we thanked her, then got into the car, waved goodbye to them all, and headed back to the highway. It was late afternoon, almost dusk, when we reached the state line. Right on the other side of the line was Memphis. As we crossed into Tennessee, Little Willie rolled down his window, looked back and waved. 'Good-byyyyye, Mississippi!' he shouted.

And I yelled: 'Hel-loooo, Tennessee!'

Then the two of us laughed. Stacey and Moe, though, didn't join in our revelry. They didn't say a word.'

Route 51, which we had taken straight up from Jackson, took us right into Memphis. The city, all aglow for Christmas, was massive and grand. Following Oliver's instructions, we remained on Route 51 until we reached Union Avenue. There we turned west and soon found ourselves in the heart of downtown Memphis, and it was a wonder. Streetlights were bright. Huge neon signs hung along the sides and on top of high buildings. Christmas decorations blinked and glistened in store windows displaying scenes of a white Christmas wonderland, the kind we seldom saw in the South. We looked for the block-long building called the Peabody Hotel and turned left. A block later we turned onto Main Street, passed Beale Street, came to Calhoun and Main and were at Central Station, just as Oliver had directed, but there was no place to park, so for several minutes we rode up and down Main and Calhoun.

Finally we found a space, parked, got out, and walked back. As we approached the station, we slowed, then stopped to observe the entrances. Like the Jackson station, the Memphis station was segregated. In Jackson white folks had their street entrance to the station, their waiting room, their gate entrances and exits to the trains, and we had ours. The same was true here. We saw some other coloured folks looking as if they were travelling and as if they knew what they were doing, and we followed them to the side of the building, and inside.

The coloured lobby of the station was crowded, so I figured the white lobby had to be too. I supposed, though, a crowded station was to be expected a few weeks before Christmas. People were hurrying in and out of the exits and up the stairs to the waiting room carrying cardboard suitcases, some held together by rope and string. Many of the folks, like Moe, were carrying shoeboxes too. Everybody I knew who ever went on a train carried shoeboxes filled with chicken, sausages, boiled eggs, corn bread, biscuits, cakes and pies, and the like. After all, tickets were expensive enough, and there was no sense in adding a food bill to the price by buying food on the train. There were plenty of coloured folks travelling and among them a number of soldiers. Outside we had seen white soldiers as well and a lot of white travellers. Ticket lines were long, and folks seemed impatient. We couldn't get near the counter. It was a huge station and Memphis was a mighty city, so I assumed it was always like this.

'So many people,' I said to Moe as I looked around. 'Hope you can get a train.'

'Got to find what time they leave from here first,' said Willie.

Stacey studied the schedule posted. 'Looks like there's a train for Chicago soon.'

'Well, it's going to leave without Moe,' I said, 'if we don't get ourselves to the ticket counter.

'Well, now!' said a voice behind us. 'Y'all younguns lookin' mighty lost! Where y'all think y'all headin' off to?'

We turned. Sitting alone at a shoeshine booth, legs crossed and looking much as if he had always sat there, was an elderly coloured gentleman. Over his clothing he wore an apron that looked once to have been white but was now heavily stained in shades of brown and gray and black; a shoebox full of polishes and brushes was at his feet. I assumed he was the shoeshine man.

173

Although it wasn't any of the old man's business where we were going, Stacey answered politely enough. 'Chicago.'

'Chicago?' rejoined the old shoeshine man; then he laughed. 'Chigaco? Shuckies! Y'all crazy? Y'all ain't goin' to no Chicago or no other place t'night. Tomorrow neither most likely not with all these folks trying to get out. Sho not with all these soldiers here! They goes first. Gots to get back to they bases. Nope! Y'all ain't goin' nowheres, not till them soldiers get to where they goin'.'

Stacey looked around. 'There always this many soldiers travelling?'

'Course not!' snapped the old man. 'But after what done happened, ya know they gots to get to where they goin'. Only make sense. All they playtime is over now.'

Stacey glanced at Willie, Moe, and me. The man was making no sense. I shrugged, feeling we were wasting our time with him. Stacey looked back to him. 'All we want to do is get a ticket for Chicago.'

'After what done happened?'

I could tell Stacey was losing patience. I knew I was. 'After what happened?'

'What – what happened?' shrieked the shoeshine man. 'Why . . . where y'all been?'

We looked at each other, not knowing why he was getting so excited. 'We just got in town – ' said Stacey.

'Y'all means t' tell me y'all ain't heard?'

'Heard what?' I said, ready to move on.

'We been bombed!'

Little Willie laughed. 'Ah, come on, man!' he scoffed.

'Don't you be laughin', boy, 'cause ain't nothin' t' be laughin' 'bout this day! Japs done bombed some little speck of a place out in that Pacific Ocean ain't nobody never heard of!'

'Well,' I said, still puzzled about why he was so concerned, 'what's that got to do with us?'

'What that got t' do with us. *What that got t' do with us?* Giiiirl, they done killed a whole buncha our soldiers over there! Done bombed a whole buncha our ships and planes and things, and these white folks is mad! Y'all see all them soldiers yonder? Well, all them's headed back to they bases. Gotta go! 'Cause we's at war now!'

174

We stared at the man, wondering if he was crazy of if we were.

'Yeah! They done bombed this place, Pearl Harbour, and we goin' to war, I tells ya that! Y'all can just take my word for that thing 'cause we sho 'nough goin' to war!'

I couldn't believe the old man's words. I didn't want to believe them. 'That what the president said?'

'Humph!' grumped the old shoeshine man, as if I had insulted him by questioning his declaration. 'The president, I ain't hearda him sayin' nothin' yet, but he ain't gotta say nothin'! Ain't nobody gonna be bombin' us and gettin' 'way wit' it! We goin' t' war, all right! Y'all can jus' take my word for that thing! Yeah, we in it now! We goin' t' war!'

The Memphis Prince

'Well, what do we do now?' said Little Willie. 'These folks are crazy! So what do we do now?'

We stood some distance from the shoeshine man, trying to figure out just what to do. Everything was upside down. We were away from home trying to be adult about things, trying to make decisions that a few days ago would have seemed impossible. We were trying to make decisions that, according to the shoeshine man, might already have been made for us.

'We going to war,' said Moe, 'what happens to me I don't 'spect much matters.'

'We don't need to hear that,' I said and turned to Stacey. 'What are you thinking on doing?'

'First, I'm thinking on trying to get a ticket for Moe to Chicago. We can't just take that man's word that there aren't any. Then we'll have to get the car checked. Can't put it on the road for anywhere until we know for certain what's the matter with it and get it fixed.' With that said, he stood in the ticket line and waited. We all did. But the shoeshine man had been right. There was no hope of getting on a train tonight, so Willie said again, 'So what do we do now?'

'We can go to Chicago,' said Stacey.

'Now, wait,' said Moe. 'Y'all ain't taking me to Chicago.'

'May be the only way you can get there,' surmised Stacey. 'That old shoeshine man, he could be right. Could be you might not get there another way, leastways not for a spell.'

'But what about Clarence?'

Stacey considered. 'He'll know to take the bus back.'

'Yeah,' agreed Willie. 'Long's his head okay and seem like it was.'

'No,' said Moe. 'I can wait here till there's a train. I can wait. I know folks here.'

'Who?' I questioned.

Moe didn't answer.

'Well, what 'bout that fella Oliver told us 'bout?' said Little Willie. 'Solomon somebody.'

'Bradley,' I finished.

Stacey glanced at me, then nodded. 'Thing is, even if Moe stays here and wait on a train, we still have to get the car fixed. Can't take a chance on the road.'

'We got money to get it fixed?' asked Little Willie. 'We gotta pay for gas and maybe Moe's ticket.'

Stacey turned to me. 'Cassie, how much money you say you have?'

'Me? I . . . uh . . .' He had put me on the spot, and for once I didn't know what to say, seeing that my money had been in the purse.

'Didn't you say you still had that money Cousin Hugh and Cousin Sylvie paid you for work at the cafe?'

'Well . . . I did have it. But I . . . I lost my purse.'

'Lost it? When?'

I looked away, trying to give myself time to say this thing right. I couldn't have him going back to that station one day on my account. 'Back at that gas station.' I looked at him again. 'Lost it in the dark when I fell back there.'

'Why didn't you tell us?'

'Boy, you forgetting all those men around that car and what I heard them say? I looked for that purse, couldn't find it, then forgot about it when I saw them. Wasn't that much money in it anyway!'

Stacey gave me a hard look, and for a moment I was afraid he would question me further. I could feel he didn't believe me, not fully, anyway; he knew me too well. I knew that one day I would tell him the truth, but not today.

'Look,' said Moe, without knowing it coming to my rescue, 'it don't matter 'bout Cassie's money. Y'all done enough spending money and losing money on my account. Now, I been thinking maybe best thing to do is for y'all to go 'head and take this ticket money and fix the car, and I'll just stay on here a few weeks and get a job. I get some money, then I'll buy my own ticket.'

Stacey refused to consider that. 'Unh-unh, you be better off in Chicago,' he decided. 'I'm going to call Uncle Hammer, ask him to wire us the money – '

'Now, look – '

'You get to Chicago and get a job, then you can pay him.'

Moe shook his head. 'It's time y'all gone on.'

'Not till you're safe.' With those words Stacey finished the discussion. Moe, tired of arguing with Stacey, said nothing else. We left the station, returned to the car, and made our way once again through the streets of Memphis. We had no trouble finding the address Oliver had given us. It was a four-storey building. Businesses were located on the ground floor and what looked to be apartments on the other three. Although lights burned brightly on the top three floors, the ground floor was dark except for one of the offices, where we could see several people hurrying about through the uncurtained windows. On the glass doors of the office was carefully painted lettering identifying the offices of Memphis Valley Enterprises. In smaller lettering were listed the various divisions of Memphis Valley Enterprises. Hanging on the inside of the door was a sign that proclaimed the offices closed until Monday at eight A.M. But we didn't have time to wait until Monday at eight A.M. Stacey knocked on the door. A couple of folks turned, saw us, shouted something we couldn't make out, then went on about their business. Stacey knocked again, this time with more urgency.

Finally a heavyset middle-aged woman looking irritated took note and came to the door carrying a stack of papers held against her chest. She didn't open the door. She merely hollered through it. 'We're closed! Didn't you see the sign?'

'Yes, ma'am,' Stacey replied. 'But we were looking for a Mr Solomon Bradley. Was hoping he might be here.'

'He's busy. We've got a newspaper to get out.'

'He works for the paper?' I said.

'He *is* the paper,' she said. 'He owns it.'

'Oh.'

Stacey looked at me as if that was of no matter, then told the woman, 'We just came up from Mississippi, and we need to talk to him. Be obliged if you could tell him we're out here.'

'Well, what's your name?'

'Logan. Stacey Logan. Tell him we're kin to Oliver Reams in Jackson.'

She looked us up and down. 'Y'all wait here.'

'Should've told her we were kin to Jasper and Jessie too,' I muttered, shivering in the evening chill. 'More folks he know we know the better.'

Stacey tapped on the glass and shouted that information to the woman. The woman glanced back, nodded, and went on. She turned a corner and was gone. A few minutes passed, and then Solomon Bradley appeared. He looked even more handsome than I had remembered. He wasn't wearing a suit jacket now and the top of his shirt was unbuttoned. He was wearing a tie, but it hung loosely. His sleeve cuffs were undone and rolled up. He looked tired but good. When he crossed the room to the door, my heart began to race, and I felt suddenly nervous. He unlocked the door and looked out. As his eyes glanced over us I stepped back, wishing I could escape so he wouldn't see me looking like this. I knew I looked a mess.

'Stacey Logan?' he said.

Stacey nodded. 'That's right.'

Solomon Bradley extended his hand. 'I'm Solomon Bradley. Oliver called this morning.' He ushered us in. I don't think he noticed me. 'Sorry you had to wait out there in that chill. What with Pearl Harbour, it's been a hectic, news-filled evening. We've had a number of people stop by for news, and I'm afraid my staff has gotten a little brusque, seeing that we're trying to get a paper out. You've heard about the bombing, of course.'

'Just heard it.'

'Well, we're a weekly newspaper and we're not supposed to publish until Friday, but we're trying to get a paper ready for tomorrow morning to let our community know how all of this is going to affect us.'

'And how you think it is going to affect us?' I asked, losing my momentary shyness.

Now Solomon Bradley looked at me, and he smiled in recognition. 'I'll let you read the paper . . . but, in short, a lot is going to be asked of us during this war, and a lot of our boys are going to have to go fight. Seeing that we don't

179

know how long it's going to last, we best prepare ourselves to fight overseas and on the homefront too.'

'What do you mean, fight on the homefront?'

'For jobs ... for the spoils of war ... or what this war could mean to us.'

'Then you figure we are at war?' said Stacey.

'Have to be,' said Solomon Bradley, sounding as sure as the old shoeshine man about the thing. 'Reports are still coming in, but the numbers are staggering. Men killed, ships, planes destroyed. Our Navy was really hit hard. We're not hardly walking away from this. Sunday, December seventh, 1941, is going to be a day to remember.'

One of the office people hurried over, waving a paper for Solomon to sign. Everybody seemed to be in a rush, everybody except Solomon. 'Sorry to be bothering you at a bad time,' Stacey apologized.

'No bother,' Solomon said after signing the paper. 'Putting together a newspaper on a day like today is what the business is all about. Course, we've never had news like this to handle before.' He moved toward a hallway. 'Come on, let's get out of all this traffic. We'll go to my office in back.' He led us down the hallway into a room removed from the commotion of the outer office. Then Stacey told him why we had come.

'We've just come up from Jackson, and we're having trouble with our car. We ran onto some rough road and – '

'Some rough rednecks too,' finished Willie. 'Had to try and outrun 'em.'

'Oh?' said Solomon. 'Well, I'm not surprised. That's a mean stretch of road coming up from Jackson. They had a double lynching along there just a few years back. Got quite a bit of attention because there was an anti-lynching bill up before Congress at the time. Of course now, the bill still didn't pass. You're lucky you got away.'

We looked somberly at him, for we all knew that was so.

'Anyway,' Stacey went on, 'we ran over a stump or something and the car hasn't been running right since. Think we'll need a new oil pan and maybe have to repair the transmission. I want to get it checked before I put it on the road again.'

'You're heading back to Jackson?'

Stacey glanced at Moe. 'Don't know yet. We might be going to Chicago.'

'Chicago? Not a good weekend for travelling.'

Stacey nodded that was true. 'Thing is, we didn't know that when we left Jackson. Had thought to put Moe on a train here in Memphis, but looks like with all the commotion it'll be awhile before he can get out.'

Solomon's eyes slid from Stacey to Moe. 'You brought him all the way to Memphis to catch a train?' None of us spoke. 'Trouble?' he questioned. 'Oliver only told me that you might be contacting me.'

'I hit a white man,' Moe confessed.

'The truth was known,' I said, 'he hit three white men.'

Solomon was thoughtfully quiet. 'Are they dead?'

Moe shook his head. 'Not far's I know.'

'Thing is,' said Stacey, 'we had to get him out. Figure he'll be safe in Chicago.'

Solomon nodded. 'Well, don't know what your situation is back in Jackson, but it seems to me that you shouldn't be staying away too long from there, especially with this war breaking out. There'll be questions asked.'

Stacey considered and said, 'We got to get Moe to Chicago.'

'You know folks there?'

'Got kin.'

Solomon looked again at Moe. 'You're welcome to stay here. I've got more than enough room. I'll see you get a train out.' Moe didn't say anything, and Solomon looked back at Stacey.

'We thank you,' Stacey said, 'but that's going to be up to Moe.'

Solomon gave a nod.

'In any case, though, we'll have to get the fan belt replaced and the car checked over before we can get back on the road. We're wondering if maybe you didn't know somebody who could maybe look the car over for us this evening.'

'On an ordinary kind of Sunday evening, maybe. But today . . . I don't know what luck we'd have. We'll give it a try, though. There's a fellow I know could do it, if I can catch up with him.'

'We'd be obliged.'

Solomon Bradley picked up the phone, dialled, and talked to someone a few minutes, then handed the phone to Stacey. 'Just tell him the problem. Name's Roscoe Smith. Folks call him Smitty. He's expecting you.'

Stacey talked the matter of the car over with the man on the phone. When he hung up, he said, 'I guess we'll be going on over there. Thank you kindly for your help. One other thing, though, if you don't mind. I'd like to put in a call to my uncle in Chicago. I'll reverse the charges.'

'Course you're welcome to use the phone for any calls you need to make,' said Solomon, 'but I doubt if you'll get through. The lines are pretty tied up.' He again handed Stacey the phone and Stacey dialled the operator, but Solomon had been right. There was no getting through, not now anyway.

'Guess I'll have to try calling him later from the garage,' Stacey said, frowning as he hung up. I knew he was worrying about the money. He looked at Solomon. 'Thanks for the use of your phone and for everything else. We're obliged.'

'It's nothing. Look, that garage of Smitty's isn't the most comfortable place in the world. You're all welcome to stay here overnight and get rested and see Smitty in the morning.'

'Well, thank you again, but we best take care of it tonight. We need to get back on the road as soon as we can.'

'All right, but the offer stands. We'll be here all night in any case, so you want to rest, you're welcome.'

Stacey looked at me, then turned back to Solomon. 'Well, I'd be obliged if my sister could stay here. She wasn't feeling so well earlier – '

'I'm fine now,' I interjected, thinking of how I must look to Solomon.

'And I'll just stay on with her,' volunteered Little Willie, eyeing one of the young women in the outer office.

'Fine,' said Solomon. 'Smitty tell you how to get over to his place?'

'Yes. Shouldn't have any trouble.'

'Good. You folks eaten? We're sending out for some fried

chicken, and there'll be plenty. You come back, it'll be waiting here for you.'

Stacey nodded appreciation, then looked at me. 'You'll be all right?'

'I'll be fine.'

'I'll watch out for her,' said Little Willie, his eyes still on the woman.

Stacey shook Solomon's hand and thanked him once again, then he and Moe left. Little Willie followed them into the outer office and didn't come back. I was left alone with Solomon Bradley.

'Would you like to rest your coat, Cassie?' he asked.

'No, I'm kind of cold,' I said. But I lied. The room was hotter than blazes, but I didn't want him to smell the vomit or to see the stains on my dress. The mud on my coat was bad enough.

He looked at me as if he could read my mind, then turned from me as a skinny young man wearing glasses came in. 'Need your okay on this, Solomon,' said the young man. 'Mag says she's ready to run it soon's you approve it.'

He pushed several pages at Solomon, and Solomon said, 'Cassie, meet my left hand, Mort Jones.'

'I got left because Mag's his right,' said Mort with a grin.

'Mort, Cassie Logan,' finished Solomon, taking a look at the papers. 'I met this young lady in Jackson yesterday reading *The Law: Case Histories of a Free Society*, a book I didn't lay eyes on until I was in law school.'

'Oh, yeah?' said Mort. 'You in college?'

'No.'

'I'm a junior at Fisk.'

'I've been thinking maybe I'd like to go to Fisk,' I said.

'That a fact?' returned Mort.

'Course, now, with this Pearl Harbor business I don't know.'

'That's something, isn't it? Never expected the war would come from the East. Always figured it would be Germany – '

'Mort, you double-check these quotes?' asked Solomon, still looking at the pages Mort had given him.

'Hazel was supposed to – '

'But you don't know if she did?'

'I can find out,' said Mort, turning for the door.

'Never mind. Something else I want to check with her anyway. Just keep Cassie company.' He left then, and my eyes followed him out.

Mort turned back to me. 'Can't hardly wait till morning. I'm going to sign up.'

'What?' I mumbled as my mind lingered on Solomon.

'I'm going to join the Army.'

I gave him my attention again. 'I was a man, I sure wouldn't, not until I got called, and then I'd be trying to figure a way not to go.'

'How can you say that? The Japs bombed us – '

'They didn't bomb Mississippi. Didn't bomb Tennessee.'

'Bombed the US of A or same as it!' proclaimed patriotic Mort. 'Bombed our ships! Killed our men!'

'I heard men got killed over there were Navy folks, and I've heard from my uncle that there weren't all that many coloured folks in the Navy, and those that were, weren't hardly fighting men. Fact, he said that's the worst branch of the service for coloured folks, so how come you want to go join up so fast for?'

'Have to! Can't let Hitler win this thing!'

'Hitler? Now, how'd Hitler get into this? Thought we were talking about the Japanese.'

'Well, Solomon says now that the Japanese have given us no choice but to fight, we'll finally be at war with Germany because, you see, Germany and Italy are all tied up in this Tripartite Pact with Japan. We fight Japan, we got to fight them, too, and Negroes got to fight Hitler.'

'Why?' I said.

'*Why?* Why? Haven't you heard his talk about the master race? Way he figure, nobody is as good as folks of that so-called superior race!'

'White folks figure the same here.'

'Yeah ... well ... it's not the same. We can't let the country fight this war without us! We sure can't stand by and let our country lose – '

'So what happens if we win? What difference would it make to us? I mean, if we win, are we going to be able to do everything the white folks can do then? We going to be able to use *their* restrooms in a gas station or eat in *their* cafes or sleep in *their* hotels or go to *their* hospitals? We going to be able to do any of that?'

'Hold on, girl! You not fighting a war with me, you know! What got you so riled?'

'I just don't believe in fighting for nothing. Just tell me we're going to be able to do those things. They're simple enough.'

'Well . . . maybe not . . . but still we got to fight, Cassie. We got to put all those differences between the white folks and us aside for the time being because we have to go fight. Can't let Hitler win. Can't let the Japs win either.' He turned as Solomon came back. 'Solomon, you tell her,' he said.

Solomon tossed some papers on his desk. 'Now, just what am I supposed to tell her, Mort? What are you two into it about?'

'He told me he's going to go sign up to fight this war, and I told him I didn't know what he had to fight for.'

'Told her the country's been attacked – '

'Ought to let the white folks fight the war. They're the ones run everything.' Solomon smiled, seemingly bemused, and I said, 'What're you smiling about?'

Now he laughed. 'You're getting pretty hot under the collar there, Miss Logan,' he said, sitting at his desk.

'Well, it's not right the way white folks do. They treat us any old way they want, and now they're in a war, they'll be wanting us to help them fight it. My Uncle Hammer fought in that other war they had, and he said when the war was over and he came back home, wasn't anything changed. Said the white folks got free in Europe, but things stayed just the same over here for us. If anything, they just got worse way coloured folks, especially coloured soldiers, were lynched after that war.' My voice rose, and I trembled. 'Here we can't even use a toilet in a gas station, and they'll be wanting our boys to go fight! Can't even stand in front of a toilet door without them making you feel like – ' I stopped. Solomon was watching me closely; so was Mort. I was saying too much. I shied away from saying more. 'Never mind,' I murmured and crossed my arms and turned away.

There was an awkward moment, then Solomon said to Mort, 'Tell Mag you can run that piece.'

Mort hesitated. 'All right.' He glanced again at me and left.

Solomon looked after him in silence, then turned to me and spoke softly. 'Just what happened out on that road, Cassie?'

'Nothing.'

'You expect me to believe that?'

'Believe what you want,' I said and looked away as the humiliation of what had happened burned at my gut like a searing iron.

'Cassie?' His voice was so soft. 'What happened? And don't tell me nothing happened. There's mud on your coat, and your stockings are torn. That didn't come from "nothing."'

Embarrassed, I backed away from him, out of the glare of the overhead light, and looked down at myself. I thought of how I had looked when I had met him yesterday. I had been pleased with how I looked then. Now I was ashamed.

'What happened? Tell me.'

I shrugged. 'I fell. We stopped at a gas station, and I fell.'

'That's all?'

I met his eyes. There was a quiet to him, like Papa. I wanted to tell him. I wanted to tell somebody what had happened. I was tired of holding it in. 'Stacey doesn't know . . .'

'I'm listening.'

I cleared my throat, growing husky with the pain of the words to come. 'We . . . we stopped at a gas station and I . . . I had to use the toilet. The gas station man, though, said they didn't have a toilet for coloured folks. Told me to use the bushes behind the station.' I glanced away from him. 'I . . . I went down to do that. Stacey and Moe and Willie, they didn't know I had gone. They were all in the store. But I never got as far as the bushes. On my way down I had to pass the restrooms they had for the white folks. Nobody was there and . . . and one of the doors was open. I thought about going in. I stopped right there in front of that open door and was trying to figure whether or not to take a chance when this white woman came over, and she saw me. She called the gas station man over on me, and two other men came with him. They . . . they talked something awful to me, and when I tried to get away, I . . . I fell and I dropped my purse and they wouldn't let me get it. They . . . scared me. They scared me something terrible and they – ' I looked at Solomon now. I looked straight at him to confess the worst part. ' – and they kicked me . . . like a dog.' Then I flicked away a falling tear. I didn't want to cry. I had done my crying.

Solomon got up from his desk as if to approach me. I put out my hand to stop him, and he stayed where he was. 'You see . . . that's how they do us. That's how they do us, and now they're in this war and our boys are supposed to go fight? My brother is supposed to go fight? My friends are supposed to go fight? It's not right. It's not right.'

Solomon Bradley studied me in silence.

'I don't want Stacey to know about what happened. Moe and Willie, they don't know, either, what happened back there, and I don't want them to know. They just think I fell. I – I figured it could've been worse, a whole lot worse, if they knew and tried to do anything about it. Please, don't tell them.'

'I won't,' he promised, and I believed him. He stood and came over to me now, despite my outstretched hand to stop him.

'Don't come near me.'

He smiled. 'Not too many young ladies tell me that.' He placed strong hands gently on my shoulders, and I tried to pull away, but he didn't let me go. Still holding me by one shoulder, he lifted my chin with the flat of his hand so that I had to look him straight in the eyes again; his gaze was intense. 'Is there something else? Anything else happened with those men?'

I folded my arms across my chest and hugged my coat closer.

'Cassie?'

'Well, if you just must know,' I snapped, 'I was so scared, I threw up on myself, and now I stink to high heaven! Okay, you satisfied now?'

'Ahhh,' he said, as if a revelation had just hit him, then he laughed. 'That's what's bothering you?'

'That's not funny!'

'No ... no, it's not,' he agreed, smiling still. Then he stopped smiling. 'But I thought maybe those men had ...' His eyes studied mine, then he squeezed my shoulder and moved away. 'We'll fix your clothes.' He went to the door, and if he had smelled the sourness of the vomit, he didn't say so. He opened the door and called the woman Mag. 'Cassie's in somewhat of a fix here,' he told her when she came in. 'She needs a change of clothes. I was just thinking maybe one of your daughter's clothes might fit her.'

Mag gave me a look up and down. Then she came closer and walked around me. I knew she smelled the vomit, but she didn't say anything either. 'Yeah, I got something she can wear.'

'Good. Then, why don't you send Mort over to your place, and you see Cassie upstairs to mine so she can wash up and change.'

'We have time for this?' asked the woman. 'I'm trying to get this story set –'

'That story can wait another five minutes, Mag. Just tell Mort what clothes to ask for.'

'Oh, all right,' agreed the woman somewhat begrudgingly, 'but we're losing precious time here. Remember, you're the one insists on getting this paper out on time.'

'Yes, ma'am,' said Solomon with a smile of mocking acquiescence.

She shook her head and returned to the outer office, calling for Mort as she went.

Solomon turned back to me. 'It'll be all right. Mag's got a bark. Actually, she's got a bite, too, but she's a rock. She keeps things on track around here. I depend on her.'

I frowned. 'What about my clothes? They need to be cleaned.'

'Don't worry. There's a cleaners in the building and I've got a little pull with them. We'll make sure you get your clothes before you leave.'

Mag stepped back into the doorway. 'I sent Mort,' she said to Solomon; then to me, 'You ready?'

I glanced at Solomon. 'Where's Little Willie? I'd better tell him where I'm going.'

'That boy's in that back room following Joanne all 'round,' said Mag. 'No need to worry about him. You'll be back before he even gets to missing you.'

'I'll let him know where you are,' said Solomon. 'Now, go on.' Despite my stepping away again, he came to me, put his hand on my back, and pushed me toward Mag with a gentle touch. 'Don't worry. We'll let him know where you are, and your brother, too, if he comes back before you finish up there. Just take your time.'

I took one more look at him, nodded, and left with the woman. I followed Mag through the office and outside, then to the end of the building, where she opened a door and led me up a flight of stairs.

'Don't get winded, now,' she told me as she reached the landing. 'I told Solomon, seeing he owns the building and just about everything in it, he ought to have a place on the second floor so folks don't have to be climbing all these stairs.'

'You mean he owns this whole building?' I said, somewhat incredulous, as I trailed behind her. 'Those other businesses too?'

'That's what I said, isn't it? He won't listen to me, though, about moving from the top floor. Says he likes the exercise. Besides that, he doesn't like to hear people walking over him.'

'This whole building . . .' I repeated in a mutter.

'Here we are,' Mag said, reaching the top floor landing. She led me down a hallway to a corner door, pulled out the keys Solomon had given her, and unlocked it. She flicked a switch as we entered, bathing the room in light. The room had a comfortable look to it. A wall of books lined one side. Paintings, certificates, newspapers, photographs, all framed, lined another, and the third wall was lined with windows that faced the street. There wasn't much of a fourth wall, for the room opened directly into a second room that looked as if it logically should have been a dining room but held instead a desk and a chair as its only furniture. Stacks of paper were on the floor, both newspapers and writing paper, and there were more books too. 'It's a bit congested in here,' said Mag, 'but you'll find your way. Solomon's a collector. I told him he's too young to be collecting all this stuff, but he pays me no attention. He's thinking about knocking out a wall into the next apartment to give himself more room, but he'll just fill that up, too, with more books and newspapers. Come on, it's this way to the bathroom.'

'Does he live alone?'

'Could hardly say alone,' said Mag, crossing the office and entering a hallway. 'He's got too many women friends to say that.'

'Oh.'

She turned on the light in the bathroom. I noticed there were two other doors along the hall. One of the doors was half-opened, and I could see the bedroom. The bed was made, but there were papers on it too.

'He reads a lot, doesn't he?'

'You could say that,' Mag conceded. She opened a drawer, pulled out some towels, and gave them to me.

'When he was in Jackson, he had a woman with him. I didn't get a chance to meet her, though. You know who she was?'

'Could've been one of a dozen young things. Here.' She slapped a fresh bar of soap into my hand and turned to the door.

'What kind of women does he bring up here?'

She looked back at me. 'Girl, you sure are asking a lot of questions about that man. Go ahead and wash up. Get in the tub and take yourself a bath if you want. Soak and relax. Nobody'll bother you. Time you get out, Mort ought to be back from my place with some clothes. I'll bring them up. By the way, you can just wrap yourself in one of these big towels hanging here when you finish.'

She left the bathroom and went back into the living room. I followed her out. 'You sure it's all right I stay here?'

'Course.' She opened the door, then looked back at me with a frown. 'You're not afraid to be here by yourself, are you?'

'No . . . What about Mr Bradley, though? Would he come up?'

There was a second of silence, then Mag laughed. 'Girl, don't you worry about Solomon. He's not thinking about you, and even if he was, he's too busy now to do anything about it. Now, there's the phone. You want something, need something before I get back with some clothes, you can call downstairs. Here.' She wrote on a pad by the phone. 'I put the number down for you. Now, just lock the door and get yourself that bath. I'll be back in just a bit.'

With that she went out, closing the door behind her. I made sure it was locked, then stood with my back to the door a moment, surveying the room. I imagined Solomon here, in this room, then left the door and walked slowly along the three walls. I looked at the paintings, studied the photographs, read a few lines of the articles, the newspapers, fingered the books, then sighed, and headed for the bathroom.

It was then that I noticed the record player and the shelf of records. I glanced through the records. There was Benny Goodman and Duke Ellington, Glenn Miller and Artie Shaw, Billy Holiday, and Cab Calloway. I longed to play one of them, but knew I shouldn't. I knew I probably shouldn't even be up here in this man's place; but it was exciting for me to be here, alone in Solomon Bradley's apartment. If Stacey knew, he would probably raise the devil; but he wasn't here, so I figured to enjoy myself while I had the chance, and the first thing I was going to enjoy was a bath.

I soaked for more than an hour. Then, wrapped in a towel, I took a book from Solomon's shelf, curled up in Solomon's chair, and read while I waited for Mag. When Mag returned some time later, she brought with her a skirt, a blouse, and a cardigan sweater. I thanked her for the clothes, then went again to the bathroom and put them on over my own still damp underwear which I had washed out and hung to dry over the heater. As we were leaving the apartment I hesitated at the door, not yet wanting to leave. Giving the room another look, I asked Mag about one of the photographs on the fireplace mantle. She looked around to see what picture I was talking about. 'Oh, that's some girl up north.'

'You know her?'

'Just seen the picture.'

'Well, is she Mr Bradley's special girlfriend or something?'

She laughed. 'Solomon's got plenty of lady friends that are special. Didn't you see them all lined up there?'

'But her picture's sitting different from the others. Sitting apart, like she's somebody special.'

Mag glanced again at the picture, then at me, and put her hands on her ample hips and gave me an odd look. 'Now, how come you asking so many questions about Solomon Bradley? How come you so interested in those pictures?'

I looked away from her, casually turning to take in the room once more. 'Oh . . . I was just wondering.'

Then she laughed. 'Well, I hope that's all you were doing, 'cause the last thing you want to do is get your mind set on Solomon Bradley. That man got too many women as it is running after him, and they got a whole lot more experience on how to get him than you do. Take my word for it. You fix your mind on Solomon Bradley, you just asking yourself for trouble.'

'I'm not fixing my mind on anybody!' I declared, looking her full in the eyes.

'Well, good, then!' she said. 'One less heart for me to have to worry about.'

'How old is he, anyway?'

'Too old for you, little country girl. Now, come on, I've got work to do.'

With that we left the apartment and went back downstairs to the newspaper office. 'Feeling better?' Solomon asked me as we entered his office. He was seated at his desk.

I nodded. 'Yes, thanks.'

'Solomon, need you to check this copy here,' said Mag, going over to him. 'Henry's ready to set the page.'

Solomon took the pages and began to read. Mag leaned over his chair, talking about cutting part of an article. As they conversed I took a better look around. There were photographs on the walls here too. All looked to be school class pictures of white folks and a boy who looked very much like Solomon. There were two college degrees hanging on the wall as well. When Mag and Solomon finished with the article, Mag took the pages to the outer office. I turned to Solomon. 'You're not from here, are you?' I said. 'I mean, you're not from Memphis.'

He glanced over at the wall. 'Guess those pictures do give me away, don't they? They were taken in Amherst. Amherst, Massachusetts. I was born there, grew up there.'

The place was foreign to me. 'You went to school with white folks?' That idea, like the town of Amherst, was foreign, too.

He shrugged. 'Amherst was a white town, so I went to a white school. My father owned a store there, and my mother was a teacher. All while I was growing up just everybody I knew and associated with was white. It wasn't a bad life.'

'Well, how did you end up here?'

He considered the question, then answered with a mock smile. 'I got lucky.'

'What was it like?'

'What was what like?'

'Being in a white school?'

'Sometimes it was rough. Sometimes it was lonely, but I got a good education. It was good enough to get me accepted into Harvard.' He looked at me as if that should mean something. It didn't. I didn't know anything about any Harvard. He laughed, at himself, it seemed. 'That's a very prestigious school. You're *supposed* to be impressed.'

'Oh. Well, what was it like there?'

'Well, again I got a fine education. But a Negro in a white school misses out on a lot of social life. Fraternities were off limits to me, white girls were definitely off limits, and there were no coloured girls nearby. It got lonely.'

'Was it worth it?'

'As I said, I got a fine education.'

'Then you came here?'

'After law school. I met a man while I was in Boston who was from here, and we used to talk a lot. I was intrigued by what he told me about the South. He encouraged me to come to Memphis and I did. I set up a law office and I've been here ever since.'

'Can I ask you something?'

He smiled. 'Now you're asking my permission?'

I knew he was teasing, so I paid no attention. 'Back in

Jackson at my cousin's cafe, I asked you if you were a lawyer and you said you figured a body had to practise the law to be a lawyer. Then you said you spent time in jail once and after that you didn't have much respect for the law. Now I know I'm not suppose to be assuming anything, but I thought from what you said, you weren't practising law, but Oliver said you were, among other things. It's confusing to me and I'd like to get it straight.'

He laughed outright. 'You know, I like you, Cassie Logan. I like how your mind works . . . among other things.' I wasn't sure how he meant that and my face went hot, but he seemed not to notice as he went on talking. 'The truth of the matter is that I use my knowledge of the law to further my business interests. I also use my knowledge of the law to advise people who come to me on a personal basis, not as clients, but just people who want some advice from a knowledgeable source. I don't charge them for any advice I might give. So you see, that's the extent of my law involvement and I don't consider that practising law.'

I glanced away from him, thinking on what he had said, then looked back. 'What was it about going to jail that made you lose respect for the law?'

'I think I've made a mistake,' he said.

'About what?'

'Allowing you to ask me so many questions.'

His tone was quiet, but I wondered if I had upset him by bringing the subject of his jail time up again. 'I was just trying to understand . . .'

'I know. As I said, I like the way your mind works.' He smiled once more. 'Maybe one day, if you continue in your persistence, I'll tell you.'

I nodded, not really satisfied with that, but knowing I shouldn't press him further about it now. Still, there were other questions I wanted him to answer, for I wanted to know everything I could about Solomon Bradley. 'So how'd you get in the newspaper business?' I asked.

'You are a curious young lady, aren't you?'

'My grandmother says I'm just nosy. You don't mind telling me, I'd like to know.'

'It's a bit of a story.'

'I don't mind.'

He sat on the edge of his desk. 'Well, to tell the truth, Cassie, things here in Memphis didn't go that well for me at first. Lot of black folks didn't much go in for settling matters in court. They figured the courts belonged to the white folks. Some of them would rather settle disputes with the old-time solution of guns and knives and fists. Finally, though, a case came up involving a land dispute, black against white, and I got it.

'Thing was, I was so hamstrung by the racial laws that the only way I could figure to educate folks about the case was to put some handbills together to explain what we were up against. I did the handbills and a lot of public speaking too. The handbills and the speaking made quite a stir. I lost the case, but I found folks were coming to me after that, because of those handbills and all that speaking. So that's how I got into the newspaper business. I figured if a few handbills and speaking to folks in a few churches and pool halls could get folks' attention, then maybe a newspaper could too. I tried it and it worked.'

'Yeah, well, that makes sense. But what about all these other businesses in the building? Mag says they're yours too.'

'That's called enterprise,' he said with a grin. 'En-ter-prise, that's the American way, Cassie Logan.' His tone was mocking. He stood and went around the desk and sat down. 'Don't you approve of enterprise?'

I shrugged. 'I just think that if you have a law degree, you ought to be practising law. If I had a degree, I'd practise law.'

'You've been thinking about what I said?'

'I've been thinking about how white folks are always falling back on the law. Maybe if coloured folks knew the law as well as they did, we could do something about it.'

He leaned back in the leather chair and studied me. 'You know, of course, that the law is written in their favour.'

'Yeah, I know that.'

'Then, what good is it being a lawyer when you know the law's written against you?'

'Mr Jamison says the law is a matter of interpretation.'

'Mr Jamison?'

'He's a white lawyer I know. He says that the United

States government law is supposed to take what he calls precedence over state law. He says that about this precedence business, it's all about interpretation. He says if the United States Supreme Court interprets the law different from the courts in Mississippi and says the United States law is right, then the United States law has to take precedence. He says that's how some things get changed. Thing is, though, right now folks in the rule of things – white folks – they aren't much calling for any interpretation about laws concerning coloured folks, and that's partly why the laws stay the same. I was thinking that if I got to know the law as well as they do, then maybe I could get some different interpretation. If we know the law like they do, then we can use it like they do.'

His eyes on me were intense. He thumped a pencil against his mouth in silence, then he smiled.

'What's the matter?' I asked.

He shook his head. 'Did you figure all that out yourself?'

I sat down on the sofa. 'Doesn't it make sense?'

'Could be it does,' he said, but he said no more than that. He studied me, then, looking at my knees, said, 'That looks pretty ugly.'

'What?'

He got up. 'Where you fell. Stay put. I'll be right back.' He left, and I looked down at my knees. When I had sat, the skirt I wore had slipped just above them; they were ugly. They were red-raw now from the bath and the loss of the scabs. Solomon came back carrying a small box. He crossed the room to the sofa, knelt in front of me, and opened the box. Pulling out some cotton and a bottle of iodine, he said, 'Scream if you want. I would.'

Then he dabbed my knees with iodine. I jerked back. I felt as if my crazy bone had just been hit.

'Sorry,' he said with an apologetic smile. He returned to his desk with the box. 'I should have told you I wasn't much of a doctor. Afraid I never developed a real bedside manner.'

I just looked at him. Despite my awe of him, I wasn't feeling too kindly toward him at the moment. All I could think on was the awful stinging in my knees.

'How's your spelling?' he asked suddenly.

I glanced up from my knees. 'Good. Why?'

'Got some proofing for you to do if you're not ready to sleep.'

'I'm not. I'd like to help. But what's proofing?'

Unexpectedly he came back to the sofa and took my hand. 'Come with me.' He led me from his office through the front office and into a back room where two men were busy running a printing press. 'This is where we print the paper. Before we go to press, though, we have to check all our copy. Have to check it for accuracy and for spelling. I'll take care of the accuracy part, you take care of the spelling. Deal?'

His eyes met mine, expecting an answer. 'Deal,' I replied.

Still holding my hand, he took me back to the front office, picked up several sheets from a basket, and said to Mag, 'These ready?'

'Ready as they're going to be,' Mag replied.

'Good.' We returned to his office. 'Here,' he said, leading me to his desk and seating me in his chair. 'Read these for me. Circle any misspellings, any typos, correct them out in the margin. Don't worry about missing something. I'll take a quick look at all of this for accuracy when you're finished.' He now released my hand and started for the door. 'Any questions you have, anything you need, ask Mag.'

'All right . . . but where're you going? Won't you be here?'

'Got business elsewhere. Don't worry about the articles, though. Mag can take care of everything.'

He reached the door and looked back. 'You all set?'

I nodded, feeling a bit let down that he was leaving, yet feeling good, too, that he was trusting me with this responsibility.

'Good. See you in a while, then.' With that said he closed the door and left.

Once he was gone, my mind lingered on him, too long in fact. All I could think about was Solomon Bradley. I left his desk and wandered about the room touching his things. Only the entrance of Mag with an armful of proofs for me to read brought me back to reality.

'You finish with any of those yet?' she asked.

'No . . . no, not yet.'

197

She tossed the papers she was holding on the desk. 'It's a rush,' she said. 'Everything's a rush.'

'All right.'

She went back to the door. 'Your brother called. He said it would be awhile yet before he gets back. He said something about having trouble getting the gaskets so they can install the oil pan. Said, too, they'll have to pull the transmission.'

'All right.'

'He talked to Willie.'

'Okay.'

She took hold of the door. 'You okay?'

'Uh-huh.'

She nodded, then closed the door behind her. I got to work. I don't know how long I worked. I just knew it was through most of the night. As I neared the end of the sheets, I found myself dozing off, but I didn't want to sleep. Solomon was depending on me and after all he was doing for us, I didn't want to fail him. I got up and stretched, then switched on the radio to see if there was any further news, but there was only music now. My mind wandered off worrying about Moe and all that had happened. I thought about the bombing, about the war folks said we were about to enter, and worried about Stacey becoming a soldier. I thought of Clarence and wondered how he was. It was already after three. Poor Clarence. If he hadn't gotten a bus back to Camp Shelby, he was probably going a bit crazy about now, worrying about that sergeant of his and what kind of detail he would be drawing because of this trip. But being good-natured, Clarence would probably figure the trip was worth it no matter what the cost and would no doubt happily do it again. I stared at the clock. Was it going to take all night to fix that car?

The music of Benny Goodman wafted from the radio, and I closed my eyes and began to sway to the rhythm. I put war and trouble at the back of my mind, pictured Solomon and how he made me feel, and swayed to that feeling. It was an awful time we had gone through and were now facing, yet I couldn't think about that right now. Solomon Bradley had swept the bad times away, and at this moment, with no one near to remind me otherwise, I

198

thought of him. I was Cinderella and he was my Memphis Prince.

'Dancing?'

I swirled around and faced Solomon. I hadn't heard the door open. 'No,' I lied. 'Well, leastways not really.' Then I confessed. 'Not supposed to dance on Sunday.'

'It's Monday, Cassie. It's way past midnight.'

'Well, it still seems like Sunday. Will be until after I sleep, I suppose.'

'Then get yourself some sleep. You can go upstairs.'

'No, I'm all right,' I said, not liking the sound of that.

He smiled, seeming to have detected my apprehension. 'You can sleep upstairs, or you can sleep down here. When Stacey and Moe get back, I'm sure they'll want to try to get some sleep before they hit the road again. You're welcome to the apartment.'

'Well, I thank you,' I said, 'but I'm not all that sleepy right now. Fact, I'm too excited to sleep. Besides, I want to help with the paper.'

'All right,' he said. Then Mort came in with some crises, and Solomon left again. I turned off the radio and waited for my heart to stop beating so fast. Settling down on the sofa, I began proofing the remaining papers. I read for some time, then pulled my legs onto the couch, put my head on the arm of the couch to rest, and was soon asleep. I woke when I felt someone leaning near. It was Solomon. I wasn't startled by his nearness, yet my breathing grew suddenly shallow.

'Didn't mean to wake you,' he said in a whisper, 'but I thought it best you have a cover. I don't want you taking a chill. Stretch out.' I obeyed. He tucked a quilt around me and smiled. 'Good night, sweet girl,' he said and walked away.

As he reached the doorway I suddenly remembered the pages and sat up with a start. 'But I didn't finish reading the –'

'It's all right,' he assured me. 'I have some time now. I'll get them. Now, sleep! That's an order!'

He flicked out the overhead light, leaving only the soft pale of the desk light burning, and went out. I fell into deep slumber.

When I awoke, it was past noon. Stacey, Little Willie, and Moe were asleep on pallets on the floor. I hadn't even heard them come in. Everything was quiet now. I got up from the sofa, went over to Stacey, and stooped beside him. Gently, I shook him. He opened his eyes sleepily. 'Is the car fixed?' I whispered.

'Man's working on it.'

'Did you get through to Uncle Hammer?'

'About an hour ago. He's sending money and he'll be waiting for Moe.' Then he closed his eyes again and fell back into sleep. I let him be and went into the outer office. Most of the people from last night were gone. Mag, however, remained.

'I think I overslept,' I said.

'You were tired,' she replied. 'All of you were.'

'Where's Solomon?'

'Not here. What do you want?'

'Was wondering about my clothes.'

'Oh.' Mag rose from behind the desk. 'They're ready. You can put them on upstairs.' She went down the hall, pulled out a couple of papered hangers, and brought them to me. 'There,' she said, then handed me a key. 'Go on up to Solomon's place and change. He's not there.'

'Thank you,' I said and turned away.

'You remember the way?'

'Yes, ma'am,' I said. 'I remember.'

I remembered the way exactly. Once inside the apartment, I changed my clothes, then lingered. I loved the thought of being here, where Solomon lived. A record was on the phonograph, and this time I didn't resist the temptation to turn on the music. George Gershwin's 'Love Is Here to Stay' was the song. As the music played I swayed across the room, holding my arms tight to my body and thinking of Solomon. The record played through but didn't reject. While it continued to spin with the grating of the needle the only sound, I just stood there in the middle of the room, my eyes closed, still swaying, humming the song.

It was then that Solomon came in.

'Does it feel like Sunday now?' he asked.

He had caught me again. Embarrassed, I rushed over to the phonograph and lifted the needle. 'I'm sorry.'

'What for? I'm the one who should be apologizing. I didn't realize you were up here. No need for you to be sorry about anything, sweet girl.' He smiled.

I managed to smile too.

He came over, picked up the needle arm, and placed it back on the record. Then he turned to me. 'May I have this dance, Miss Cassie Logan?' I didn't say anything, and he smiled that magnificent smile, slipped his right arm around my waist, took my hand in his, and as 'Love Is Here to Stay' again floated from the speakers, he danced me across the room. At first he held me some distance from him, his eyes smiling into mine, then he pulled me closer, and I could feel his heart beating. I knew he could feel mine.

I swirled in a daze.

I was a princess.

And he was a prince.

The world was at war.

Moe was in trouble.

But for the moment none of that mattered. Solomon Bradley had me in his arms.

I was dizzy.

I was reeling.

The world was a dream.

Then he kissed me.

Solomon Bradley . . . kissed me.

He kissed my forehead.

He kissed the bridge of my nose.

He kissed my mouth . . . and I returned his kisses.

Within seconds, before I was ready, he pulled away. But those few seconds had been enough to make me feel what I had never felt. My legs were weak. My body was trembling. My thoughts were racing. My head was in a cloud and all my thinking was blurred.

I wanted more. But he wasn't giving.

As he let me go he laughed in a good-natured way, as if he had kissed no more than an infant. 'I shouldn't have done that,' he said.

'Why . . . why not?'

'Because I know better,' he confessed. 'But there's a way about you, Cassie Logan. A way about you that's a cut between a sassy little girl and a most outspoken woman, and that's a dangerous combination for an old man like me, who ought to know better.'

'What do you mean?' I asked earnestly.

Again he laughed. 'I mean I best be careful if I don't want your brother coming after me with a shotgun.' He then took my hand and pulled me toward the door. 'I think we'd better get back downstairs. Your brother's probably wondering about you.'

I didn't want to leave, not yet, but I followed him anyway. As we reached the door someone knocked. Solomon opened the door and Moe was standing there. The sound of the needle still spinning on the record scratched the silence. Solomon released my hand. Moe spoke hurriedly. 'Stacey figure to be ready to go soon, Cassie. Just got a call from the garage. The car's fixed.' He turned to go back down the hall.

The phone rang inside the apartment, and Solomon said, 'I'll get that. Cassie, you go on with Moe.'

My eyes lingered on Solomon a moment, then I hurried after Moe. 'The money from Uncle Hammer get here?' I asked, catching up with him.

'Yeah. Stacey and I'll be going down to pick it up, then he'll go for the car.'

'Then we're going to Chicago?'

Moe slipped his hands into his pockets. He didn't look at me. 'No. I told Stacey I want to stay here in Memphis and wait for the train. Solomon said he'd put me up.'

I felt somewhat disappointed about our not driving to Chicago. Driving to Chicago meant spending more time with Moe. I wasn't yet ready to let him go, but I didn't tell him that. 'You have any idea when you can get a train out?'

'Soon's I can,' he said.

As we reached the stairway Solomon called out to us, and we looked back. His apartment door was still open, and he was holding the phone. He motioned us to return. When we entered the apartment, he put the receiver against his chest and said to Moe: 'Good news. I'm talking to a fellow I know who's been able to get a ticket for you.'

'Ticket?'

'Yes, a train ticket to Chicago. He'll be bringing it over. You can leave tonight.'

Moe looked uncertain. 'Tonight?'

'That's right.' Solomon smiled, pleased. But Moe didn't smile. He said nothing.

'Now, you don't have to worry, Moe,' I said, taking his hand and squeezing it. 'You don't have to wait here. You'll be in Chicago with Uncle Hammer before too long now.'

Moe nodded. 'I'm obliged,' he said to Solomon.

'Glad I could help.' Solomon put the receiver back to his ear and continued making arrangements. Moe and I left and went back downstairs to tell Stacey and Little Willie the news. We reached the bottom of the stairway, and I took Moe's arm before he could push the door open.

'Moe, I want to talk to you about just now upstairs. About me being in the apartment with Solomon. My clothes came back, and Mag said I could change them up in Solomon's place –'

'She told me.'

'Well, Solomon didn't know I was there, and he came –'

'You don't have to explain nothing to me, Cassie.'

'But I want you to know –'

'Cassie, I told you, you don't never have to explain nothing to me. Never.' I knew Moe meant what he said. Still he looked away, out to the street, so I couldn't see his eyes.

'Moe?'

He pushed the door open to the sidewalk. I wanted to talk, but I knew Moe didn't. I felt bad that he had seen me with Solomon. Moe cared something special for me, and I didn't want that to change. Ever. He didn't make me feel the way Solomon Bradley was making me feel, but he was my friend, and that was a good feeling too. I didn't want to lose that. He extended his hand to me. 'Come on,' he said. 'Stacey's waiting.'

It was early evening by the time we prepared to leave for the train station. Moe had wanted Stacey, Willie, and me to head back to Jackson right away, but Stacey insisted upon seeing him on the train. He wanted to make certain that Moe was safely on his way north; so did Little Willie and I. If it would ensure that, a few hours one way or the other didn't make much difference to us now. If Clarence hadn't gotten himself a ride back to the base by now, he was already absent without leave and there was nothing we could do about it. Besides, we figured he would want us to see Moe on the train.

'I figure you should be all right if you follow the way I marked on the map for you,' Solomon told Stacey as we went out to the car. 'Once you're in Mississippi you can avoid Route 51 after leaving the town of Grenada by taking that short stretch of back road I've marked, and bypass that gas station where you had trouble. You shouldn't have any trouble going back through at night, though. Folks should be asleep.' He smiled. 'Course, I know you went through at night before.'

'Maybe we'll be luckier this time. We sure do thank you for all your help.'

'Glad to do it,' said Solomon, and the two shook hands.

'You, too, Mort.' Stacey shook his hand as well. 'Good luck with the Army.'

'You, too, man,' said Mort.

'Yeah, sure. You take it easy.'

The woman Mag came over to me and to my surprise gave me a hug. As she held me she whispered, 'Now, you take care, girl, and don't you be thinking on Solomon. You forget about him. He's too much for you.' She let me go. That was all she had to say. I glanced over at Solomon saying good-bye to Moe and Willie, then I said my good-bye to Mort, to the others, and got into the back seat of the Ford, without saying anything to Solomon. Little Willie got in front with Stacey. As Moe stood at the back door thanking Mort and Mag, Solomon came over to my window. I rolled the window down. He smiled, and I trembled.

'You going without saying good-bye?'

I didn't answer. I was afraid to answer, afraid my voice would betray how I was feeling.

The smile remained, as if he understood. 'Look, I have something for you. Actually two somethings for you. A book with the chapter called 'A Woman in Green and a Man in Grey' and a Sherlock Holmes mystery. Take them. I'll pick them up my next trip to Jackson.'

I touched the books with my fingertips as if they were gold. 'When will that be?'

He laughed. 'Who knows? Maybe a year from now ...maybe next week. Anyway, you read them. We'll talk about them when we meet again.'

I took the books from him. 'Thank you,' I barely whispered.

He leaned into the car and kissed my cheek. Then he said good-bye again to the others and stepped away from the car.

'Listen, thanks again for everything,' Stacey said.

'Don't mention it. Just take it easy on that road.'

'Good-bye,' I said, my voice low.

'Good-bye, sweet girl,' said Solomon Bradley with a smile that shared a secret.

Stacey started the car. Moe sat beside me. I wanted in that moment of leaving for Moe to go back home with us. I wanted in that moment of leaving for Solomon to kiss me again. Neither was to be. Stacey pulled away. Solomon's eyes met mine in silence. Nothing more was said. We left the folks of Memphis Valley Enterprises behind and went on to the station.

At the station Stacey, Little Willie, and I walked with Moe up the stairs and out onto the crowded platform. We could see many white travellers at the other end. We stood talking for a few minutes, then Moe took my hand, and said he wanted to talk to me, and we left Stacey and Little Willie and walked down the coloured section of the platform. When we were some distance away, he released my hand. He glanced up the platform at Little Willie and Stacey. Then he looked back at me. 'Cassie, you remember when we were stuck in them woods and I was going to ask you something and those men came along?'

'I remember.'

'Well, it had to do with how I feel about you. I ... I ain't never said it before, how I feel. Always figured there to be time, but now ... there ain't no more time.'

A porter hurried by with some luggage, and Moe glanced at him before continuing. 'I feel ... I feel so strong for you, Cassie,' he said, looking at me once more. 'Been feeling like this a long while now. But all this time I been saying to myself, she got her schooling yet. She's gonna be somebody and I want her to be somebody. Maybe that's why I wanted to be somebody too.' He paused, as if expecting me to say something. I didn't, and he went on. 'I was thinking maybe after you finished high school, I could tell you how I was feeling, maybe make plans for getting married . . . if you'd have me. I was thinking I could help put you through school. I was dreaming . . . all kinds of dreams. But, Cassie, I got no more time for thinking and dreaming. I'm going to have to get on this train and leave from here, and I got no idea when I'm gonna see you again. I wished there'd been some time. Wish I'd spoke this way long time back, but I guess . . . I guess I wanted to get to be somebody first. Now I got to say it. I seen the way that man Solomon Bradley was looking at you. I seen how a lotta other fellas been looking at you. I know I don't speak my mind now, it's gonna be too late.'

I stared at him, not knowing what to say.

'I just want you to know how I feel and want you to think on me. I know I got me no education, got nothing like that Solomon Bradley – '

'Now, how did Solomon Bradley get into this?' I asked defensively.

'Because he's the kind of man girls fall for, fall for hard and fast. Won't be long 'fore men all over the place be asking you to marry 'em, Cassie, 'specially with you going off to school – '

'May not be going any place now, what with this war – '

'You'll go. Thing is, I just wanted you to know how I feel and . . . one of those fellas ask you 'bout marrying, just think on me, will you, 'fore you say yes. Think on me right now, saying what I'm saying. I promise you, Cassie, I'm gonna make something of myself, 'spite all this. I'll make you proud, I promise you. You'll see. I'll make you proud.'

'You always make me proud, Moe.'

He shook his head. 'I ain't wanting to leave from here. Like to be going on back home with y'all.'

'I wish that too.' I took his hand. 'It'll be all right.'

'Cassie . . .'

'Yeah, Moe?'

He stepped closer, slipped his arms around my waist,

and kissed me. As he pulled back, his lips brushed my cheek and he whispered, 'I love you, Cassie. I love you so.'

At that moment there was an announcement over the speaker. The train for Chicago was getting ready to pull out.

'You're going to have to go,' I said, knowing those words were not what he wanted to hear.

'I know.' He glanced up the platform. Little Willie and Stacey were waving him over. His eyes on them, he spoke softly. 'I don't want to leave.'

'But you're going to have to.'

"Ey, hoss!' hollered Little Willie, heading over. 'Sorry to be breaking this up, but the train's 'bout to move out, man! Can't have you missin' this here train after all the trouble we done had getting you here. 'Sides, that scound Clarence probably fit to be tied 'cause we ain't shown up yet. You get on out of here so we can go get that boy!'

'Yeah, I 'spect you right,' said Moe, letting me go. Then, hand in hand, we walked back up the platform with Willie.

When we reached Stacey, he glanced at me as if he knew what Moe had told me; then he half smiled at Moe. 'Well, this is it, I guess.'

'Yeah ... guess so. Look, Stacey,' said Moe, 'I want you to know, want all of you to know, that I'm gonna pay y'all back for everything. Stacey, every penny you had to spend on this trip, every penny you had to spend on your car, I'm going to pay you back.'

Stacey nodded as if none of that mattered. He held out his hand; Moe shook it, then they hugged each other.

'All aboard!' called the conductor.

Stacey pulled away. 'You best get on the train.'

Moe nodded, then said good-bye to Willie and hugged him too.

'Man, get on outa here!' ordered Little Willie, failing to cover a shaky voice. 'Get on up to Chicago!' He pushed Moe toward the train and gave him the shoebox of food.

'Y'all'll tell my papa I'm all right?'

'Don't worry now about that,' assured Stacey. 'We'll talk to him. Say hello to Uncle Hammer for us!'

'Yeah, sure, and y'all tell Clarence I hope he's getting

along better and he don't be bothered with no more of them headaches. Tell him we missed him up here.'

'Yeah, we'll do that.'

Another porter passed by. 'Best get on board, boy, you going on this train, 'cause we's 'bout to move on out.'

Moe nodded and, holding his shoebox, stepped onto the train. Looking back, he said, 'Don't forget what I said, Cassie.'

'I won't. You just take care of yourself in Chicago now, you hear?'

'I hear,' he said, gazing at me. 'I hear . . .'

The train began to move. He waved good-bye from the doorway. He stayed in the doorway and we stayed on the platform watching in silence until the train was out of the station. We stayed until Moe was gone.

'Well, guess that's that,' said Willie.

'Yeah . . . that's that,' said Stacey, turning away.

As we were leaving the station the old shoeshine man whom we had seen the day before yelled at us from his stand. "Ey! Ain't y'all the young folks I done seen down here yesterday?'

We went over to him. He had three customers sitting on the stand. 'Yes, sir,' said Stacey, 'we were here yesterday.'

'Come back, huh? Get a train?'

'We got lucky.'

'Yeah, y'all sho did, y'all got one,' said the shoeshine man, rhythmically slapping a shine on a customer's shoe. 'Well, what I tell ya?'

'Sir?'

"Bout us goin' to war? What I tell ya? I know'd it yesterday, soon's they bombed that place Pearl Harbour. Know'd it! Just done took the president this long to say so.'

'The president?' I said.

'Yeah, the president! Ain't y'all heard? Y'all don't never hear nothin', do ya? He just done spoke up. Said we at war! Yeah! Sho did! Know'd it yesterday!'

'When you hear this?' asked Stacey.

'Just now. President just been talking on the radio. We done declared war on Japan! And from what folks been sayin', we gon' be at war with Germany and Italy, too, 'fore too long 'round here. You two boys, y'all best enjoy these here last few days y'all got, 'cause sooner or later y'all gonna be like them boys y'all see yonder in them uniforms. Yeah, y'all gonna be soldier boys! Y'all gonna hafta go fight this war!'

We looked somberly at the old shoeshine man, so sure of his own words, and turned away. 'Y'all take care now,' he called as his rag popped. 'Y'all take care.'

Stacey looked back. 'Yes, sir . . . thank you.' Then the three of us hurried from the station, got into the Ford, and left Memphis, Tennessee.

It was near midnight when we arrived at Ma Dessie's. As we drove into the yard we saw a lantern shining in the night, then someone called: 'Who that?'

Stacey answered. 'The folks from Jackson. We're here about Clarence. He still here?'

'Yeah . . . he here.'

We got out of the car. The lantern came toward us now. Holding it was the old man whom we had seen yesterday sitting on Ma Dessie's steps. His arm was outstretched, holding the lantern, and his eyes were squinted. 'Yep, that's y'all, all right,' he confirmed. 'We was wonderin' if y'all was comin' back. Wasn't rightly sho what we was gonna do, y'all ain't.'

Stacey apologized. 'Sorry to take so long, but we had car trouble. We told Ma Dessie, though, we was coming back.'

Little Willie laughed. 'Yeah, couldn't hardly go leave ole Clarence without no way home. Shoot! He probably put out with us. Hope, anyways, he got plenty of sleep, 'cause we gonna hafta burn some rubber to get him back 'fore he misses another day from that Army without leave.'

'How's he doing?' asked Stacey of the old man. 'His head still giving him trouble?'

The old man shook his head and was silent. Then he motioned to the house with the hand holding the lantern. The light swung eerily across his face.

'Bet the boy's mad, though,' said Little Willie. 'Course, now, can't blame him none for that, we getting back so late.'

When the old man didn't say anything, Stacey, too, looked at the house. 'He sleeping? Know it's late, and we

209

hate bothering you this time of evening, but it couldn't be helped, us getting back just now. All of us, we got to be back in Jackson before morning, so if Clarence here, we best wake him on up and – '

'That boy, he done got the headache bad,' said the old man in a sudden burst of words. 'The boy was cryin' and screamin' something terrible. He done had the headache bad.'

'Thought he was better,' I said.

The old man hung his head. 'He just give way – '

'Give way? What you mean?'

The old man looked at me in silence.

'What?'

'Ma'am,' he said, his voice soft, so soft. 'Ma'am, that . . . that boy's dead . . .'

The night blackened and nothing was the same.

'Naw,' murmured Little Willie. 'Naw . . .'

'Sister Dessie in there, she say y'all comin' back, but we ain't know'd y'all was or you wasn't. That boy, he give way late last night, and he been lying up there dead all the day. We been looking for y'all, but we just ain't know'd if y'all was gonna come. Sho didn't.'

'Where is he?' Stacey's voice was no more than a whisper. My tears were already falling.

'He on in here,' said the old man, turning and leading the way with his lantern. He climbed the steps of the shack, then told us: 'Was thinking for a while maybe we was gonna hafta bury this boy up at our church graveyard, but then we got to thinking him being a soldier and all, maybe we best tell the sheriff 'bout it. But Sister Dessie, she said y'all was gonna come back for him. Sister Dessie, she say it's the Lord's will. Sister Dessie say that boy, he ain't got no war to fight now. He got no war to fight.'

A Final Farewell

The old man opened the door, and we went in. Ma Dessie, Tesda, the woman from the hospital, the girl Maylene, and some people we didn't know were gathered there. The room was lit by one single kerosene lamp, and its light reflected on Clarence, laid out straight and neat on a board that rested on the bed. He looked soldier-perfect. His clothes were newly pressed. His hair was combed and parted, just right; his fingernails were dirt-free clean, and his face looked as fresh-washed as a newborn babe's. He didn't look as if he was sleeping at all. He lay too straight, too perfect, for that.

'We done bathed him,' said Ma Dessie. 'Know'd it ain't our place t' do it – that place belong t' his family – but seein' he done passed on here and y'all ain't come back, we figures it the best thing 'fore the death chills set in. Ain't know'd what his mama'd want him buried in, so's we just done bathed him wit' scents and washed out that uniform and underclothes he done had on and put 'em back on him.' She glanced at us and was quiet.

For the longest time we just stood there staring at Clarence, but I didn't know what to feel. It was as if something had turned off in me, making it difficult to feel anything. Too much had happened. I felt all drained inside.

Ma Dessie pulled a piece of folded paper from her pocket. 'This here, we done found this here in that boy's pocket.'

Stacey reached for the paper, but I took it. 'I know what it is. It's that letter for Sissy.'

'Y'all sit on down,' said Ma Dessie.

We sat on crude chairs around the bed, our eyes on Clarence, as if expecting him to suddenly jump up, grin, and strip away the pallor of grey that had settled over him. But Clarence didn't move.

Stacey spoke quietly. 'We'll have to call down home. And we'll have to call the Army.' His voice was dreamlike. Everything was dreamlike.

Neither Little Willie nor I said anything.

'Need to call tonight – '

'I don't think so, boy,' said Tesda, standing behind him. 'Not t'night. Ain't nothin' open t' go makin' no phone calls, and ain't no coloured folks 'round here got no phones.'

Stacey turned and looked at her. 'But . . . we got to see to Clarence.'

Tesda shook her head. 'Can't nothin' be done till mornin'. Y'all might's well settle in for the night.'

'We've put you out enough – '

'The Lord done brung y'all here,' said Ma Dessie. 'Now, the Lord done worked his will. Can't go questionin' the ways of the Lord, so y'all jus' settle on down and don't worry none 'bout us. We got food here. Can fix y'all a place t' sleep.'

'We obliged to you, but if we can't get a telephone till morning, may be best for us to go back to Jackson. We can do our calling from there.'

Little Willie kept his eyes on Clarence. 'Then, that'll be you, hoss,' he said. 'You go on back, you and Cassie.'

'What about you?'

'I'll stay on here . . . with Clarence.'

Stacey shook his head. 'I don't know – '

Little Willie turned to him now, and his eyes were bleary. 'Should've done stayed with him before. It was me should've done stayed with him, but I . . . I had to see Memphis – '

'Willie – '

'Naw, ain't gonna talk 'bout it now. Y'all just go on, call the Army, make arrangements. You better at that kinda thing than me. Then y'all can go on home and tell Mr and Miz Hopkins 'bout what done happened. You know I'm making sense, man.'

'Yeah . . . I know . . .' Stacey's voice faded. He lowered his head and closed his eyes. Little Willie nodded, then suddenly got up, knocking his chair backward upon the floor, and, crying, rushed out onto the porch. I remained by the bed with Stacey, gripping Clarence's letter to Sissy in my hand.

Before dawn Stacey and I were back in Jackson. We went straight to Rose Street and told Oliver, Cousin Hugh, and Cousin Sylvie about Clarence, then we called the Army. The Army said they had to verify Clarence's death and that they would send a vehicle for his body. They said that they would take him home. Shortly after calling the Army, Stacey and I got back into the Ford, left Jackson, and once more headed south for home.

Before noon we were back in Strawberry. Nothing had changed in the town during our few short days away, though I supposed, because so much in our lives had changed, that it would be changed too. We drove past the Dueeze Garage and the Barnett Mercantile, past the old grey men sitting in the morning sun, and everything was the same. Outside Strawberry the land, too, was unchanged. The forest, the fields, everything was the same as before we had left, and that seemed strange to me, for our lives had changed so that they would never be the same again.

As we approached Soldiers Bridge Crossroads we saw the sheriff's car parked in front of the Wallace store. Several pickup trucks and wagons were parked there, too, and a number of people, all of them white, milled about the crossroads.

'Looks like trouble,' Stacey said, then pulled over to the side of the road and stopped the car.

I looked at him. 'Well, what you stopping for? It's not our trouble.'

Stacey cocked his head toward a truck parked on the other side of the gas pump. Sitting in the rear of the truck was Harris Mitchum. His arms were behind his back, and his feet were tied. Sissy sat beside him, but there were no ropes on her. 'Ah, no,' I groaned and shook my head at the madness of it all.

Stacey looked at me, and his eyes told me he was feeling the same. Then he opened the door and got out, and I followed. We started across the road to the truck, but before we reached the gas pump, Sheriff Dobbs met us. He gave us a good stare up and down, then he said: 'Now, jus' what y'all doin' back here? Thought y'all had jobs up there in Jackson.'

'Yes, sir . . . we do,' answered Stacey. 'But we had to come back . . . We got bad news about Clarence Hopkins.'

'That soldier boy?'

'Yes, sir. He . . . Clarence, he's . . . he's dead.'

The sheriff stared at us in silence for a moment, then he shook his head and sighed. 'Well, what happened?'

'Don't rightly know. All we know is he had this terrible headache, and he said it was killing him. I suppose he was right because . . . because he just up and died. The Army, they're supposed to bring him down, but his folks don't know about it yet. Figured it'd be better if we told them anyway, and seeing we got no phones down here, we thought we come on back with the news.'

The sheriff again shook his head. 'Sorry to hear 'bout this. That Clarence, he was a good boy. Ain't never give me no trouble. Course, I s'pose we gonna be losin' a lotta you boys now we in this war.'

'Yes, sir . . . I suppose so.' Stacey looked across the road at Harris. 'We were just headed over to talk to Harris and Sissy – '

'May be best y'all jus' go 'head and stay way from them.'

'They in trouble?' Stacey asked, as if he hadn't already figured that out.

'You could say that. That boy Harris, he helped that boy Moe get away. Drove him out of Strawberry after he done took that crowbar to the Aames family. Mr Caret Jones and his boys jus' done caught up with him hidin' down in them woods with his sister.'

With eyes still on Harris, Stacey nodded; then he looked back at the sheriff. 'How're the men got hurt? They pulling through?'

'They survivin', I reckon. Mr Statler Aames, he up and walkin' 'round, and so is his brother Leon.'

'What 'bout the other one?' I questioned, butting into the conversation I knew was best left between Stacey and the sheriff. 'The one they call Troy?'

The sheriff gave me a look, and Stacey, after a quick glance my way, reasked the question. 'He going to pull through?'

214

'Still touch and go with him.'

'Then you mean he could die?' I asked in a hiss of a whisper.

The sheriff looked at me again, and this time he answered me. 'That's 'xactly what I mean.'

I looked away, giving up a word in silent prayer, for if Troy Aames died, it was all over for Moe down here. He could never come back again. He would be lost to us forever. I also gave up a word in silent prayer for us all, for if people like Sheriff Dobbs got to checking, there might be more questions to answer, questions such as why Clarence was so many miles north of Jackson when he died, while Camp Shelby where he was due to report was a number of miles south of Jackson; questions such as why Stacey and Little Willie weren't at work on Saturday night when they had told the sheriff that's why they were in a rush to get back to Jackson. Hard questions to answer. All I could do was pray that they were never asked.

Stacey cleared his throat. 'Mr Dobbs, you don't mind, we'd like to go on over and talk to Harris and Sissy. We been long friends with them, you know . . .'

The sheriff was silent for so long considering, I turned back to them and found him studying hard on Stacey. He studied me again too. 'Long as y'all don't get no bright ideas 'bout tryin' to cut that boy loose,' he said finally. 'Y'all jus' stand put there at the back of that truck, and don't y'all go gettin' on.'

'Thank you, Mr Dobbs.' Stacey touched my arm, to walk on with him, but then he hesitated and looked again at the sheriff.

'What is it?' said Sheriff Dobbs.

'Just . . . just that Sissy and Clarence were going to get married, and she . . . she doesn't yet know 'bout him being dead. Appreciate you don't mention it to her till we get a chance – '

'I got no need to tell her nothin',' said the sheriff gruffly and stalked off toward a group of men standing at the corner of the store.

We watched him, then headed for the truck. As soon as Sissy saw us coming, she jumped up, ran to the edge of the truck bed, fell to her knees, and grasping Stacey's hands, sputtered, 'Oh, Lordy, Stacey! Lordy, I'm so glad t' see y'all! They gonna take Harris away! They gonna put sweet Harris in jail!'

I studied Harris. 'Harris, you all right?'

Harris nodded mutely, but he didn't look all right. He looked as he had that night on the Rosa Lee.

'How they get you?' I said.

Harris shook his head, as if he didn't understand that himself. Sissy spoke for him. 'They come before and gone all over the place, but we had done hid Harris. Then they come back just now, and they got him, and Harris, he so scared! Ma and Auntie, they gone to try and find y'all's daddy, see if he couldn't talk for Harris. But I already done told them men come for Harris it wasn't him. Told 'em it was that white boy Jeremy Simms took Moe out. Told the sheriff that too!'

'Ah, Sissy,' I said.

Sissy turned spitfire eyes on me. 'Don't you "Ah, Sissy" me! I seen Moe get in that white boy's truck! Cassie, you seen him too! You tell 'em you seen him!'

'Sissy . . . we can't – '

'What you mean, we can't? They gonna take Harris!'

Stacey gripped her arm. 'Sissy, listen,' he said quietly, 'it's best we keep Jeremy's name out of this – '

'How come? Y'all carin' more 'bout that white boy than Harris?'

'Course not, Sissy. But we've got to think about Moe too. Now, listen to what I'm saying to you – '

'There he is!' cried Sissy; then, despite her bulging stomach, she wrenched away from Stacey, leapt off the truck, and before we could stop her, she headed straight for the Simmses' truck, pulling in front of the store. The truck came to a halt, and as Charlie Simms, Statler Aames, and Jeremy got out Sissy ran right up to Jeremy, poked an accusing finger into his chest, and yelled, 'You the one done it! You the one! Tell 'em it was you!'

Jeremy stepped back, the colour draining from his face.

'Tell 'em – '

Statler slapped Sissy's arm down and shoved her away. Sissy came back at him, yelling for Jeremy to confess, and this time Statler laid his flattened hand right into her

216

chest and knocked her back with such force, she fell hard upon the ground. Stacey and I both rushed to Sissy's side as Mr Simms looked from her to Jeremy, then faced off with the sheriff. 'Hank, what this here nigger gal talkin' 'bout?' he demanded.

Sheriff Dobbs came over. 'She the sister of that boy Harris yonder.'

Charlie Simms turned to the truck. 'Well . . . see y'all done finally got that nigger. He done told y'all where he took Moe?'

The sheriff glanced at the men standing near, then looked back at Mr Simms. 'Well, Charlie . . . he sayin' . . . he sayin' he ain't took Moe no place.'

'Let me at him!' shouted Mr Simms and headed straight for Harris like some charging bull. 'I'll make him tell where he done took that nigger!'

'But it wasn't Harris!' Sissy screamed. 'Wasn't Harris! I seen it! I seen the whole thing! It wasn't Harris! It was a white boy took Moe out!' She pointed a finger straight at Jeremy. 'That white boy, right there!'

Jeremy seemed to go smaller as all eyes, including his father's, turned on him. Then Charlie Simms started for Sissy. The sheriff intervened. He stepped in front of us and caught hold of Mr Simms's shoulders and halted him.

'You let go of me now, Hank!' Mr Simms ordered. 'Let go of me right now! That gal, she lyin' on my boy! You oughta know how these niggers lie!'

Sissy had her back up now. She showed no fear for herself, not with Harris in trouble. Holding her stomach and leaning against Stacey for support, she got up. 'I ain't lyin'!' she declared. 'You ask your boy, you think I'm lyin'! I seen Moe get onto the back of his truck, and he seen him too! Harris, he was already gone when Moe got onto his truck! Ask him! He standin' right there! Ask him!'

The sheriff looked at Jeremy. Charlie Simms jerked away, turning to the other men. 'Ain't nobody askin' my boy nothin'! Any one of y'all believe the word of a nigger and go questionin' my boy, they ain't no friend of mine!'

The men shook their heads, murmuring that they weren't thinking of such a thing.

'Don't you go worryin' yourself none, Uncle Charlie,'

consoled Statler, gripping his uncle's shoulder. 'We know who done this thing! That nigger Harris over there been vengeful ever since that accident of his! His way of gettin' back at us. Couldn't've been nobody but him took Moe out!'

'Well, that be the case,' said Sheriff Dobbs, 'I'm gonna take him on with me. Harris! Get on down from that truck, boy. You goin' to town!'

Harris looked around perplexed, as if he didn't know what was going on. Two of the men jumped onto the truck and jerked him up, and he shuffled to the edge.

'No!' Sissy screamed again and ran back to the truck. 'Wasn't him, I tell ya! Wasn't him!' Then she turned to me. 'Cassie, you tell 'em! You seen it!' She pointed right at me. 'That girl there, she seen it too! She seen Moe get in Mr Jeremy's truck! Whole buncha us seen it! Now, Cassie, you tell 'em! You tell 'em, Cassie!'

The judgment was now on me, and I didn't know what to do. I didn't know what to say. If I denied I knew about Jeremy, these men would take Harris away. If I told them what Sissy said was true, they most likely wouldn't believe me anyway, and they would still take Harris. I didn't think that whatever I said would make any difference to what happened to Harris. The thing was, though, that I would make an enemy of Sissy by not telling the truth, and I would betray Jeremy if I did. I didn't want to make that choice. I looked at Jeremy, saw the awful fear in his eyes, then looked at Stacey, who saw my fear and stepped forward. 'Sheriff – ' he started, but then Jeremy spoke up and cut him off.

'It's ... it's the truth ... That girl Sissy, she ... she speakin' true.' There was only silence as all eyes turned on him. 'She speakin' mostly true 'bout Moe on the truck, 'ceptin' for ... 'ceptin' I ain't seen Moe get on. She mistakin' that ...'

Sissy started to deny that hotly, but Stacey tightly clutched her arm and laid a look on her that warned her into silence, and she said nothing more.

'I ain't know'd ...'

The silence was deafening.

Then Charlie Simms tore it. He stormed over to Jeremy and stood like a mountain before him. 'What you sayin'?'

Jeremy bowed his head, unable to speak with his father opposite him. Mr Simms jerked Jeremy's head upward and clinched his chin with fingers like a vice. 'What you sayin', boy?'

Jeremy looked again at the men around him, and I knew that his world was crumbling. 'I – I ain't know'd Moe was on the truck, Pa . . . I ain't know'd . . . not till I done got to Bogganville and . . . and I seen him jump off. I ain't know'd . . . and – and I was fearful of tellin' . . . scared to tell ya, Pa! I was scared . . .'

Mr Simms emitted a horrendous scream and slammed his enormous fist into Jeremy's jaw. Jeremy slumped but his father caught him by the shirt collar, held him and slammed his fist into his stomach, then again into his face. This time Jeremy went flat to the ground. Mr Simms raised his leg to kick him, but the sheriff grabbed hold of him. 'Let him be, Charlie! Let the boy be!'

Charlie Simms, in his rage, knocked the sheriff backwards and tried to get at Jeremy again. This time some of the other men intervened and pulled him off. They kept hold of him as the sheriff recovered and came back to face him. 'Now, Charlie,' he said, 'we been knowin' each other all our lives and I know this here ain't easy for you, what this here boy's sayin'.' He looked around at the other men. 'But I figure we oughta believe him, what he's sayin'. That he ain't know'd that boy Moe was on his truck. We gotta believe that, all of us. We know he wouldn't be turnin' his back on his own. We know that!' He looked pointedly at Statler. 'You know it, too, Stat. Jeremy's your blood!'

Statler studied Jeremy and turned away from him without a word.

The sheriff looked back to Mr Simms. 'Charlie?' he said.

The men helped Jeremy to his feet. Jeremy, his face bleeding badly, looked at his father and tried to speak. He grimaced with pain, then mumbled, 'Pa, ya . . . ya gotta believe me. I – I ain't know'd – '

Charlie Simms set a dead-eyed stare on his son. Then, in a voice as chill as well ice water and as low and quiet as a winter still night, he said, 'Get outa my sight. Don't know where ya got it from, but you always was a nigger lover. Never thought I'd live to see the day I said that 'bout my own flesh, 'bout my own son, but it's so. I done tried to beat it outa you since you was knee-high, done tried to make ya see right, but you jus' had t' be 'round niggers. Well, ya might's well be one your ownself, 'cause you ain't white no more. Not after what you gone and done 'gainst your own kin. Your own blood, boy!' Jeremy's lower lip quivered, and I knew he was fighting back tears. 'Don't you never again let me see you in this life, boy. Can't stand the sight of ya.'

I shivered, feeling Jeremy's pain, feeling the stabbing jabs of his father's anger, for the chill of that anger – and that hate – was enough to arouse the devil.

'But, Pa – '

Charlie Simms spat upon the ground in front of Jeremy, the spittle landing on Jeremy's shoes, turned his back on his son, and headed for his truck.

Weakly Jeremy held out his hand, upraised, in a plea to him, then let it drop and lowered his head.

'Get this boy to my car,' Sheriff Dobbs told the men. 'I'll take him on home.'

Mr Simms turned wildly. 'Not t' my house, you won't!'

'But, Charlie, this boy need tendin' to. His ma need t' take a look at him – '

'Far's I'm concerned, he got no ma, no pa neither. He got no family now. You wanna see t' him, that's up t' you. But me and mine, we got no further use for him. None in this world.' He set his eyes on Jeremy one last time. 'He dead t' me.' Then Charlie Simms got into his pickup truck with his nephew Statler, and they rode off down Soldiers Bridge and across the Rosa Lee.

As the truck sped away nobody said a word. Finally the sheriff sighed and turned to the men holding Harris. 'Y'all let that boy go on home now,' he said.

The men looked at the sheriff with questions in their eyes, but they cut the ropes anyway, and we helped Harris down. The sheriff didn't say anything to Harris or to us. He just gave Stacey a nod, indicating for us to leave. He waited until we had gotten Harris across the road and into the Ford, then he helped Jeremy into his car and drove off toward Strawberry. As the sheriff's car passed us we glanced over at Jeremy, but his eyes were downcast, and he didn't look back.

We left the crossroads and headed south toward home. Just past Jefferson Davis School, we met Papa in the truck headed for the crossroads and the Wallace store. Ma Batie and Mrs Sarah Noble sat beside him. Stacey braked, and so did Papa. Papa, seeing Sissy and Harris seated in back, said, 'Everything all right?' He seemed not surprised to see Stacey and me.

'Yes, sir,' Stacey said. 'Jeremy . . . Jeremy told them he took Moe out, left him in Bogganville . . . We were just on our way to take Harris and Sissy home.'

Ma Batie leaned across Papa and cried, 'Harris! Harris, they hurt ya? Answer me, boy!'

Harris looked around but said nothing.

Then Mrs Noble hollered: 'Harris! You sure you all right, son?'

'He fine, Auntie,' answered Sissy, holding tight to Harris. 'Don't you be worryin', Ma, he jus' scairt, that's all. Otherwise he be fine. He be fine.'

'Stacey, Cassie,' said Papa, 'you two all right?'

Stacey nodded. Papa looked at me, waiting on my answer. I couldn't lie to Papa. I never could. I wasn't all right, and there was no sense in saying I was. But I couldn't say what I needed to say about Clarence, not yet. I couldn't blurt that out in front of Sissy. I couldn't blurt out all that had happened since we had started on our road to Memphis, so I just gave a nod too and kept my silence. Papa studied us both as if he knew there was something more, but all he said was 'We'll follow you back.'

Papa turned the truck around and Stacey drove on. Once at Ma Batie's place, Stacey and I stayed outside with Papa as Sissy, her grandmother, and aunt helped Harris into the house. As soon as they were inside, Stacey told Papa about Clarence. He told him about Moe as well. When he finished, Papa sighed a deep, tired sigh and looked out to the field north of the house, as if not wanting to believe, yet believing still. 'I was with J. D. Hopkins the day Clarence was born,' he said. 'We were out hunting when we got the word. Clarence was J.D.'s first born and he was so proud . . . so proud.' Papa was silent for some moments gazing at the field before he turned again to us. 'When we leave from here, we'll go get your mama and Big Ma then go over to

221

the Hopkins place. We'll go over and see Mr Turner after that.' He sighed once more and looked at the house. 'Cassie, you go in with Sissy and send Ma Batie and Miz Noble out so we can tell them 'bout Clarence. Best we let them tell Sissy.'

I did as Papa said, and after Ma Batie and Mrs Noble were gone, I watched in silence as Sissy stood protectively beside Harris who sat on a stool in the corner staring at the floor and saying nothing. 'He be all right,' she told me, patting his shoulder. 'He be all right.' I nodded, then listened to her coo and fuss over Harris until Ma Batie and Mrs Noble came back in. Papa and Stacey came with them.

Ma Batie stood motionless for a moment, then went over to Sissy and placed a strong hand on both her shoulders. 'Sissy, child . . . Sissy – '

Sissy smiled brightly. 'Don't worry, Ma. Harris, he be all right. He be just fine.'

'Girl, listen to me. Got some bad news here. Clarence . . . Clarence, he's dead.'

Sissy laughed, then pulled away and sat down in the rocking chair beside Harris.

'Girl, you hear what I said?'

'I heard. You oughta be shame of yourself, Ma, telling me something like that.' She put her arm back around Harris, who now looked at her.

'Child, it's the truth! The boy's dead!'

Sissy gave her grandmother a hostile stare then, gripping the arms of the chair, settled back and began to rock vigorously. 'Y'all funnin' me.'

Stacey went to her, placed his hand on the chair, and stopped the rocking. He stooped in front of her and softly said, 'Clarence wrote you. He was thinking on you all the time.' He looked at me. 'Give her the letter, Cassie.'

I did.

Sissy took the letter, glanced at us both with suspicion, and read it. Then she looked up grinning. 'Clarence, he said we gettin' married! He said we gettin' married come Christmas!'

Stacey folded her hand in his. 'He's dead, Sissy.'

Sissy's hand tightened around the letter. 'Naw . . . naw, he ain't. What y'all tellin' me that for?'

Stacey kept hold of her hand. 'Something . . . something was wrong with his head, Sissy. He had all these awful headaches.'

Sissy shook her head. 'Y'all funnin' me and I don't like it. Clarence, he put y'all up to this, ain't he? He jus' wantin' to get back at me 'cause I done give him a hard time 'bout this baby I'm carryin'.' She rubbed her stomach. 'Well, he done had his joke, but I ain't findin' it funny.'

I, too, stooped beside her now. Gently I laid my hand on her arm. 'Sissy, it's so . . . It's true. Clarence . . . is dead. He died Sunday night.' It was the first time I had spoken the words myself. It was the first time I had admitted it myself. 'The Army's supposed to bring him here tomorrow sometime.'

Sissy stared at me, then at Stacey, then stared straight ahead at nothing and was a long time silent. Ma Batie and Mrs Noble came closer. Harris pondered us all in silence from his stool. Then Sissy pulled her arm from my grip. She pulled her hand from Stacey's. She calmly folded her letter and got up. 'I got work to do.'

'Sissy – ' I said, unable to stop my own tears from welling up.

She put out her hand to stop me from saying more. 'My Clarence, he ain't gone no place. Me and him we gonna get married, he come back Christmas. Me and this here baby, we gonna wait for him and he come back, we gonna be us a family. We gonna be us a family and we gonna be just fine. Just fine.'

Ma Batie took hold of her by the shoulders again. 'Ain't you heard what we been sayin'? Sissy, you gonna hafta accept this, girl! That boy, he gone! He gone!'

'I know, Ma, that's what y'all said,' Sissy replied quietly. 'You s'pect me to cry 'bout it? Well, I got no cause to cry 'bout what y'all say. I know the truth.' She placed her hand on her stomach again, smiled, and then turned and went out the back door, across the porch and into the yard.

Both Ma Batie and Mrs Noble started after her, but Harris reached for his crutch and spoke for the first time. 'I get her,' he said, pulling himself up. 'I get her.' Leaning heavily against the crutch, he limped onto the porch and followed Sissy across the yard and into the woods.

No longer able to see them, Papa, Stacey, Ma Batie, Mrs Noble, and I stood staring across the yard after them anyway. Then Ma Batie shook her head and sank into a chair and put her hands to her head. 'Lord, what's gonna come of that child now?' she wailed. 'What gonna come of her?'

A short while later we heard Sissy scream Clarence's name, and her scream was like a knife that rent the afternoon asunder.

I had hardly slept since Memphis. That first night back at home I did sleep, but the sleep was hard. There were dreams, so many dreams. There were dreams of Clarence and dreams of Moe. Jeremy was in those dreams, and so was Solomon Bradley. I couldn't keep them all straight. They faded in and out, popping up in places where they shouldn't have been. It was Moe who was dead and not Clarence. It was Solomon who was in love with me, not Moe. It was Jeremy who was the soldier. I couldn't make sense of it.

There was music in the dream, the music of George Gershwin. There was Clarence's coffin laid out in an all-night wake, and Sissy was screaming and crying, and I was there floating in the arms of Solomon Bradley, holding him tight as 'Love Is Here to Stay' played across my mind. It didn't make sense, but it seemed so real.

Then Clarence walked across my dreams all tall and soldier-handsome, and I wanted to shout, to tell everybody that everything was all right, and that Clarence was alive. But then I saw Moe laid out in a coffin, and the dream turned sour. When one dream became too difficult, I forced myself to wake and shake it off, but then I dozed off again and the dreams came back. They would not go away, and all night long, in every dream, Sissy kept screaming on and on.

It started raining on Wednesday. It rained throughout the all-night wake at Great Faith, and on Thursday morning, when we buried Clarence in the Great Faith graveyard, it was raining still. It rained all the day. After the burial folks for the most part sat with Clarence's family at their home trying to comfort them, but there seemed to be no comfort now. As the day drew toward night folks went home to tend to chores. Animals had to be fed and locked up for the night. Supper had to be eaten and bodies rested for another day. After all, life went on, or so it was said.

After the chores and supper, after Oliver, Cousin Hugh, and Cousin Sylvie headed back to Jackson, the boys and I with Mama and Papa and Big Ma sat before the fire, not yet wanting to part, despite the weariness of the last days. In the morning Stacey would be returning to Jackson, too, but I wasn't yet ready to go. Papa would take me back in the truck on Sunday. With the kerosene lamps and the fire our only light, with the rain pounding down hard on the tin roof, we listened to the latest news on the radio, listened to it and thought of Clarence and the days ahead. The news wasn't good. On this day, while we had buried Clarence, Germany and Italy had declared war on us too. On this day it was reported that the government was proposing to lower the age of young men being drafted to fight from twenty-one to eighteen. There seemed to be no question now that Stacey would have to go fight.

'War last another year and a half,' said Little Man, 'and I'll likely be going too. Heard on the radio about maybe being able to volunteer at sixteen.'

'Hush up that talk!' ordered Big Ma.

'But I'll be sixteen then – '

'You won't be going,' Mama said absently, her eyes on Stacey.

'But I want to go! I want to fight those Germans!'

Mama turned now. 'There's nothing we can do to keep Stacey here, but we won't be letting you go, you nor Christopher-John, not until we have to.' There was finality in her voice.

'Pray to the good Lord, this war don't be goin' on that long,' said Big Ma. 'Couldn't stand for 'em t' go take these boys like they done took Kevin and Mitchell and Hammer. I done lost two of my boys to they war. Couldn't stand t' lose these boys here.'

I looked around suddenly, fearfully. It hadn't occurred to me that Christopher-John and Little Man would ever have to go fight. I had worried about Stacey but not them. Now the very thought of them going made me tremble. Christo-

225

pher-John was sitting next to me. Impulsively I placed my hand over his. He looked at me, understood, and managed a smile. Then he looked at Stacey, and his eyes were so intense, I thought he was going to cry. He didn't. Maybe, despite what he was feeling, he was figuring he was too old for crying. I didn't figure I was; but I refused to cry, for I feared if I started up again, I would cry forever.

Papa looked around at us, got up and slowly stirred the fire. He put a new log on, too, then he turned and looked long upon us once again. Then, in his strong, calming way, he said, 'Seeing that Stacey's leaving for Jackson come morning, I think it's time we prayed.'

'Yes, Lord,' agreed Big Ma.

Mama rose as if in a dream and went to Papa. She hugged him, took his hand with her own, and reached out for Stacey. Stacey got up and went to them. Big Ma stood as well, and so did Christopher-John, Little Man, and me. We formed a circle, and we held each other's hands. Then we bowed our heads and prayed. Each of us prayed in turn, Papa, Mama, Big Ma, the boys, and me. We prayed for the days ahead. We prayed for all those we loved. We prayed for Clarence's family and for Moe and his family. We prayed for our family too. As we said our amens there was a knock on the door.

'Now, who could that be this time of night?' questioned Big Ma, dabbing at her eyes.

Papa looked at her, touched her shoulder gently, and went to the door. When he opened it, Jeremy Simms was standing in the doorway. His hair was plastered down from the rain, the jacket he wore looked soaked, his face was badly swollen, and his lower lip was busted. Jeremy apologized. 'I . . . I know it's late,' he said, 'but I seen ya light – '

'Come in,' Papa said, 'out of the rain.'

'No, sir . . . I thank ya, but I just wanted to talk to Stacey a minute . . . that be all right.'

Papa looked back into the room at Stacey. Stacey looked at him, too, then he crossed the room and went out onto the porch with Jeremy. 'How you doing?' we heard Stacey ask as they left the porch.

'Oh, I'm all right, I s'pose,' Jeremy answered, though he didn't sound all right. His words were somewhat mumbled.

Papa closed the door behind them and came back to the fire. As soon as he was seated, I got up and headed for the door.

'Cassie, where're you going?' Mama asked. 'Jeremy didn't say anything about wanting to talk to you.'

'But I want to talk to him. Please, Mama.'

Mama glanced at Papa, who nodded, and I went out too. Christopher-John and Little Man followed me. The rain had let up now, and there was only a drizzle. Stacey and Jeremy had walked down the lawn and now stood near the road. I stepped off the porch and went as far as the magnolia tree. Christopher-John and Little Man stayed on the porch. Stacey glanced back at us but didn't admonish us to leave. Jeremy glanced back, too, but he seemed not to mind our being there. 'I . . . I was right sorry to hear 'bout Clarence,' he said.

Stacey looked off into the night. 'Yeah . . .'

'Heard it was a real hard funeral. Folks faintin' and screamin' and all . . .'

'Well, that was to be expected, I s'pose. Who'd've thought Clarence would've just up and died like that?'

'Yeah . . . yeah.'

They both gazed into the night.

Finally Stacey turned back. 'Thought you were in Strawberry.'

'Yeah, I was. Come back tonight to try and see my ma. Pa . . . Pa, he wouldn't let me, though.'

'I'm sorry,' said Stacey. 'I'm sorry 'bout this whole mess.'

'You got no cause. Wasn't never your fault.'

'But I asked you – '

'That don't matter none. I ain't had to do it. Wouldn't've done it I ain't wanted to. 'Sides, it was what was right, and I ain't sorry.'

'But you losing everything because of it.'

Jeremy shrugged. 'I don't know. Me and my family, you know we done had a parting of the ways long time ago. Onliest one I'm feeling sorry 'bout is my ma. Wanted to see her 'fore I go, wanted to see her real bad . . . I'll be writin' her, though, lettin' her know where I am.'

Stacey nodded. 'Where you heading?'

'Army. Figure to join up. What with us at war with

Germany and Italy, too, now, figure they need even me.' He attempted a smile and grimaced from the pain.

Stacey took note of his pain, but he shared the smile.

'You gonna join up?' asked Jeremy.

'Figure to wait till they call me.'

Jeremy nodded as if he understood why.

'When you leaving?'

'Soon as I can. Going up to Jackson on the bus.'

'Sheriff not holding you?'

'Naw. He said he got no choice but to believe what I was saying, that I ain't know'd Moe was on the truck. Said it was too hard not to believe me. 'Sides, only folks in the jail are Negroes and he said he couldn't stand to put me in 'side of them.' He glanced at Stacey as if checking whether or not he should have spoken that truth, but Stacey understood it as well as Jeremy. 'Sheriff, he the one brought me down here. I been stayin' at his house.'

'That a fact?'

'He said he ain't wantin' me goin' off without seein' Ma. He even gone and talked t' Pa, but ya know how Pa is . . .'

'Yeah . . . I know.'

Jeremy sighed, wiped at his nose with the back of his hand, and looked out into the night before speaking again. 'How's Moe?' he said, turning back. 'He all right?'

'He's safe.'

'Good . . . good.' He did not ask more. Now he turned to leave. 'I best go.'

Christopher-John and Little Man came from the porch and down the lawn. Jeremy glanced back at all of us. 'Want y'all to know I ain't never gonna forget them days we used to spend fishin' down there on the Rosa Lee and layin' back on the banks of the Caroline. Gonna think 'bout y'all whenever I be thinkin' on home 'cause . . .'cause them was good days, spite of everything. They sure was . . .'

'We're not going to forget those days either,' promised Christopher-John in a soft, sad voice.

'Naw, we not,' agreed Little Man, and there was no questioning that.

Jeremy nodded and extended his hand to Stacey. Stacey took it, and it seemed a lasting handshake. 'Look, Jeremy,' Stacey said as Jeremy turned away once more, 'I can take

228

you to Strawberry – Jackson for that matter. Willie and I, we going back to Jackson in the morning.'

'I thank ya, but no need. Sheriff Dobbs, he waitin' for me up front of Jefferson Davis School. He gonna take me back to his house for the night, and I . . . I figure after all the trouble it be best I jus' go on take the bus up.'

'You're most likely right. But leastways let me take you on up to the school. This rain could start pouring again.'

'Kinda like t' walk, Stacey. Army take me, gonna be a long time 'fore I go to walkin' these roads again. Be good to walk 'em one last time. Hope you understand.'

Stacey did understand. He gripped Jeremy's hand once more, and this time the handshake was like an embrace. 'You take care of yourself, Jeremy . . .'

'You do the same . . .'

'We'll be thinking on you and all you done.'

Jeremy smiled. 'You ever play that ole wind pipe I made, you think of me, hear?'

Stacey smiled too. 'Yeah . . . I'll do that.'

Jeremy backed away. He held up his hand in farewell, and looking again up the slope, he called, 'Cassie! Christopher-John! Man! Y'all be good, now!'

I wanted to cry but refused to do so. I wanted to run down and hug him, too, but something kept me from it, that same something that had always stood between us. Instead I took a few steps toward him, stopped, and said softly, 'You take care of yourself, Jeremy.' My voice betrayed me. It cracked with the tears I was feeling, and I cleared my throat to go on. 'Jeremy . . . don't . . . don't you go getting yourself killed!'

He managed a grin, despite the busted lip. 'Gonna try not to, Cassie,' he promised just as softly, and there were tears in his voice too. 'Gonna sure try not to.' He backed away, then stopped. He took one more long look at us, and he said, 'See ya in the Army, Stacey.'

Stacey nodded. 'Yeah . . . see ya there . . .'

Then Jeremy held up his hand in a final farewell, turned, and walked away into the misty night. As he headed up the road he looked such a lonely figure, but then, again, he always had. We hadn't always understood Jeremy Simms, and I had often wondered if he even understood himself.

He had made us uncomfortable with his presence and his offer of friendship, and we had hated him for his betrayal; yet now his leaving tugged at my heart. I whisked away an errant falling tear. So much had changed. Clarence was dead. Moe was gone, and now Jeremy was leaving. I didn't know much of anything about this war we were in. I didn't know much of anything about Japan or why they'd attacked us. For that matter, I didn't know that much more about Germany or Italy either. All I knew was that people who had always been a part of my life, people I loved – and that included Jeremy Simms – were leaving, and some were not coming back. All I knew was that my brother soon would be leaving, too, and that I was fearful of what was to come.

We watched Jeremy pass the cotton fields, watched him pass the old oak, watched him until the road changed its course, rose and wound away. We watched until there was no more of him. For some time the four of us just stood there staring up the deserted road. Then we shared our feelings in one glance, returned to the house, and went inside.

Later, as I lay in the comfort of the feathered bed beside Big Ma, I awakened to the fluted sounds of an awkward music. I glanced out and saw nothing, but I knew Stacey was out there. I knew he was out there playing that wind pipe.

I rose from the bed. Opening the door, I went onto the wet porch and just stood there in my long cotton nightgown, staring across the blackened lawn. The music played on. Then, as suddenly as it had awakened me from my sleep, the music stopped, and soon Stacey came walking from the forest and across the road and up the damp grass, a box in his hand.

'Cassie?' he said. 'What're you doing up?'

'Are you all right?' I asked.

'Yeah . . . yeah, I'm fine.' He stepped onto the porch and looked down at the box.

'You were playing it,' I said.

He smiled. 'You can call it that?'

'You don't think he's coming back, do you?'

'What?'

'Jeremy. You think he's gone for good.'

Stacey shook his head, sighed, and looked out into the night., 'I can't say.' Then he looked again at me. 'Hope I didn't wake anyone else.'

'You see I'm the only one came out.'

'Yeah ... yeah ...' He looked long at me, then, doing something he very seldom did, he folded me into his arms and hugged me. After a moment he let me go and moved toward his room. At the door he turned. 'You go on back inside now and go to sleep,' he said.

'You still leaving in the morning?'

'Have to. I got a job to go to ... I think.' He reached for the knob. 'Night, Cassie.'

'Good night,' I said and went back down the porch. I opened the door to my room, took one more look out at the rainy night, out at the misty road, then at my brother. He smiled at me, went inside, and took the box with him. I went inside too and lay down beside Big Ma, and I slept.

The night passed.

The morning came.

Stacey left.

We did not see Jeremy Simms again.

ALSO IN

General Editors: Anne and Ian Serraillier

Chinua Achebe Things Fall Apart
Douglas Adams The Hitchhiker's Guide to the Galaxy
Vivien Alcock The Cuckoo Sister; The Monster Garden; The Trial of Anna Cotman
Michael Anthony Green Days by the River
Bernard Ashley High Pavement Blues; Running Scared
J G Ballard Empire of the Sun
Stan Barstow Joby
Nina Bawden The Witch's Daughter; A Handful of Thieves; Carrie's War; The Robbers; Devil by the Sea; Kept in the Dark; The Finding; Keeping Henry
Judy Blume It's Not the End of the World; Tiger Eyes
E R Braithwaite To Sir, With Love
John Branfield The Day I Shot My Dad
F Hodgson Burnett The Secret Garden
Ray Bradbury The Golden Apples of the Sun; The Illustrated Man
Betsy Byars The Midnight Fox
Victor Canning The Runaways; Flight of the Grey Goose
John Christopher The Guardians; Empty World
Gary Crew The Inner Circle
Jane Leslie Conly Racso and the Rats of NIMH
Roald Dahl Danny, The Champion of the World; The Wonderful Story of Henry Sugar; George's Marvellous Medicine; The BFG; The Witches; Boy; Going Solo; Charlie and the Chocolate Factory; Matilda
Andrew Davies Conrad's War
Anita Desai The Village by the Sea
Peter Dickinson The Gift; Annerton Pit; Healer
Berlie Doherty Granny was a Buffer Girl
Gerald Durrell My Family and Other Animals
J M Falkner Moonfleet
Anne Fine The Granny Project
F Scott Fitzgerald The Great Gatsby
Anne Frank The Diary of Anne Frank

Leon Garfield Six Apprentices
Graham Greene The Third Man and The Fallen Idol; Brighton Rock
Marilyn Halvorson Cowboys Don't Cry
Thomas Hardy The Withered Arm and Other Wessex Tales
Rosemary Harris Zed
Rex Harley Troublemaker
L P Hartley The Go-Between
Esther Hautzig The Endless Steppe
Ernest Hemingway The Old Man and the Sea; A Farewell to Arms
Nat Hentoff Does this School have Capital Punishment?
Nigel Hinton Getting Free; Buddy; Buddy's Song
Minfong Ho Rice Without Rain
Anne Holm I Am David
Janni Howker Badger on the Barge; Isaac Campion
Kristin Hunter Soul Brothers and Sister Lou
Barbara Ireson (Editor) In a Class of Their Own
Jennifer Johnston Shadows on Our Skin
Toeckey Jones Go Well, Stay Well
James Joyce A Portrait of the Artist as a Young Man
Geraldine Kaye Comfort Herself; A Breath of Fresh Air
Clive King Me and My Million
Dick King-Smith The Sheep-Pig
Daniel Keyes Flowers for Algernon
Elizabeth Laird Red Sky in the Morning
D H Lawrence The Fox and The Virgin and the Gypsy; Selected Tales
Harper Lee To Kill a Mockingbird
Laurie Lee As I Walked Out One Midsummer Morning
Julius Lester Basketball Game
Ursula Le Guin A Wizard of Earthsea
C Day Lewis The Otterbury Incident
David Line Run for Your Life; Screaming High
Joan Lingard Across the Barricades; Into Exile; The Clearance; The File on Fraulein Berg
Penelope Lively The Ghost of Thomas Kempe
Jack London The Call of the Wild; White Fang
Lois Lowry The Road Ahead; The Woods at the End of Autumn Street

How many have you read?